Changing the Rules

Changing the Rules

The Politics of Liberalization and the
Urban Informal Economy in Tanzania

AILI MARI TRIPP

University of California Press

BERKELEY   LOS ANGELES   LONDON

University of California Press
Berkeley and Los Angeles, California

University of California Press, Ltd.
London, England

© 1997 by
The Regents of the University of California

Library of Congress Cataloging-in-Publication Data

Tripp, Aili Mari.
    Changing the rules : the politics of liberalization and the urban
informal economy in Tanzania / Aili Mari Tripp.
        p.   cm.
    Includes bibliographical references and index.
    ISBN 0-520-20278-3 (alk. paper). — ISBN 0-520-20279-1 (pbk. :
alk. paper)
    1. Dar es Salaam (Tanzania)—Economic conditions.   2. Informal
sector (Economics)—Tanzania—Dar es Salaam.   3. Tanzania—
Economic policy.   4. Government, Resistance to—Tanzania.
I. Title.
HC885.Z7D377   1997
330'9678—dc20   95-53702
                                                        CIP

Printed in the United States of America
9 8 7 6 5 4 3 2 1

For Warren and Leila

Contents

Illustrations

Tables

Maps

Preface

Given the explosion of informal economic activity in Africa in the 1980s, the study of the informal economy by social scientists appears to be woefully slow, trailing developments. In Zaire, Janet MacGaffey (1987) noted that one consequence of the growth of the informal economy has been the emergence of a new mercantile class that has been changing class configurations in that country. Naomi Chazan (1983, 196) argued that in Ghana the degree of internal organization in the informal economy reflected the degree of disarray in the formal system. Robert Bates (1981), Frank Ellis (1983), and others have described the magnitude of evasion of official crop-marketing boards and the predominance of parallel market trade in the African context.

If one considers the far-reaching political and economic consequences of the informal economy suggested by these authors, it seems remarkable that so few political scientists and economists have found the informal economy in Africa worthy of greater attention. Instead, scholars have generally been content with making the perfunctory observation that the informal economy creates problems in the use of official statistics, without fully exploring the implications of such claims.

Yet since the late 1970s the informal economy has become an increasingly significant political, economic, and social phenomenon in many African countries. People have become increasingly forced to rely on their own resources while lessening their dependence on the state and the formal economy. In Tanzania, informal economic exchanges are more common than are similar transactions in the formal economy. For urban dwellers, employed and self-employed alike, the informal economy accounts for what the majority of people do to make most of their income. During periods of commodity shortages and hiked prices, the official figures on real incomes could not possibly have been accurate, because they were generally based on consumer price indexes that primarily reflected official prices rather than the higher unofficial prices. Ratios of highest to lowest income levels generally only consider formal salaries and wages, not the large gaps between real incomes derived from informal businesses. Similarly, figures on crop exports reflect only those crops sold through official marketing bodies and not the large quantities that are channeled through parallel markets. Even many of the recent studies of the informal sector, amazingly, do not capture in their samples the largest numbers of microentrepreneurs who work in individually owned businesses; nor do they always include the large numbers of women, whose household tasks, farming, and business activities may be so intermeshed that they elude survey categories. These observations clearly have enormous implications for any conclusions drawn about economic growth, equity, and resource distribution.

This study focuses on the political challenges of the informal economy rather than on problems related to accounting, as important as those problems are. Some have characterized the informal economy as a form of disengagement from the state and of resistance to the state (Azarya and Chazan 1987, Bayart 1986, Chazan 1988). This book, however, shows that the informal economy is more than simply disengagement from the state. Under extreme economic duress, people have challenged the existing political and economic order by engaging in activities that in themselves became new economic and institutional resources. In doing so, they helped bring about changes in the rules of the game. The study explores these new economic resources (for example, new products, services, sources of credit, and savings). At the same time, this study looks at the moral code within which much of this informal economy operates and shows how it came into conflict with the existing political order and ideology in Tanzania. The strengthening and creation of alternative institutions reflecting a different set of rules became in itself a form of resistance.

My own interest in the informal economy started, in part, with an empirical problem when I began to question how urban dwellers in many African countries were surviving on the reported official wages when the cost of living was many times greater than those wage incomes. When I returned to Tanzania (I had grown up there from 1960 to 1974) to carry out my fieldwork in 1987, the discrepancy was all the more incomprehensible. Official wages did not correspond even remotely to the cost of living regardless of the level of formal wages. As I had suspected and as all Tanzanians knew, informal incomes made up the difference. But what I had not expected was the extent to which people relied on informal incomes.

What I also did not anticipate was the interest Tanzanian people I interviewed had in understanding the informal economy. Individuals knew how they themselves were making ends meet, and they had some idea of how their relatives, neighbors, and friends were surviving; but few had a sense of the broader picture, and many expressed their curiosity about this to me. In fact, in many of the poorest neighborhoods where I carried out a survey, many people, some of whom could barely read, requested a copy of my report and gave me their address. This interest in the research topic and the importance people themselves placed on the informal economy gave added urgency to the study.

As I began to fathom the enormity of the informal economy and its centrality to the Tanzanian economy, I was forced to consider its broader political, economic, and social implications. To begin with, participation in the urban informal economy had resulted in the Tanzanian case in massive reversals in dependencies and reversals in the direction of resource flows at many different levels: away from the state and toward private solutions to problems of income, security, and social welfare; away from reliance on wage labor and toward reliance on informal incomes and farming; and a gradual shifting of migration patterns with increasing new movements out of the city into the rural areas. Similarly, relations and patterns of obligation in the household were being transformed, with greater resource dependencies on women, children, and the elderly, where only a decade earlier urban women had mostly relied on men for income, children on their parents, and the elderly on their adult children.

 Women's heightened economic activity also gave greater prominence to alternative logics of economic decision making, which emerged among the poor to confront government policies that worked against them in their struggle to survive. The struggle against the harassment and bribing of vendors by the militia, against unjust licensing policies, and against re-strictions on sideline businesses and other such conflicts brought to the fore competing economic rationales. The embeddedness of narrowly de-fined economic activity in social and cultural life, in household activities, and in activities involving the regeneration and sustenance of life made the state's intrusions all the more oppressive.

The informal economy helps explain some of the internal circumstances that allowed Tanzania to embark on a program of economic reform and austerity at a time when urban dwellers, in particular, were suffering enormous hardships. People's reliance on their own solutions explains how they were able to cope when the government launched economic restructuring programs that involved cuts in social-service expenditures and in food subsidies, continuing low wages, and some layoffs. Although this study does not attempt to justify these cutbacks, it shows how informal economic strategies meant that people did not experience the full force of these austerity measures.

At the same time, urban dwellers resisted policies that infringed on their ability to carry out informal income-generating activities through strategies of noncompliance and "quiet, everyday resistance," to borrow a term popularized by James Scott. In response, policy makers made a number of concessions to people operating in the informal economy, making it easier for them to pursue such activities. This loosening up came at a crucial time, when international donors were pressuring the government to adopt austerity measures that otherwise would have made life, especially for urban dwellers, virtually untenable. Most of the pressures for liberalization, privatization, and legalization of various informal economic activities discussed in this book, with a few exceptions, were distinct from the economic reforms pushed by international financial institutions. Rarely has the discussion of economic reform in Africa considered these internal pressures and domestically initiated reforms.

These developments inevitably had repercussions for the political order. Key tenets of Tanzania's statist and socialist orientation began to unravel in the face of pressures for greater political inclusiveness and local control through the legitimation of informal economic activities. For example, the 1991 Zanzibar Declaration effectively undid the Arusha Declaration, which had been promulgated by the ruling party, Tanganyika African National Union (TANU), in 1967. TANU had sought through the Arusha Declaration to eliminate bases for class inequality by discouraging foreign investment and by forbidding capitalist practices of party members, middle- and higher-ranking civil servants, and government officials.

The study of the informal economy adds a new dimension to the study of state-society relations, which in the literature on African politics has been dominated by state-centric approaches, even given the emphasis on civil society and nongovernmental actors in the 1990s. Much of the current debate has focused on the demise and weakness of the African state, and less emphasis has been placed on why people themselves have withdrawn from the state and have resisted state policies and development programs through strategies of noncompliance. Instead, scholarship has focused on elites and their abuses of power, on patterns of personal rule, and on patron-client relations.

The approach of this study is to look at the whole network of interactions between various social actors, from households to networks, voluntary associations, the ruling party, government institutions, the military, the formal private sector, international lending institutions, and all of the other significant actors on the political stage in Tanzania. Politics in this context involves struggle, negotiation, and accommodation over how resources will be allocated and what values, ideologies, symbols, and institutions will predominate. The challenge is not to replace past top-down approaches to the study of politics or development with an approach that would make the state irrelevant. The aim is to focus on areas where "constructive reciprocities," as Goran Hyden (1992) calls them, have been established and to learn from the experiences of those who have challenged and overcome existing structural limitations.

It is, of course, much easier to identify and focus on the myriad economic constraints people face in their daily lives and on the obstacles that stand in the way of making the state responsive to the needs of people. What the study of the informal economy shows is how people have adapted and persevered amid extreme adversity. People did not wait for the government, the ruling party, donor agencies, or anyone else to solve their problems. They took matters into their own hands and tried to reconstruct the world around them to the best of their ability to suit their needs. They did so even when it meant having to skirt laws that undermined their ability to pursue a livelihood. The government eventually had to take note of some of these forms of resistance. More than once I heard government authorities say that the people led the way with their strategies and that the leaders followed behind with their policies, by legalizing, privatizing, and legitimating activities that had already been "sanctioned" by the people. Aspects of these economic pressures even contributed to some of the political liberalizing trends that were under way by the early 1990s, as Tanzania sanctioned multipartyism, the press gained greater freedom, nongovernmental organizations were being encouraged, and other signs of political openness became visible.

As such new reciprocities were being forged, new conflicts, in the form of tensions between religious and ethnic groups and between classes were surfacing. At the root of these conflicts lay the debate over how best to attain equity and economic justice, issues that confront most societies attempting to reverse decades of heavy state-directed top-down approaches to development and growth.

The book begins with a discussion of the informal economy as a manifestation of societal noncompliance with the state, as a tool for institutional change in challenging state norms of fairness and economic justice, and as a means of creating new institutional resources. Chapter 1 grapples with the problems of using reified categories of "informal-formal economy" and "state-society." It also explores some of the ways in which understandings of the informal economy have not sufficiently differentiated licit activities from illicit ones. Similarly, ideologically charged notions of the informal economy have not adequately taken into account the diversity that exists from one part of the world to the next regarding the informal economy, the reasons for its existence, and its potential.

Chapter 2 provides a historical context for the rapid changes that took place in the 1980s in Tanzania with the decline in real wages, flight from wage employment, intensifying rural and urban linkages, the growth of income-generating projects, and the growing importance of informal incomes in families with wage earners in the formal sector. The chapter also provides a general background for Dar es Salaam and for Manzese and Buguruni, the two parts of the city that were the focus of the study. Chapter 3 gives a general outline of the shifting boundaries of state control of the economy. It shows how the postindependence state expanded its jurisdiction, only to retreat in the 1980s as a result of economic crisis, a loss of state resources due to failed government policies, pressures from international donors, and popular pressures of noncompliance that created spaces for people within which to establish new institutions.

The next chapter explores some of the conflicts between coalitions that polarized party and government leadership over the direction and pace of economic reform. It identifies the societal winners and losers in the reform process and explores the paradox of urban workers who had the most to lose from these reforms yet seemed relatively unaffected by the various austerity measures that were imposed on them. The informal economy, which had already emerged in response to economic crisis, becomes an important reason in explaining this relative urban immunity.

Chapter 5 looks at the changing household dependencies in which women, children, youth, and the elderly have taken on greater responsibilities in providing income, while male wage earners no longer are the main source of income for the urban household, as they were prior to the 1980s. The chapter also explores alternative economic decision-making strategies that characterize much of the informal economy but are especially apparent in the way women go about their business activities. Chapter 5 highlights the embedded nature of economic activity in the totality of life experiences and in society.

Chapter 6 shows how the state's rules of the game are challenged and changed by people who refuse to comply with bans on microenterprise activity, on sideline activities, on the operation of private buses, and on other activities that are basic to their efforts to gain a livelihood through what they consider legitimate means. The chapter shows how the state retreated and changed the rules in the face of such popular pressures. Chapter 7 shows how these pressures manifested themselves in conflicts among the country's rulers, bringing to a head an ideological conflict between the party and government leadership that led to the dismantling of the key ideological tenets. The concluding chapter suggests some of the institutional conflicts underlying the changes that occurred in the 1980s regarding the informal economy. It explores the implications of these dynamics for understanding state-society relations and problems of local governance.

Map 1. Regional boundaries of Tanzania.

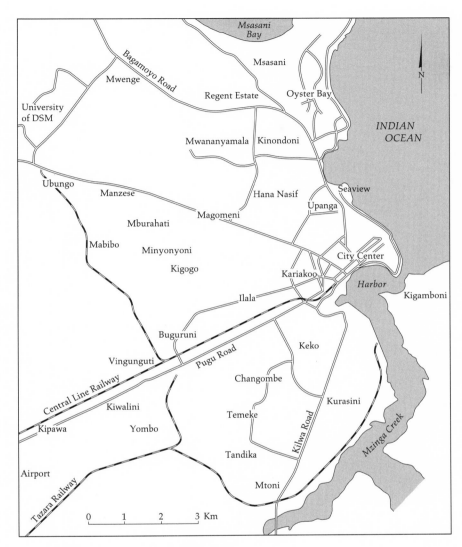

Map 2. Major wards of Dar es Salaam.

Acknowledgments

This book has been a labor of love. It is the product of countless hours spent talking to street vendors, market sellers, and small-scale entrepreneurs who told me their stories and shared their insights and woes. Without them the book could never have been written. I am more grateful to them than they will ever know. They have given me so much more than a book to write. They have left me with an enduring admiration for the incredible perseverance of millions who toil daily to make a livelihood in the face of enormous odds.

I owe a debt of gratitude to my husband, Warren Tripp, for his endless patience, support, and confidence in me. His enthusiastic assistance with every computer-related problem I confronted in writing the book was greatly appreciated. Our daughter Leila, born in the middle of writing the book, presented a happy challenge to my work and a delightful distraction when I was not writing. She gave me a first-hand appreciation for how women's work is embedded in daily life and how inseparable the regeneration of life is from the rest of life and work.

I thank my parents, Marja-Liisa and Lloyd Swantz, who first took me to Tanzania when I was two years old and raised me in that country, fostering in me a deep sense of appreciation and respect for its people. I was privileged to be able to draw on my parents' rich experience and knowledge of Tanzania in my research and writing.

In Tanzania, I have Salome Mjema, my research assistant, to whom to offer my most sincere gratitude. Having had her as a childhood friend made our reacquaintance all the more special. In the course of interviewing more than a thousand people together, we shared the daily adventures, joys, thrills, and embarrassments—not to mention frustrations—of carrying out fieldwork.

Because so many people in Tanzania generously contributed to the research project in one way or another, it would be impossible to thank them all individually. Nevertheless, I would like to mention, in particular, Benno Ndulu, Kuthbert Omari, and Mboya Bagachwa, who, in addition to Marja-Liisa Swantz, made up the research team I was privileged to work with. We were studying grass-roots strategies of development in a project sponsored by the Helsinki-based World Institute for Development Economics (United Nations University). I also am grateful for the friendship of William Mjema, Barbro Johansson, Kati Vuori, and Mrs. Mwakansandile. I am especially grateful to Camillus Sawio for his helpful comments on various chapters.

I owe much to Ronald Herring, Evelyne Huber Stephens, Karen Tranberg Hansen, Crawford Young, Michael Schatzberg, Michael Lofchie, Robert Charlick, and many others who provided detailed suggestions and criticisms of chapters, offering their rich comparative perspectives in Latin America, the Caribbean, Asia, and other parts of Africa. Many heartfelt thanks to Karen Andes, Kathleen Mulligan-Hansel, and Peter Kupaza, who provided research assistance at different stages. In writing the book I enjoyed the support and intellectual stimulation of my dear friends Antonia Maioni, Pierre Martin, Paula Holmes, Grace and Mark Thomsen, Heather Thiessen, and Valerian Laini. Similarly, colleagues at the John D. and Catherine T. MacArthur Foundation, where I worked as a visiting research associate, were extraordinarily supportive. I know I have left unmentioned many of you who deserve my gratitude: please accept my apologies and know that your contribution is appreciated.

Finally, I am grateful to the United Nations World Institute for Development Economic Research, the Northwestern University Alumnae Fellowship Program, the Institute for the Study of World Politics, and the American Council of Learned Societies for their generous financial support of my fieldwork and writing.

1 Introduction

A group of about forty Dar es Salaam passengers had boarded a privately owned *daladala* minibus to go to work. On their way they were stopped by a police officer. At the time this incident occurred in the early 1980s, privately owned buses were illegal. Informal transport had increasingly come into greater use as the needs of the population reached crisis proportions, far exceeding available public services. Realizing they would be in trouble, the passengers, who up until that moment had been perfect strangers, spontaneously transformed themselves into one big, happy family on its way to a wedding and started singing, clapping, and making shrill, ululating sounds, as is the custom for people on their way to celebrations. The police, unable to charge the driver for operating a bus on a commercial basis, had no choice but to let them go.

This vignette represents one of the innumerable actions that were characteristic of daily life in Tanzania in the 1980s. It tells a story about noncompliance and resistance, of small and anonymous ways in which people skirted institutional restrictions believed to be harmful to their immediate interests.[1] As a result of an ongoing economic crisis that began in the late 1970s, the Tanzanian government did not have sufficient foreign exchange to purchase adequate numbers of buses. Nevertheless, the government had banned the use of private buses. Clearly the effect of thousands of individuals flaunting the law, using informal taxis called *taxibubus* and minibuses called *daladala* or *thumni,* had a collective impact that did not escape the authorities. The authorities were finally forced in 1986 to allow the private use of buses in the city, alleviating some of Dar es Salaam's transport problems. Thus actions like those taken by the minibus passengers became especially significant when seen as part of broader forces for institutional change. So commonplace were these tussles between minibus drivers and police that one journalist dubbed them the *"daladala* war."[2] They highlight, as this book attempts to show, noncompliance as not only a means of resistance to old institutions but also the way in which social forces in Tanzania brought new resources to bear in creating alternative institutions.

Daily evasions of state control affected virtually every sector of the society and the economy. These activities included eluding licensing and taxation of microenterprises; buying and selling food crops on parallel markets;

1

ignoring party restrictions on pursuing sideline income-generating projects; and engaging in other such activities that could be considered part of
the informal economy. By informal economy, I am referring to economic
activities that are subject to regulation but that, in fact, operate outside
government controls.

In this study I relate these kinds of evasions of state policy to broader
political and economic changes in Tanzania that began around the mid-
1980s in the direction of greater economic liberalization and legalization of
various economic activities. I focus on some of the domestic dynamics that
shaped these specific economic reforms in Tanzania, while recognizing the
importance of external pressures from the international financial institutions and foreign donors. My focus on the internal politics of economic
liberalization is, in part, an attempt to shed light on a debate that has, with
a few important exceptions (Callaghy 1989, for example),[3] largely focused
on economic reform as a consequence of International Monetary Fund
(IMF) and World Bank pressures (Lancaster 1990, 115). Insufficient attention has been given to the impact of local forces on the direction, pace, and
nature of economic reform and, in particular, on reforms that were not tied
to donor conditionality. It has been acknowledged that forces within the
Tanzanian government as well as within the academic community were
pressing for economic change (Barkan 1994, 29; McHenry 1994). Nevertheless, little attention has been given to the complex societal pressures
that influenced Tanzanian leaders to begin moving away from a situation
in which the central government and the ruling party, Chama Cha Mapinduzi (CCM),[4] were the sole arbiters of development policy.

After Tanganyika's independence from Britain in 1961 the party gradually came to dominate the government, and the lines between the two were
often unclear. Part of the explanation for the impetus for economic reform
lies with the state itself. The CCM and the central government gradually
increased their control over the economy and over local political participation by absorbing, coopting, eliminating, or curtailing the activities of key
independent organizations and economic institutions. However, as Tanzania fell deeper into economic crisis in the late 1970s and early 1980s, the
state increasingly lost its capacity to regulate social relationships and to
extract and appropriate resources, to borrow Joel Migdal's definition of
state capacity (1988, 4). State leaders seemingly devised their own agenda
with little concern for accountability or popular compliance. In the 1980s,
as the economic crisis deepened, the regime found itself in danger of losing
what little credibility and legitimacy it still retained. Thus Tanzania's statist

policies gradually began to give way to economic liberalization as state boundaries of economic and political control were pulled back.

Pressures from donors forced Tanzania to conclude an agreement with the IMF in 1986. In fact, these external pressures sped up the process of economic reform and were influential in shaping and determining the direction they took. It is doubtful that the reform measures would have been as extensive or as rapid without such external demands. The 1986 agreement also bolstered forces for economic reform within the Tanzanian leadership at a crucial time.

Opposition to the changes came from the party leadership and public-sector managers who were tied to the party patronage system, from sections of the military, and from various party mass organizations. Private manufacturers held the middle ground, opposing only some of the reform policies, like trade liberalization, and sought to speed up other reforms. Those leaders who supported reform aligned themselves primarily with the government. They were backed mainly by exporters and importers. Urban dwellers, who were more dependent on the state for jobs, social services, and security than were their rural counterparts, potentially had the most to lose from the retreat of the state. Surprisingly, they were by and large indifferent to most of the economic reform measures. The quiescence of urban dwellers, whom authorities often considered a potentially volatile population, was a key factor in facilitating the imposition of austerity measures.

Thus the actors within the informal economy affected economic reform in Tanzania in two important ways. On the one hand, they forced the government to ease restrictions on their entrepreneurial activities and legalize various economic pursuits to make it easier for people to make a living under extremely difficult circumstances. At the same time, people's involvement in informal sector activities served as a cushion, albeit a thin one, against the hardships brought on first by economic crisis and later by austerity measures that were part of structural adjustment in Tanzania. This study, therefore, accounts for the seemingly paradoxical position taken by city dwellers, who like urbanites in many parts of Africa, were operating within exceedingly narrow economic constraints, heightened by the crisis of the late 1970s and 1980s. As real wages in Tanzania fell by 83 percent between 1974 and 1988, urban dwellers and their kin expanded their pursuit of a variety of survival strategies, including reliance on farming and increasing their involvement in small income-generating projects, such as making pastries, carpentry, or tailoring.

The growth of the informal economy is probably one of the most important developments in Africa in the 1980s, affecting virtually every social stratum of society from children, to the elderly, to women, high-income and low-income groups alike. In Tanzania the agricultural sector was affected by the sale of crops on parallel markets. Wage workers were living primarily off their sideline incomes. Education programs were affected by absenteeism as children increasingly involved themselves in income-generating projects. Teachers frequently obtained their main source of income from tutorials after classes. Physicians resorted to their private sideline practice as the demand for health care grew and doctors found their official incomes below subsistence levels. The extent of urban women's involvement in income-generating activities reached unprecedented proportions. In short, few areas of life in Tanzania were untouched by these informal strategies.

From the mid 1970s through the 1980s Tanzania experienced a shift in the direction of resource flows and of dependencies at two different levels: in individual households and in society's relations with the state. The economic crisis meant that the reliance of household members on wage incomes in the formal sector was replaced by a reliance on the informal income-generating activities of women, children, and the elderly. Former financial obligations of men to women, parents to children, and adult children to their parents were in the process of being reversed because informal projects had generally become more economically rewarding than were wage earnings in the 1980s. For example, because most wage earners were men, the burden frequently fell on women in the household to become the main breadwinners through their various income-generating activities. In creating these reverse dependencies, the new direction of resource flows gave women and even children a greater amount of freedom and autonomy within the household than in the past as a consequence of their economic leverage.

During the crisis of the 1980s, the state's increasing inability to provide basic social and public services, to ensure livable incomes for the employed, and to offer viable police protection, for example, had made it necessary for local organizations and individual initiatives to fill some of these voids. In fact, the resiliency of society and its ability to reproduce itself with considerable autonomy from the state is one of the reasons the entire fabric of society did not fall apart during years of unprecedented hardship, to the amazement of many Tanzanians. One airline pilot I spoke with observed: "Any other country would have had riots if they had gone through what we have gone through in the past years."[5] As a consequence, urban dwellers were relatively unaffected by state policies that had an impact on their formal salaries; hence there was virtually no visible opposition to the austerity measures that accompanied structured adjustment. The blow of receiving a small pay raise was somewhat softened by the fact that more than 90 percent of household income was coming from informal businesses, primarily operated by women, children, and the elderly. By providing alternatives to the state's diminishing resource base, these strategies diverted demands that otherwise might have overwhelmed the state, possibly causing an even more serious legitimacy crisis. In the end, little was demanded of a state that had placed itself at the center of the nation's development agenda and established itself as the guarantor of society's welfare.

However, the state did encounter resistance to policies that threatened people's means of obtaining a subsistence through the informal economy. These included issues of how to define productive work; what kinds of businesses should be licensed; levels of taxation; where microentrepreneurs could carry out their business; whether teachers could teach tutorials; whether doctors could legally practice private medicine; the sale of food crops on parallel markets; and moonlighting.

NONCOMPLIANCE AND INSTITUTIONAL CHANGE

People's nonengagement strategies frequently brought them into conflict with government regulations and party edicts, in much the same way that James C. Scott has depicted "everyday forms of resistance" in his books *Weapons of the Weak* (1985) and *Domination and the Arts of Resistance* (1990). Scott shows how such quiet strategies of noncompliance defy popular notions of resistance, which generally emphasize purposeful collective action and organization. Scott argues that the traditional scholarly focus on riots, revolutions, strikes, and other overt manifestations of resistance captures only a small fraction of the whole spectrum of resistance, which ranges from small, individual acts of resistance in response to immediate problems to highly organized movements with clear ideological goals, sustained over a long period of time. The minibus protest in the vignette was not highly organized, nor was it premeditated in the sense that the actors had identified a broad, common goal they were pursuing. Yet all the *daladala* passengers, fully cognizant of the illegality of their action, responded out of their own interest in getting to work in a situation in which there was no other means of transport.

In some instances the state responded to this kind of opposition by legalizing various activities—privatizing minibuses and loosening controls on internal trade, for example. In other cases the state merely turned a blind eye to practices it was not prepared to condone because to do so would have involved a more sweeping change in the state's ideological orientation.

The reforms began in 1982, when the government reintroduced local governments and cooperatives with the intent of shifting control of marketing and local administration away from central government. In the 1980s the government also effectively dropped its *ujamaa* villagization policy in rural areas and abandoned its campaigns to resettle unemployed or self-employed city dwellers in the countryside. Around the mid-1980s party members and civil servants engaging in sideline income-generating projects became less fearful of being "found out" and of facing possible recrimination. Still, not until 1991 was the Leadership Code of the Arusha Declaration repealed in what was known as the Zanzibar Declaration. This declaration allowed employees to engage in second incomes without fear of losing their jobs or job-related benefits. It also represented the beginning of ideological concessions and a backing away from the socialist legacy of the country's first president, Julius Nyerere.

In the late 1980s, economic liberalization was followed by political liberalization, as the hegemony of the ruling party began to unravel. Parliamentary debates, for example, became livelier and more open as representatives began to freely discuss issues that once would have led to a quick demise of their political career. Around the end of the 1980s the press began to experience greater freedoms, although it still faced harassment, and by 1992 the country had officially embraced multiparty politics.

This study builds on the work of Margaret Levi and James C. Scott to argue that noncompliance can be seen an act of resistance and the basis for institutional change, which occurs through the process of developing alternative structures and institutions that eventually may come to replace many of the most problematic state rules. Levi (1990) outlines one of the most useful ways of explaining this kind of institutional change in her work on contingent consent. She argues that the most effective form of compliance is informal internalized rules, including moral principles, but more frequently, the "norm of fairness." The norm of fairness generates contingent consent, which means that people comply with an institutional arrangement they deem fair and that is collectively informed and adhered to. Compliance is contingent on approval of the social bargain and the compliance of those providing the service, such as the provision of promised benefits by institutional managers. Compliance is also predicated on the assurance that others are holding up their end of the bargain.

Noncompliance can be used as a bargaining tool to change an institution. This happens when a group has increased resources at its disposal that permit it to reject the current institutional arrangement, when the dominant institution loses resources, when a change in consciousness occurs, when people believe that others are failing to comply, or when those wielding institutional power break their end of the social bargain. According to Levi, noncompliance thus results from an assessment of the effectiveness of a norm of fairness, of the probability of achieving a desired outcome, and of whether others are also complying. Even the most oppressive institutional framework, Levi argues, contains a contractual element, so that those not receiving their end of a bad bargain may resort to noncompliance, thus forcing the institutional leaders to resort to costly enforcement, resulting either in a weakening of the institution or its transformation through revolution or reform (Levi 1990, 413). However, as Scott has argued, collective action by the relatively weak is extremely difficult because they lack the resources, organizational skills, and mechanisms through which to organize. Therefore, noncompliance often becomes the preferred and initial form of resistance, which reduces the bargaining power of those in control of the institution they are seeking to influence.

This framework for explaining institutional change is useful in explaining the dynamics described in this study. Popular noncompliance with the dominant economic institutions regarding micro- and small-scale enterprises and the pursuit of sideline incomes eventually led to the state's ignoring various activities it was not prepared to condone openly, to legalizing, to liberalizing, or even to recognizing economic activities it had previously considered illegal or undesirable.

In his 1981 book *Markets and States in Tropical Africa,* Robert Bates described African state leaders' practice of pursuing economic irrationalities to secure political objectives. My study looks at the limits of these practices. I argue that by the mid-1980s these economic irrationalities were being challenged by popular noncompliance and resistance to economic policy. The state's legitimacy had been severely undermined by the authorities' own economic and political strategies, while declining state resources made them increasingly untenable. What Bates's theory does not help explain is why the Tanzanian state began to change its economic and political orientation in the mid-1980s. By the early 1980s the government was no longer able to appease the urban dwellers through food subsidies because unofficial price hiking, known as *ulanguzi,* had kept food prices high and because government control of internal and external markets had resulted in hoarding and scarcities of commodities. Moreover, life for the average urban dweller had become so difficult by the 1980s that rural agricultural production began to look increasingly attractive by comparison, while notions of urban bias more accurately described an earlier period in Tanzania's economic history.

Scott's pathbreaking work on noncompliance helps explain the significance of the informal economy within the broader picture of state-society relations. The informal economy as a form of noncompliance falls under Scott's array of "weapons of the weak"—foot dragging, dissimulation, false compliance, pilfering, feigned ignorance, arson, sabotage, slander, and tax evasion. Scott's focus on these forms of noncompliance makes it possible to link several important themes in explaining changes in state-society relations. First, it allows for agency—that is, the capacity to act—in a context in which people are resisting a perceived injustice while they are acting in order to fulfill immediate material needs. By focusing on quiet, everyday forms of resistance, Scott gives agency to the so-called invisible majorities who do not wield the weapons or have the organizational capability of the elites, intelligentsia, and middle classes, who can more easily afford the risks of open confrontation. At the same time, Scott shows how the nature of the resistance is conditioned in part by the parameters of resistance set by the institutions of repression.

My study is limited to quiet strategies of resistance in the form of economic noncompliance; it does not deal with actions that involve active sabotage, banditry, arson, and other forms of resistance that Scott lumps together, perhaps too easily. As mentioned earlier, tax evasion, trading in parallel markets where trade is highly regulated, and carrying out business in unauthorized areas are tactics of noncompliance vis-à-vis the state. But noncompliance can also include more subtle forms of gossip, slander, the pretense of compliance and ignorance, and resistance through music, art, dance, theater, and ritual. Such resistance can serve to foster autonomous norms and values, creating a culture of noncompliance and creating an alternative ideological vision among nondominant actors.

The evasion of official channels for the conduct of business, politics, and the law is the least active form of resistance but potentially can have as much effect as any overt display of opposition. The larger the number of people who refuse to comply, the less risk there is for others who do not comply and the greater the incentive to join their ranks. Noncompliance is less threatening to the powers that be because it avoids direct confrontation and thus does not require a direct response (Scott 1985, 29).

Even though Scott accurately warns against overromanticizing every-day forms of resistance, I think the greater danger has been the tendency of social scientists to ignore them completely.[6] What remains puzzling is why these quiet forms of resistance have received so little attention within the research agendas of political scientists when the little documentation there is clearly suggests that they are an important form of opposition and a significant force for change. Certainly, they pose more methodological challenges to the researcher than do strikes, riots, or demonstrations, which are more likely to be photographed or filmed, written about in the press, and recorded in primary historical sources. It is easier to find out in the case of an overt protest action who was involved, what occurred, where it happened, and how many were involved in the action, even if with great difficulty. Nevertheless, the lack of data is not the main reason why non-compliance has been generally overlooked. I believe it has to do with a more fundamental problem with the way in which politics and power relations are perceived as nonreciprocal and asymmetrical.

I contend that focusing specifically on issues of noncompliance allows us to look both more broadly and more closely at the interactions between the dominant and nondominant forces in a way that permits greater agency to those who act within larger constraints. This focus is especially important in the context of the urban poor in Tanzania, who are operating within economic and political circumstances fraught with limitations. Focusing on noncompliance permits a more multidimensional look at the dynamics between dominant and nondominant forces. It allows for a range of tactics that go beyond the Marxist framework of oppression and resistance or the pluralistic notion of citizens' pressing demands through collective and individual action whereupon the government responds like an independent arbiter, sifting through the competing demands, weighing them against each other (Dahl 1971).

The general neglect or even outright dismissal of these activities as forms of resistance has to do with a narrow perception of politics and a preoccupation with formal political structures (parties, governments) and processes (elections). Two noted anthropologists, Jean and John Comaroff (1987, 192), have even questioned whether Western social scientists, in both the Weberian and Marxist traditions, had been looking for expressions of collective consciousness (resistance) in the wrong places; that is, in formal institutions rather than in the texture of the everyday.

Similarly, many economists and others disregard the broader social circumstances within which informal economic activities take place. They focus on the unregulated character of the informal economy—on tax evasion and smuggling, for example—but they frequently ignore its broader political, economic, social, and historical implications, tending to regard such activities simply as criminal behavior (Bawly 1982; Gutmann 1977; Ray 1975). But as Migdal (1988, 31) suggests, when significant numbers of people refuse to comply with key regulatory measures established by the state, noncompliance can no longer be considered an aberration or an isolated case of deviant criminal behavior. Today, in many countries, societal noncompliance is a struggle over whether the state has the right to make the rules over and above societal actors. Widespread noncompliance and a burgeoning informal economy are indicative of this disjuncture in society-state relations over who makes the rules of the game and what they should be.

DISENGAGEMENT, EXIT, AND WITHDRAWAL FROM THE STATE

Disengagement, exit, and withdrawal from the state are prominent themes in recent writing on African politics. In the earliest of such discussions, Goran Hyden, using Tanzania as a case study, argued that the principal constraint on the development of African economies was the African rulers' inability "to make the peasants effectively dependent on their policy measures"; that is, the peasantry remained "uncaptured" by the state, withdrawing into an "economy of affection" (1980, 33). Others later described the informal economy as part of the process of disengagement on par with sectarian religious cults, exile, criminal networks, witchcraft and sorcery, fundamentalist social movements, smuggling, independent churches, millenarian movements—all of which were said to have arisen in the context of diminishing opportunities and increasing economic insecurity. Representing "counter-symbolic systems of authority," as René Lemarchand refers to them, these phenomena of disengagement from the state also express themselves culturally in cynicism, satire, and ridicule of the state and even of the everyday struggle to survive (Azarya and Chazan 1987; Hyden 1980, 1983; Lemarchand 1992).

In a similar vein, Jean-François Bayart has argued that the constant pressure of social groups has undermined and reduced the scope of state power and contributed heavily to its economic failure. These pressures included tactics of "revolts, refusal to grow certain crops, declining productivity, strikes, abstention from elections, migrations, religious revivals and even the creation of theocratic communities outside state control, smuggling, the flourishing of informal exchange, distribution of information outside the official media, satirical, religious messianic or revolutionary attacks on the legitimacy of the state, and sabotage of the instruments of political control" (Bayart 1986, 113).

Although I share many of the concerns of Scott and also of those who comment on problems of disengagement and withdrawal in the African context, I depart from the emphases of these analyses of societal responses in a number of ways. I would argue that the informal economy represents more than simply evasion of the state. It has involved the creation of new resources, both economic and institutional. Survival strategies have also created economic resources that have enabled people to sustain themselves as the state has failed to provide social and public services, to maintain security, and to ensure adequate formal wages. These strategies have deflected demands on the state, to which the state was in no position to respond. At times they provided a safety valve for the state, allowing people to find ways to survive without further undermining the legitimacy of the state. This is a functional rather than a dysfunctional role of the informal economy, which does not necessarily undermine the state in the way that some purport.

Another important contribution to the discussion of societal withdrawal from the state has come from those who suggest that kinship groups compete with the state for legitimacy. Peter Ekeh (1975), for example, argued that there are two public realms. The "primordial public realm," made up of kinship groups, is considered moral and legitimate. The state constitutes the second "civil public realm"; it lacks legitimacy and is characterized by corruption. Hyden echoes this in arguing that the state is corroded by a society that values family and other "primordial" ties over civic obligations. Ultimately the "economy of affection" drains the state of resources through communal ties and leads to corruption, nepotism, tribalism, and the primacy of narrow parochial interests (1983, 17).

Certainly, family and kin are important to the cohesiveness of society in Africa, and African sociability is a key feature of the African social landscape. Nevertheless, there are several difficulties in seeing the conflict as one between kin and the state. First, patronage, nepotism, and corruption pervade African politics, but African governments are not unique in this respect. In most countries, when rent seeking and the illegal diversion of resources from the state occurs, these resources usually find their way to kin and friends. African societies are not structurally and inevitably constrained by ties of affection, even though, as Hyden argues, smallholder production provides exceptional opportunities for evasion of the state and reliance on kin. African societies are constrained, however, by political systems and weak institutions that are not conducive to good governance.

Second, for most wage laborers or self-employed people, their occupations do not present opportunities for siphoning off resources or funds from the state; nor do most have relatives in such positions who could, through corruption, obtain resources to divert to family members. Such distinctions suggest the importance of being clear about which classes and which individuals benefits from patronage, especially at the local level.

Third, the emphasis on the "primordial" realm as the key source of all immorality in the state bureaucracy perpetuates a state-centric view of state-society relations. The basic disjuncture between societal and state visions of justice means that people have evaded the state because its policies have undermined their interests or because they have found state policies repressive and reprehensible. When resources are scarce and relying on people one trusts is paramount, it is only natural that these are the people one turns to first.

Finally, and most important for this study, the "kinship-first" argument ignores the fact that people have sought communitarian solutions that draw on familial ties to deal with their problems in ways that have not undermined the state. They have relied on their own resources and built their own institutions where the state has failed to meet their needs. Rather than seeing these ties simply as a constraint, it would be useful also to consider how they facilitate not only survival strategies but also in the accumulation of capital, and investment and savings, in Africa and elsewhere.

NEW INSTITUTIONAL RESOURCES

Noncompliance in Tanzania not only constituted a form of resistance, it also involved the creation of new resources. These new resources are visible at every level in virtually every sector of society, involving the creation of formal and informal associations and the expansion of primarily informal but also formal business enterprises.

The basic provision of security in both urban and rural areas has changed: today it is carried out at the local level through *sungusungu*, or local defense teams. The authorities officially recognized them in the late 1980s, although no official laws were changed to accommodate them. After the *sungusungu* were recognized, violent robberies dropped from 655 to 382 between 1989 and 1990 alone.[7]

Hometown development associations became visible in the late 1980s as urban dwellers sought to provide assistance to the rural towns from which they originated. They used these associations to build schools, orphanages, libraries, roads, and clinics; to establish projects to conserve the environment; to provide solar electricity and water; to disburse soft loans to women's groups engaged in business; and to raise funds for flood relief and other such causes.[8] These new associations resemble the early, ethnically based welfare and burial societies that formed in Dar es Salaam in the early 1900s to help new migrants adjust to city life, except that their focus today is to assist people in their rural towns and villages.

The decline in formal medical services in the 1970s and 1980s resulted in a narrowing of options for medical care. At the same time, it caused greater reliance on traditional medical practitioners and midwives, who were able to reconstitute themselves in the Tanzania Traditional Healers Association, which had dissolved in 1980. Local healers reported a significant expansion in the numbers of patients in the 1980s in interviews I conducted in Dar es Salaam during my field research.[9] In urban areas in 1988, only 40 percent of women gave birth in hospitals; the majority relied on local midwives.[10]

Parents lobbied to expand educational opportunities for their children and finally won the right for local community groups to form private secondary schools in the late 1970s. By 1988 the number of private schools equaled the number of government schools. Some areas, like Kilimanjaro Region, were especially aggressive in organizing and building new private schools (Hyden 1989, 14). Unofficial, extralegal school-organizing committees made up of local community residents led by local prominent individuals took on the responsibility for raising the funds and building the schools (Samoff 1989, 8).

Central to this book is the heightened involvement in income-generating activities and in urban farming, especially by workers, women, children, and the elderly. For women it has meant increased demands on their time, but at the same time it has given them greater decision-making leverage within the household. Informal savings groups of women have emerged alongside this informal economy.

This study also indicates that the informal economy has provided opportunities for capital accumulation and class formation independent of the state, as Janet MacGaffey (1987) has shown in the case of Zaire. In Tanzania, women in particular have taken advantage of these new opportunities most aggressively, and one now finds for the first time a small but growing number of women who have been able to move from small, informal businesses into larger, formal enterprises.

These are just a few examples of how the informal economy and informal associations have increasingly assumed greater importance in the lives of urban dwellers. The informal economy also operates within a set of institutions, norms, and rules that often represent alternatives to those advanced by the state. For example, one's own survival is seen as inseparable from that of one's community. Therefore, survival strategies are collective efforts rather than individual ones. They involve reciprocity and mutuality, both the reliance on and support of kin and friends in times of hardship. Moreover, the egalitarian ethic dictates that everyone is entitled to a subsistence. This is, in essence, a claim of redistributive justice, in which those with the means are obligated to assist the less advantaged.

Norms associated with small, local communities that are often described in terms of James Scott's "moral economy" are extended in the urban setting to people with whom they are not related through kinship, ethnicity, or other primary affiliation. Primary associations are maintained, but new ties are also created. Sometimes fictive kinship ties (that is, the extension of kinship obligations to nonkin) are established.

There is also a flexibility or a willingness to bend the rules in favor of those who are not as well situated, even if they are not kin. Welders, tailors, carpenters, market sellers, and medicine men or women, for example, prefer to charge according to the means of the customer rather than fixing one price for their goods or services. Under difficult economic circumstances, trust is of paramount importance, but this trust in the urban context does not necessarily involve one's kin, as it might in rural areas. In fact, as my study shows, these ties have been built across ethnic lines and involve people who work together (who might form savings clubs), or neighbors who share cooking and childcare responsibilities, or market sellers who watch each others' stalls. Mechanisms of accountability are pursued vigorously even in the smallest, most informal associations.

Other norms suggest that the profit motive is tempered by other considerations. A mother may dip into her business savings to pay for the medical treatment of a child. Business owners may hire extended-family members out of welfare considerations rather than considerations of economic efficiency. Entrepreneurs consciously look for ways to lessen market competitiveness by cooperating, networking, and seeking new markets as well as new commodities to produce and sell.

All of these norms represent potential bases for institutional reform that would be more in line with the way in which society values self-reliance, redistributive justice, and communitarianism. This study suggests that what exists in Tanzania is a conflict between at least two existing types of institutions, one formal and the other basically informal. It is a conflict between different, coexisting sets of rules that are competing to assert themselves, with the consequence that, in many instances, the informal ones have prevailed even where the state has failed to concede openly that its rules no longer hold sway.

PERSPECTIVES ON POWER AND THE INFORMAL ECONOMY

The most common theoretical approaches to power relations (those of Thomas Hobbes, Max Weber, Robert Dahl, and Steven Lukes) tend to see power as absolute and asymmetrical, where one actor prevails over another in a zero-sum fashion. To understand how strategies of noncompliance can bring about political changes, it is necessary to look beyond conventional conceptions of power and to develop more reciprocal understandings of power. It is necessary to redefine political participation as a process of decision making in which negotiations take place, conflicts are worked through, and accommodations are made. These distributions of resources and power are not only located within particular places or events like elections, coups, or revolutions; they are part of a process of negotiation that constantly permeates social relations at many different levels in different contexts.

The interaction of power relations is evident when one considers that even the most invincible claimants to power depend on others to make them powerful (Arendt 1986, 62). For example, power vested in the state is ultimately fleeting if members of society, subjugated through coercion, quietly and inconspicuously refuse to comply with state regulations. A more fluid concept of power and politics is thus necessary to capture the full range of power relations, granting the possibility for agency and power to both dominant and nondominant actors.

Anthony Giddens (1984) argues, for example, that the autonomy of nondominant forces can influence the dominant forces in a two-way arrangement. In fact, built into structures of domination are structures that can erode that same domination. Thus autonomy can be exercised by a nondominant actor in ways that affect the manner in which a dominant actor exercises power. If power involves the human capacity to act and to change a set of circumstances, then the assertion of power is not necessarily zero-sum, where a gain for one is a loss for another. A gain in institutional resources within society, therefore, does not necessarily mean a loss for state power. It may, in fact, enhance state strength by allowing the state greater legitimacy.

Power is not inherently conflictual, either. In fact, power can be exercised within a reciprocal relationship based on cooperation and consensus. I would go as far as to argue that power is most suspect and vulnerable at the moment of coercion. Massive noncompliance indicates that confidence and legitimacy have already diminished considerably, and coercion in this context implies an even greater loss of power at a greater cost and risk for the actor. Coercion in a situation where noncompliance has not occurred implies an anticipation of resistance. In either instance, the capacity to influence through consensus or persuasion has been curtailed through noncompliance or the threat of noncompliance; therefore power, or the capacity to act, has been diminished.

Levi makes this same point in *Of Rule and Revenue* (1988), arguing that if an institution relies simply on coercion to implement policies, the cost of enforcement cannot be sustained, and other means of compliance will eventually have to be sought. Similarly, Wunsch and Olowu argue in the African context that sustained development cannot emerge in a context of coercion, because people can find many ways to resist such force (1991, 10).

A related premise of my study is the recognition that politics in formal arenas represents only a small part of the negotiations, accommodations, and redistribution of resources and power within society. Informal organizations and networks can be equally important to the conduct of politics in many contexts. A study of nonformal institutions and arrangements can help clarify how widespread acts of noncompliance can affect formal political structures. Such a focus makes it possible to explain the role of societal pressures on policy change where no clearly visible and overt resistance has challenged the status quo, although ultimately I show how the changes were institutionalized through visible formal mechanisms, such as parliamentary action.

THE INFORMAL ECONOMY AND THE STATE

Although there are many important ways in which Tanzanian society evaded and resisted state regulations and created alternative structures, I have chosen to focus on the informal economy because it brings into sharp relief some of the most antagonistic conflicts between state and society. The fact that these differences center around one of the most basic human activities—pursuing a livelihood—makes them all the more significant.

Given the considerable interconnectedness of the informal economy and the state and given the divisions within the informal economy, some argue that dichotomies like the informal economy/state duality obscure the complex, overlapping fluid "structures, forces, alliances, traditions and ideologies" that can more appropriately explain African economic and political realities (Bangura and Gibbon 1992). Others have suggested focusing on the symbiotic nature of the informal and formal economies as an alternative to seeing informal economies as being defined by the state and existing only as reactions to failures of the state and the formal markets (Roitman 1990). Larissa Lomnitz has shown how informality is intrinsic to formality and is a mechanism for adapting to shortcomings in modern, heavily bureaucratic and regulated states. Informal modes of exchange thrive in the "interstices of the formal system," as she puts it (1988, 43). Michael Schatzberg gets to the heart of the matter when he asks the pointed question: "Where does state end and civil society begin?" (1988, 4). Central to this study is an attempt to grapple with these ambiguous interrelationships. But, at the same time, the informal economy—state relationship is preserved for the purposes of outlining the contours of rules and institutions that are being contested in the context of political and economic reform. This is by no means an attempt to reify these notions in the abstract. In trying to make sense of the daily struggle to survive, I use the formal-informal economy, state-society, and legal-illegal templates to capture many of the key dimensions of people's own realities as they experience and interpret them.

This study focuses on the relationship between the informal economy and the state, because this is one way of zeroing in on the shifting boundaries of government control and a way of analyzing the limits of compliance with state regulation and the extent of state legitimacy over time. For the analytic purpose of showing how people's economic strategies have been at odds with state policy, I draw sharper-than-necessary lines between the informal economy and the state. Lomnitz, who argues for the inseparability of informal and formal systems, recognizes the simultaneous dissonance between competing economic logics. "Informal activities are socially embedded transactions that obey a symbolic-cultural logic that differs from (and often clashes with) economic rationality or the formal ideology of the state. The rules of sociability that govern informal exchange vary from culture to culture" (1988, 43). Recognizing these conflicting economic visions should not in any way detract from the complex connections and interrelations that often blur the boundaries between the state and the informal economy or between the formal and informal economies.

The main reason why the state–informal economy distinction is preserved in this study is that such a distinction exists in people's minds and language in culturally defined frameworks. I found in my study of Dar es Salaam that people were extremely clear about when their livelihood was being threatened by a particular government policy or agent. But such distinctions are also evident in more benign, less conflictual contexts. One example from the coastal region near Mtwara illustrates this distinction well. In the recent past, if a woman was delivering a child, usually the mother's relatives provided hot water, a razor, a bed or mat, and a plastic sheet to the local midwife. After the delivery the midwife would be given beer to drink and, later, gifts and money. In a particular village, several midwives had gone for a one-week training course at a government district hospital to improve their knowledge of hygiene. After the midwives completed this short course, the women no longer provided them with the equipment they needed for the delivery, nor with any of the usual gifts and money. In one week these midwives had been moved conceptually to another category, were thereafter associated with the government (*kiserikali*), and were said to have adopted modern methods. Reciprocal obligations of gift giving were no longer required, and the midwives were no longer seen as community members, but rather as part of a "formal" institution tied to the government (M.-L. Swantz 1994, 101–3).

The distinction the Mtwara villagers made with respect to the midwives is typical of popular, everyday conceptualizations of state-society relations. When seen through the lens of conflicts between microentrepreneurs and the state over the right to subsist, the lines between state and society become even more sharply defined.

THE INFORMAL ECONOMY IN COMPARATIVE PERSPECTIVE

In spite of much agreement on the importance of the sector, *informal economy* remains one of the most elusive terms in social science. It is frequently also known as the black market, the informal sector, the second economy, the parallel economy, the underground economy, and the hidden sector. In Africa it is referred to by even more terms, including *magendo* in East Africa, *l'économie de débrouillardiese* or *système D* in Zaire, *kalabule* in Ghana, and *as-suq al-aswad* to Arabic speakers. Given the many ways in which the informal economy is conceptualized, it is not surprising that there is little agreement on its definition. Scholars of the informal economy have spent inordinate amounts of time and paper in defense of their particular definitions. It would, however, seem that the words and meanings one chooses to describe the informal economy should correspond to the problem with which one is concerned. For the purposes of this study, the informal economy is defined by the state parameters of legality, the borders of which have been shaped by the social, political, economic, and legal context within which they are found. What varies, however, are the different conditions that give rise to such activities, which in turn determine the forms these activities take.

Our understanding of the informal economy today represents a considerable advance from the early 1970s, when Keith Hart (1973) and an International Labour Organisation (ILO) study of Kenya (1972) first popularized the term *informal sector*. The ILO report characterized the informal sector by its ease of entry, reliance on indigenous resources, family ownership of enterprises, small scale of operation, labor-intensive and adapted technology, skills acquired outside the formal school system, and unregulated and competitive markets. The report contrasts this sector with the formal sector, which has "difficult entry; frequent reliance on overseas resources; corporate ownership; large scale of operation; capital intensive and often imported technology; formally acquired skills, often expatriate and protected markets (through tariffs, quotas and trade licenses)" (1972, 6). The dualism of the ILO report came under sharp criticism by theorists like Ray Bromley (1978), Chris Gerry (1977), Colin Leys (1973), T. G. McGee (1978), and Caroline Moser (1978). Their overriding criticism was that it is not possible to draw hard and fast lines to demarcate the two sectors. Case studies showed the relationship between the two sectors to be far more fluid than implied by the dualist theories. They pointed, for example, to the difficulty of entering the informal sector, just as one might find it difficult to enter the formal sector.

Today it is widely recognized that the informal economy is an integral part of modern economies. It is not an atavistic legacy of past centuries, nor simply a reflection of the so-called backwardness of developing economies; that is, it is not restricted to the sweatshops of nineteenth-century London or to the poor urban dwellers of Bogotá. The informal economy does not exist simply to absorb urban unemployment or to serve as a source of income for poor migrants, as earlier studies indicated. It can be as much a source of additional income for well-paid consultants who "neglect" to report their total income as it can supplement wages for low-income workers who moonlight.

In a city like New York a large portion of the construction, apparel, electronic, and furniture industries are carried out on an informal basis (Sassen-Koob 1989, 60). It is well known that people working in the U.S. service industries, like automobile repair, hairstyling, childcare, and moving, frequently evade taxation either partially or completely. Likewise, a 1983 survey in Denmark found that one-fifth of Danes sought informal painters and repair people, childcare workers, gardeners, cleaners, and hairdressers on a regular basis (Mogensen 1988, 6). In fact, Sweden, Denmark, Belgium, and Italy were reported to have the highest levels of informal activity in Europe (Frey and Weck-Hanneman 1984).

Approximately 11 percent of all households' total income in Russia came from informal sources. Similarly, in Georgia (of the former Soviet Union), incomes from the informal economy surpassed official wages. In Poland informal enterprises accounted for 32 percent of the money income in 1983. In Hungary three-quarters of the population obtained supplementary income from the second economy (Sampson 1987, 126). As in many parts of Africa, the spread of the informal economy in Eastern Europe over the past two decades has been attributed to persistent and growing shortages of desired goods and services, rising consumer aspirations, lack of fear of state repression under the communist regimes, coupled with even greater lack of confidence in state institutions, which had proven to be incapable of meeting basic needs for housing, goods, and services (Sampson 1987, 134). The uncertainties brought about by regime change in the former Soviet Union and Eastern Europe in the late 1980s suggest even greater reliance on the informal economy.

In many Latin American countries the growth of the informal economy has been attributed to economic crisis and foreign debt, which increased their vulnerability to foreign penetration and resulted in the weakening of organized labor and an increase of the informal sector. Many companies faced heightened difficulties in trying to remain competitive, forcing them to resort to the increased use of subcontracting to informal workshops or to homes (Safa 1987).

Thus the informal economy is clearly an international phenomenon. What form it takes and the various reasons people engage in these activities vary from country to country. Evidence, however, indicates that the informal economy is growing faster than the formal economy in many parts of the world as a consequence of the process of worldwide economic restructuring that followed the economic crisis of the 1970s and early 1980s (Castells and Portes 1989b, 32).

Differences over definition may suggest deeper disagreements over how the informal economy is to be regarded, however. For example, Manuel Castells and Alejandro Portes (1989a, 1989b) have identified some of the main factors giving rise to the informal economy. In general, according to the authors, informalization has been a consequence of economic restructuring that aimed to cope with the structural crisis of the 1970s. More specifically, businesses have informalized in response to organized labor, to make up for decreases in profits due to wage-increase demands; to increased state regulation of the economy in the provision of social-welfare benefits and the imposition of health and environmental controls; to the intensification of international competition as labor costs have been diffused and lowered; to the sanctioning of informalization by the state in special economic zones that exempt businesses from abiding by regulations that govern business outside these zones; and to economic crisis and austerity measures promoted by international financial institutions that have made people pursue whatever means they can to earn a living.

In addition, Castells and Portes argue that informalization may be a consequence of the very existence of state monopolies of various institutions, where restrictions are manipulated for private gain. Those in authority can, for example, use their positions to sell exemptions from state-imposed controls (Castells and Portes 1989a, 299). In centrally planned systems where official prices for various commodities have sometimes purposefully been kept low, bureaucrats with access to the distribution system have been able to use their positions to sell commodities at higher prices, especially where shortages are prevalent or have been artificially created.

Castells and Portes's analysis, which has become widely accepted, accurately describes many of the dynamics that have given rise to the informal economy in many parts of the world. Nevertheless, in many respects the debate has become highly ideological, often to the detriment of many of the participants in the informal economy. It has pitted scholars like Hernando de Soto (1989), who see the informal sector as a seedbed of capitalism and the ultimate free market, against those who see it as a strategy of big business to suppress wages and thus retain market competitiveness. Both of these positions obscure some of the most important aspects of this economy, which need to be disaggregated and specified according to locale. The informal economy needs to be looked at in the specific historical, economic, social, and political context within which it has emerged, rather than as an abstraction that exists for the same purposes in all time and place.

In some parts of the world, such as most of Africa, informalization has been not a strategy of large capital but rather a response of workers and their household members to falling real wages as a result of general economic decline. Wages are so low in a country like Tanzania that self-employment, whether full-time or part-time, almost inevitably is a more reliable way of making a living than is holding a job in the formal economy. In many countries in Africa the crisis has resulted in seriously depressed living conditions. The stabilization programs of the 1980s frequently compounded many of the hardships, resulting in inflation induced by devaluation and massive layoffs due to closures of uncompetitive industries. The inability of the state, generally the major source of employment, to provide adequate incomes and employment prompted individuals, groups, and mutual-aid organizations to seek alternative solutions to their worsening economic situations. The decline in real wages, coupled with rising rates of unemployment, led many urban dwellers to seek informal sources of income to supplement their wages or to leave their jobs altogether and go into private business or farming. This growing pattern is evident not only in Tanzania but, as case studies show, throughout contemporary Africa (Azarya and Chazan 1987; Chazan 1983; MacGaffey 1987; C. Newbury 1986; D. Newbury 1986).

Conventional definitions of the informal economy, like that of Castells and Portes, typically fail to distinguish between different kinds of activities that fall under the umbrella of the informal sector in one important respect. They fail to distinguish activities that create new products and provide real services, transport, sales, and trade from those that involve the illegal diversion of resources that belong to the state or to formal companies or from those activities in which people use their official positions to enrich themselves through bribery, for example. Many like Reginald Green (1981) simply define the informal economy as including corruption and patronage—even violence, in the case of Uganda—without at the same time making some clear distinctions between activities that have created new resources and those that involve illegal diversions of state resources and international aid.

The state determines whether various activities are legal and what (such as a license or a tax) is required to make them legal. Since the 1970s the informal economy has been conceptualized in relation to the state. For example, the 1972 ILO report referred to the informal sector as activities that operate outside government regulation and are mostly ignored and often aggressively suppressed by the authorities. John Weeks (1975, 2) and Janet Bujra (1978–1979, 49) distinguished between the private sector, which was recognized, nurtured, and regulated by the state, and the informal sector, which was characterized by its economic insecurity of operation, operating outside the system of benefits and regulations of the government and without access to credit and technology transfer.

Obviously, people operating in the informal economy do not choose to be labeled as informal, and they have many objectives, interests, and rationales in going about their economic activities that have nothing to do with the state. This has been one of the characteristics of the informal sector. But if one accepts that the state draws the lines of legality for economic activities, one can divide the informal economy into at least two forms. Illicit activities have no legal counterpart in the society in question. Depending on the social and political context, illicit activities might include embezzlement, bribery, extraction of rents, kickbacks, and other forms of criminal activity. The informal economy also includes licit or legitimate activities, which do have a legal counterpart in the society in question. For example, selling peanuts without a license in Tanzania is a licit informal activity because one could potentially obtain a license for the same activity. The line between licit and illicit forms of informal economic activity is fine, and there are many gray areas and, most importantly from an empirical standpoint, many connections between various kinds of licit and illicit activities. But it is important, in terms of understanding the potential of the informal economy, to make these distinctions in order to separate those aspects of the economy that undermine the functioning of the economy and the state from those that include productive activities. This study focuses on these licit activities within the informal economy, in order to examine the conditions under which state boundaries expand and contract with respect to the economy and in response to societal pressures.

It is also important to distinguish between the regulation of informal activities that genuinely accomplishes what it is intended to do and the kind of regulation that simply places unnecessary burdens on the poor, who are forced to pay bribes to government officials in charge of issuing licenses and permits. If the regulation genuinely ensures safety and cleanliness, protects children from undue exploitation, and serves to increase revenue in order to enhance the provision of social services and infrastructural supports, it should be condoned and promoted. But if it simply serves as a mechanism for bureaucratic officials to extract bribes from those applying for business licenses and other registration requirements, it undermines the very purpose it was intended to serve and acts as a deterrent to those who would otherwise try to obtain legal authorization for their enterprises. Moreover, it undermines the legitimacy of the state for those who are most affected by these government institutions; that is, the poorest members of society. In countries like Peru, where the informal economy makes up approximately 45 percent of the labor force and creates 38 percent of the GDP (gross domestic product), opening up a "legal" business is a virtual impossibility without going through endless red tape and without payment of bribes in order to become registered (de Soto 1989). Although the Peruvian case is one of the best documented, similar situations exist in other parts of Latin America, Africa, and Asia. My study in Dar es Salaam also bears this out.

The argument that labor is disadvantaged and threatened by the growth of the informal economy also needs to be looked at in its long-term and short-term contexts. In Tanzania it is not foreign capital that has caused the informalization of labor but, rather, general economic decline. Ideally, it would be desirable if wages surpassed the cost of living for workers and their families. In the short run, given the precariousness of the formal sector and, in particular, the state's lack of resources and industry's weakness, the prospects that the formal economy will provide adequate wage increases appear relatively dim. But even more problematic is the continued policy emphasis on the formal sector and the greater support given to formal industries relative to the informal sector. This creates serious distortions in a country like Tanzania, where the balance sheet is quite simple. To support labor in Tanzania at this time in essence would involve creating an economic environment more conducive to small-scale and microbusinesses.

There are other, straightforward reasons to prioritize the informal sector. Among them are the fact that micro- and small-scale entrepreneurs grew at a time when much of the rest of the economy was on a downward spiral. According to a 1989 survey of the Bureau of Statistics, the number of microenterprises tripled from the mid-1980s to 1989. A 1989 World Bank survey compared the 1986 output of small and large firms with 1985 data and found that most larger firms contracted, while 60 percent of the small and medium-sized firms expanded in this short period (Bagachwa 1991, 69). Small businesses have been a major source of employment where the formal economy has been laying off workers and imposing freezes on hiring. Similarly, a 1990 World Bank survey found that microenterprises doubled their employment levels between 1984 and 1990 (Bagachwa 1991). Because informal activities tend to be labor intensive, employment takes place at relatively low capital cost (International Labour Organisation 1992, 5).

The informal economy has provided opportunities for sectors of society, like urban women, youth, and the elderly, who have limited opportunities for formal employment. In fact, informal incomes represent the major source of nonagricultural incomes. My survey showed that in 1988 nine-tenths of the urban household income was obtained from informal income-generating projects and that one-tenth came from formal wages. Thus the informal economy provides people with incomes that come much closer to meeting their needs than do formal wages. The fastest-growing wages are in the informal economy.

Small-scale and microentrepreneurs rely primarily on local inputs, unlike formal industry, which is heavily dependent on foreign exchange and the importation of inputs. Small-scale entrepreneurs serve primarily local markets, although their exports of sea products, spices, charcoal, and other such items have become an important source of foreign exchange in recent years. Small-scale entrepreneurs provide local consumers with affordable products, often tailored to meet individuals' specifications.

In terms of productivity, small-scale producers have proven to be at least five times more effective than their large-scale counterparts in terms of output measured per unit of investment (Kim 1988, 96). Although individual accounts may be small in scale, when the many accounts are aggregated they represent substantial amounts of internal investment and saving.

Because of the structure of micro- and small-scale enterprises, capital and resources do not remain in the hands of a few but are more widely distributed among a larger segment of the population, whereas large-scale enterprises tend to concentrate capital in the hands of the state or a few capitalists.

Carpenters, tailors, mechanics, blacksmiths, hairstylists, and others provide training on an apprenticeship basis, adding to the country's pool of skilled and semiskilled workers. Commonly, once an apprentice has mastered a skill, he or she may opt to start his or her own business and create employment for others.

In spite of all these realities, however, the formal, large-scale industrial sector continues to claim by far the majority of government supports, even though it is unlikely that the sector can be shored up in the near future to increase productivity to the point that wages can be raised to meet workers' needs. It is incomprehensible that in this context of deindustrialization, emphasis continues to be placed on large-scale industry, when in fact it is the micro- and small-scale producers who are sustaining the urban population. These entrepreneurs continue to operate with virtually no supports and in a hostile regulative environment.

Arguments that informal activities are simply survival strategies (such as Stein 1992, 93) tend to see large-scale industry as a goal in itself. They run the danger of overlooking the reality of millions of low-income people, including, perhaps ironically, industrial workers who themselves depend almost entirely on sideline micro- and small-scale enterprises (manufacturing, trade, and service enterprises) for their livelihood. Most will never become large-scale industrialists, nor can they hope to. But with the necessary skills, inputs, and capital, they can make a living for themselves and their families, which is better than the alternative.

There is also a tendency to underestimate the agency of individuals operating within the informal sector. When one considers the enormous constraints this sector faces, one is constantly reminded of Marx's dictum that people make history but not in conditions of their own choosing. Naturally, there are limitations to the openness of entry into various occupations. Markets in this informal sector are often constricted. The capital is not always available to keep businesses afloat, and people move from one business to the next when one fails. These are the realities of working in the informal sector. But it is important, at the same time, to bear in mind that people have drawn on their own resources and have come up with creative, flexible, and viable solutions to the problem of survival under extreme duress. This in itself should command the respect of academics and policy makers. Those concerned with the policy implications of a study of the real economy need to begin with the actual economic activities of people and not an idealized version of what the formal economy ought to look like. Arguing that people just take what they can get in the informal economy and that they operate simply out of necessity ignores how people have actively involved themselves in this parallel economy to improve their situation. It ignores the dynamic decision-making processes and institution building they have had to engage in within the informal economy.

Ultimately, participation in the informal economy pertains to questions of governance. When large numbers of people participate in economic activities that defy regulation, they may be asserting their power and their notion of what the rules that govern them should be. They may be asserting a different vision of economic justice and of how resources should be redistributed. Or they may be expressing their view of what should be considered productive economic activity to challenge what activities the state has deemed of value. This means that there needs to be more real dialogue that takes local viewpoints into account rather than simply governmental orders and decrees based on unfounded assumptions and biases that affect the livelihood of people. A greater understanding of the constraints that micro- and small-scale entrepreneurs face would undoubtedly lead to a revision of unnecessary and cumbersome tax and licensing regulations that invite abuse by officials at the expense of the self-employed. More importantly, it would result in changes in the legal environment so that the rights of the micro- and small-scale entrepreneurs might be better protected. Discrimination against the informal sector in favor of large-scale industry would diminish as greater recognition is given to this dynamic sector and its important role in creating employment and in enhancing domestic investment and savings. It would result in increased training, credit, and other programs to assist this sector.

METHODS

My study seeks to explore the relationship between human agency and the structural factors that inhibit or enable action in the context of the growth of the informal economy. The methods I chose reflected this need to employ interpretive methods to understand people's own motives and decisions as well as the constraints and opportunities they encountered, including limitations imposed by the authorities, by the economic situation Tanzania faced, and even by the world economy.

My fieldwork methods were selected based on the premise that I would need to combine a variety of methods to obtain the insights and data necessary to understand the role of the informal economy, especially because many of these activities were by definition not sanctioned by the authorities. However, the prevalence of these activities made my task easier, for they carried little if any social stigma. Sometimes I had to adopt an anthropologist's eye for significant details and to incorporate close observation. Other questions regarding household income and demographic data on participants in the informal economy required that I carry out more systematic cluster surveys. Civil servants who feared being exposed to the party for having second incomes were interviewed through a snowball survey, in which we established trust by interviewing friends of initial contacts, then friends of those friends, and so on. Similarly, government and party perspectives were gleaned through interviews with leaders from the cabinet and Central Committee levels down to the regional, district, and branch levels. Appendix A details the methodology employed, and Appendix B lists some of the people interviewed in the study.

I carried out my initial fieldwork on the urban informal economy in Tanzania's largest city, Dar es Salaam, between 1987 and 1988 and returned for brief research visits in 1990 and 1994. The study was concentrated in two parts of the city, Manzese and Buguruni, populated primarily by workers and small-scale entrepreneurs. In these areas, a research assistant and I carried out 300 interviews with local party leaders at the lowest level of ten-house cells and a cluster survey of 287 residents. Having obtained a list of party cell leaders (each leader represents ten or more houses that make up a geographically determined cell), we interviewed every other leader on the list and the first resident (over the age of 18) we encountered in the house to the left of the cell leader's house. The sample generally corresponded to census data with respect to gender, age, and marital status. In Manzese and Buguruni I made a special effort to talk to local religious leaders, teachers, and other important community figures, as well as leaders and members of local organizations, both formal and informal. These included women involved in the Union of Tanzanian Women (UWT) projects, members of the party's youth organization (VIJANA), Moslem imam and Ahmadiyya brotherhood leaders, Catholic and Lutheran ministers and laypeople, organizers of local-defense teams, people running manufacturing and market cooperatives, members of dance societies, educators at a City Council–sponsored nutrition center, women involved in *upato* rotating credit societies, managers of football clubs, and many others. We carried out all of these interviews in Swahili. We also spoke with national leaders of the Women's Union and its small projects branch (SUWATA), the Young Women's Christian Association (YWCA), the Family Planning Association (UMATI), the Tanganyika Association of Chambers of Commerce, the Dar es Salaam Chamber of Commerce, the Association of Tanzanian Employers, and the Tanganyika Tea Growers Association, among other groups.

Prior to carrying out the cluster survey, we conducted unstructured interviews citywide with about 300 self-employed entrepreneurs and a snowball survey of 51 middle- and upper-income residents engaged in sideline businesses.

2 Dar es Salaam in Transition

Farming is the backbone of our country. Even the government considers it this way. In any case, you always end up going back to farming.

> Crane operator at the Tanzania Harbor Authority, whose wife and children farm eighty kilometers north of Dar es Salaam

Since 1729 Omani sultans had controlled settlements along the Tanzanian coast and had even transferred Oman's capital from Muscat to Zanzibar in 1840 to accommodate the expansion of their commercial links with East Africa. Thus Dar es Salaam was founded by Zanzibar Sultan Seyyid Majid in the 1860s at a time of increased contacts between the mainland and Zanzibar, with Swahili, Arab, and Indian traders transporting copal (resin used in varnish) and produce to Zanzibar markets. Caravans brought slaves and ivory through the area from the interior, although primarily to the trading center at Bagamoyo, sixty-four kilometers north of Dar es Salaam.

As Dar es Salaam (Arabic for "haven of peace") grew, it engulfed local Shomvi and Zaramo settlements along the coast that subsequently were to become centers of the city's suburbs. In 1957, 36 percent of the city's population was Zaramo, with the Rufiji and Luguru representing the second- and third-largest ethnic groups, respectively (*African Census Report 1963*, 47). However, migration and intermarriage among a large number of ethnic groups diffused the influence of the Zaramo over the next decade. By 1967 the Zaramo made up roughly 27 percent of the city's population (Sporrek 1985, 32). Although their numbers have dwindled over the years, the Zaramo remain the largest ethnic group in Dar es Salaam, making their influence felt especially in the city's cultural and economic life. Even though official statistics are no longer gathered on ethnic background in Tanzania, it is obvious to observers that one of the main characteristics of Dar es Salaam is its heterogeneity: it brings together large numbers of Tanzania's 120 ethnic groups. Even in my small survey of 287 residents in Buguruni and Manzese, I came across people from 45 different ethnic groups. People of various ethnic origins were concentrated in different parts of the city: the Zaramo in Ilala and Buguruni; the Nyamwezi in

Magomeni and Kinondoni; the Ngoni in Kiwalani; the Luguru in Manzese; and the Ngindo, Matumbi, and Ndengereko in Temeke.

With the onset of German rule in 1891, Dar es Salaam was the natural choice as the administrative, commercial, and communications center of German East Africa. It remained the administrative center of the British-controlled territory from 1919 to 1961, when it became the capital of independent Tanganyika (Sutton 1970, 7). It still serves as the effective capital of the country, although efforts have been under way since 1973 to shift the capital to Dodoma.

Today, Dar es Salaam has about 1.4 million people, making it the largest city in Tanzania, the population of which reached 23 million with the 1988 census (Bureau of Statistics 1989). The city covers an area of 1,100 square kilometers and is the most densely populated area in Tanzania (Kulaba 1989, 206). It has the country's largest harbor and is also the industrial, commercial, and communications center of Tanzania.

At the center of the city are the administration buildings, the main commercial and shopping areas, and the Asian residential area, which is divided between the main Asian communities: Hindus and Muslims (mostly Ismai'li but also Ithnasheri and Bohora). Asians in Dar es Salaam also belong to other religious communities, including Jains and Sikhs (sects that are offshoots of Hinduism), Parsees (Zoroastrians), and Catholics. The industrial centers are located along a railroad that extends from the harbor through the two main industrial areas. Warehouses and light mechanical and construction industries are located along Pugu Road; the newer textile, beer-brewing, and dairy plants are situated along Morogoro Road in Ubungo. Pugu Road also runs through Buguruni and Morogoro Road through Manzese, the two areas that were the focus of my survey. Lime quarries and brickworks are found on the northern outskirts of the city, especially near the Wazo Hill cement factory (Sutton 1970, 12).

Of the living quarters, only Kariakoo, Ilala, Magomeni, Kijitonyama, Mwananyamala, and parts of Keko, Chang'ombe, and Temeke can be considered planned. Kariakoo has the most sizable concentration of workers and the largest wholesale market. It also has more stores and restaurants than does any other part of the city (Sutton 1970, 13–14). Most of the city—60 percent, according to Stren—sprang up in unplanned fashion, often out of already existing villages surrounded by farming areas (1982, 78).

According to 1991 labor-force survey figures, wage earners accounted for 36 percent of the urban working population. In a 1986–1987 survey of 600 Dar es Salaam residents, Kulaba discovered that 60 percent of the adult population was self-employed or working with family in a small business (1989, 212). These figures generally corroborate the findings of other, concurrent surveys (Tibaijuka 1988), including those of my 1987–1988 research, in which I found that 68 percent of Manzese and Buguruni residents in Dar es Salaam were self-employed, 59 percent farmed, and only 5 percent had no income-generating enterprise, employment, or farm (Table 1). Of the last group, most were young wives or students not seeking employment or self-employment. In other words, I found few truly unemployed people. Kulaba likewise found no unemployed respondents in his survey. This is not to say that they did not exist: many young people wandered the streets of the city center, some of whom were engaged in petty crime. However, these survey results suggest that many of the studies may have exaggerated the problem of unemployment by automatically considering street vendors and others engaged in similar occupations as unemployed (Ishumi 1984).

Most city dwellers (83 percent) were tenants, according to Kulaba's survey (1989, 213). Even in the mid-1950s, Leslie found that 81 percent of the 5,000 Dar es Salaam residents he surveyed were tenants (1963, 261). According to my 1988 survey, rents in typical neighborhoods like Manzese and Buguruni averaged around TSh 260 per household.[1] About four households lived in every house, generally renting from one to two rooms each. According to the 1988 census, the average household in Dar es Salaam was composed of 4.3 people; in Buguruni, 3.6 people; and in Manzese, 4.2 people (Bureau of Statistics 1989).

In the planned as well as the unplanned neighborhoods, houses are built in what is called the Swahili style. Each house has a porch in the front that is used by all members of the household for sitting and chatting with visitors or neighbors, for preparing food and weaving mats on occasion, and (for men, usually) for playing cards or *bao*, a game on a large board with four rows of holes. Some rent their porch to a tailor or launderer. Others sell pastries, flour, or charcoal (retail) from their porch or turn it into a food stall for selling vegetables and fruit. A central hallway separates the two or three rooms on each side. The hallway leads from the front entrance to the back courtyard, which is used for cooking and washing clothes. These courtyards are frequently closed off with a fence of thatched palm fronds called *makuti*. In the back courtyard is a pit toilet that is also used as a washroom.

Each house is built on a foundation of a mixture of stones and cement. The walls are made of mangrove poles, which are tied together and filled with mud, often covered with a *makuti* roof or a *mabati* tin roof. The

Table 1 Percentages of Occupations among Dar es Salaam Residents, 1988

	Women	Men	Total
Employed			
with no other source of income	4	11	7
and self-employed	1	9	5
and farming	2	9	5
and self-employed and farming	2	5	4
Total employed	9	34	21
Self-employed			
with no other source of income	13	35	24
and employed	1	9	5
and farming	53	15	34
and employed and farming	2	5	4
and retired	0	2	1
and retired and farming	0	3	1
Total self-employed	69	69	69
Farming			
with no other source of income	15	8	12
and employed	2	9	5
and self-employed	53	15	34
and employed and self-employed	2	5	4
and retired	0	2	1
Total farming	72	39	56
Retired			
without any source of income	0	1	1
and self-employed	0	2	1
and farming	0	2	1
and self-employed and farming	0	3	1
Total retired	0	8	4
No occupation	10	0	5

N = 272

SOURCE: Survey data I collected in Manzese and Buguruni in 1987–1988. For the methodology used, see Appendix A.

borders of doors and windows are often strengthened with small stones and cement. By 1995 most houses in Dar es Salaam had nonearthen floor and iron roofs. Half of the houses had electricity, but kerosene was the main source of lighting fuel for 49 percent of city residents (Ferreira and Goodhart 1995, 26).

HISTORY OF THE CITY'S INFORMAL ECONOMY

From the earliest times, the local Zaramo inhabitants of the coast traded food staples, fruit, vegetables, fish, and poultry with the growing urban center of Dar es Salaam. They also traded firewood, charcoal, and gum copal, which was sold to Indian traders and exported to Europe for varnishing ships (Beidelman 1967, 16–17). The gum copal trade decreased as wooden ships fell into disuse.

Informal income-generating activities grew as the city expanded, providing residents with cheap services and goods. Arab cultural influences were evident in coffee vending, one of the earliest small enterprises in Dar es Salaam. Much like today, coffee vendors would walk the streets, clicking together their small coffee cups to let people know they were passing by. They sold a strong coffee from a *mdila* (large brass pot) that was carried around on a frame with a base filled with hot charcoal pieces to keep the container warm. Some added ginger to the coffee to spice it up. Small coffee- and teahouses called *mikahawa* and *hoteli* were also popular gathering places for workers in the postwar period. At these places, a variety of refreshments and snacks were sold, including tea, often spiced with cardamom or cloves, fruit juices, and *sambosa, chapati, vitumbua, maandazi* and other such fried pastries popular to this day (Anthony 1983).

By the mid-1950s Leslie (1963) found people involved in diverse income-generating activities in addition to the ones already mentioned. These included large traders, shop owners, vehicle owners, and small vendors of fruit, *mshikaki* (roast meat), fish, coconuts, charcoal, onions, *tembo* (palm wine), water, milk, old bottles, tin cans for roofing, old clothes, and peanuts. Like today, some walked the streets with their wares; others sold from *magenge* (stalls) outside their home or just off their front porch. People reported profits of up to 50 percent from such activities. Iliffe describes thousands of young boys and young men who collected scrap, sold oranges, and sought odd jobs like loading and unloading trucks at the harbors (1979, 388–89). Rickshaws were in use until the 1950s, when they gradually gave way to buses. Prostitution increased with the expansion of the docks and industry in the 1930s. However, as more women found their way into the city, their income-generating activities expanded to endeavors like cooking and selling beans, local beer, pastries, rice, or porridge. Some women would buy wood scraps from sawmills, builders' yards, and furniture makers and resell them as firewood (Anthony 1983, 158; Leslie 1963, 135, 232).

Having such sources of income often put women in a position to build a house. At the end of the 1960s, as many as 18 percent of the houses in Dar es Salaam were owned by women (M.-L. Swantz 1985, 166). Leslie reported that in 1956–1957, when Magomeni, a large section of the city, was opened up for applications for plots to build houses, 19 percent of the applicants were women. In the Kisutu section of the city, as many as 45 percent of the houses were registered in a woman's name; and a sample taken in Kariakoo and Ilala, older parts of the city, showed that 40 percent of women owned houses. Although the majority of these women inherited houses from their deceased husbands, parents, or brothers, as many as one-third had been able to build houses from income they obtained through small enterprises like selling cakes, beans, coconut ice, and fried fish (Leslie 1963, 168–69).

Ethnic groups differed in their inheritance practices. The Zaramo, who comprised the largest ethnic group at the time of Leslie's study, integrated aspects of Islamic law into their inheritance practices, dividing the land and property of the deceased, with 25 percent going to the spouse, 50 percent to the father's side, and 25 percent to the mother's side of the family. The children inherited from the father's side, as did the father's brothers and sisters. If the children were minors, the father's brothers would hold the property until they were adults. There is evidence that even in the late 1960s family courts or extended-family courts were almost solely responsible for adjudicating inheritance cases (M.-L. Swantz 1970, 89–91). It is also noteworthy that in 1957, around the time Leslie was making his observations about home ownership, the male-female ratio in Dar es Salaam was 1.31; in 1978 it had been reduced to 1.15, and by 1988 it was only 1.11 (Bureau of Statistics 1986, 1989).

After independence the Asian and European communities, which had more capital at their disposal, were largely responsible for initially developing the small industries in areas like food processing and in the manufacture of clothing, furniture, soap, and shoes. Similarly, the largest shopkeepers were of Asian or Arab descent, and half of all shopkeepers were Asian (Anthony 1983, 5; Leslie 1963, 135).

Throughout the 1960s and 1970s self-employment continued to provide cheap food and goods for Dar es Salaam's residents. At that time, unlike the 1980s, the self-employed earned incomes that were lower than those of wage earners, with the exception of a few lucrative activities, such as healing, wholesale charcoal trade, and shopkeeping.[2] A 1971 study of urban incomes found that 45 percent of those who were self-employed earned less than TSh 150 per month at a time when the minimum wage was TSh 170. One-quarter had incomes greater than TSh 350, and 10 percent earned more than TSh 1,000 per month (Bienefeld 1975, 57–59). Up until the 1970s, the rates of urban formal-sector employment appear to have kept pace with the growth of the urban labor force. This may have been why there were fewer street traders in Dar es Salaam than in some other African cities. One study in 1968 found that more than 77 percent of wage earners were migrants, whereas of the self-employed only 62 percent were migrants, indicating that those coming to the city were primarily seeking employment (Sabot 1974, 50). These demographics changed dramatically in the 1980s as self-employment began to offer better prospects than wage employment. As I will show in this chapter, employment declined significantly, in part due to factory closures but also because people left employment to farm and to engage in income-generating projects.

The following two sections give a short background to Buguruni and Manzese, the two areas of Dar es Salaam I focused on in the study (see Appendix A).

BUGURUNI

Prior to colonialism, Buguruni was known for its coconut plantations, which were owned by Asians, Arabs, or Africans. One of the largest estates, the Daya Estate, was in the hands of an Indian planter. The first settler who moved from the city's coastline to Buguruni was called Momba. He parceled out land to others who followed, many of whom married into his family. These new settlers included names like Kirumba, a fellow Zaramo, and two Pogoro ex-slaves, Feruz Ambari and Farhani. Some of the most important figures in Buguruni's recent history derive their stature from being descendants of these early settlers and from owning coconut plantations. Two of them, Binti Madenge and Mwinyi Amani, had Chama Cha Mapinduzi (CCM) Party branches named after them in Buguruni (Leslie 1963, 65; Mwijarubi 1977).

During German colonial rule, Buguruni grew out from a Zaramo village into an unplanned settlement on the outskirts of Dar es Salaam. In the late 1960s its population was 10,000. Since then it grew nearly fivefold, to a population of 48,247 in 1988 (Bureau of Statistics 1989). Leslie

Table 2 Chama Cha Mapinduzi, Buguruni, Dar es Salaam, 1988

Party Branch	Population	Number of Party Members	Number of Ten-House Cells	Number of Households
Madenge	9,966	526	35	2,813
Mnyamani	12,680	633	57	3,474
Malapa	10,263	509	46	2,978
Kisiwani	15,378	503	70	3,935
Total	48,287	2,171	208	13,200

SOURCE: Bureau of Statistics 1989; records from Manzese and Buguruni CCM branches.

found that 68 percent of Buguruni residents were Zaramo in the mid-1950s (1963, 258); today almost half the residents are Zaramo. As a renowned Zaramo area, Buguruni attracted people from throughout Dar es Salaam in search of its famed Zaramo Mdundiko dance troupes and medicine men.

The Ward of Buguruni belongs to the Ilala District of Dar es Salaam Region. The ward is made up of four branches: Madenge, Mnyamani, Malapa and Kisiwani, which are divided into 208 ten-house cells (Table 2). In the late 1980s about 2,171 CCM members lived in Buguruni (4 percent of the population), according to local party records. Buguruni had three schools: Buguruni Primary, Buguruni Moto, and Buguruni Visiwi, with a total enrollment of around 4,177 pupils (52 percent of whom were girls).[3]

The ward remained primarily Muslim in the late 1980s, with eleven mosques, fifteen *madarasa* (Koran schools) and an Ahmaddiyah brotherhood that is growing in strength. It also had a Lutheran church (500 adult members), started in 1967, and a much smaller Assemblies of God church.[4] In addition, there is a YWCA hostel for women, an Anglican-run hostel for young women, and an Anglican Theological College.

Buguruni's laborers work along Pugu Road in nearby factories like Metal Box, Mitsubishi, and Sunguratex. Others are drivers at Wazo Hill, or workers at the harbors, or in the army. Buguruni's residents farm in the nearby valleys of Chanika and Msimbazi, although many have farms farther away in the Coast Region—in Kisarawe District, for example—or other, more distant parts of the country. Buguruni's Zaramo residents maintain strong ties with relatives in nearby areas where they go not only to farm but also to participate in puberty and other rites, as well as marriage and burial ceremonies, to give birth, to make *tambiko* (ritual offerings to ancestor spirits), and for divination and medical treatment. To this day, patrons in Buguruni derive much of their prestige from their ability to manipulate rural-urban links. They take advantage of the urban areas' dependence on the countryside for produce, bringing into the city charcoal, fruit, wood, and fish from the coastal villages (L. Swantz 1969).

MANZESE

Like Buguruni, Manzese grew during German rule from a small village into an unplanned settlement approximately ten kilometers outside the city limits. In fact, it is the largest unplanned settlement in Dar es Salaam and in Tanzania (Kulaba 1989, 245). It began as a settlement of Zaramo, Nyamwezi, and Manyema agriculturalists. Many of the Nyamwezi and Manyema were descendants of porters during the height of the Arab trade. Manzese grew after World War II, as the colonial government forcibly moved people out of areas like Muhimbili and the Technical College for purposes of construction. Even more important to Manzese's growth was the establishment of industries in the nearby Ubungo area in the late 1960s and 1970s. In 1967 the population of Manzese was 4,630; by 1978 it had grown to 28,522. The population had nearly doubled ten years later, reaching 59,600, according to the 1988 census. Manzese flourished, in part, because it originally evolved outside the city limits and hence outside the jurisdiction of city licensing regulations, where it was easier to brew beer and carry out other illicit commercial activities like prostitution.

Today most Manzese workers are employed in the nearby Urafiki Textile Factory, Chibuku breweries, Fishnet factory, Coastal Dairy Industries, Portland Cement, Ubungo Water Supply, the University of Dar es Salaam, Wazo Hill, and the Transport Institute (Mashisa 1978; Sporrek 1985, 71).

The Ward of Manzese belongs to the Kinondoni District of Dar es Salaam Region. The ward is made up of nine branches: Mnazi Mmoja, Mferejini, Muembeni, Midizini, Uzuri, Mwungano, Mvuleni, Kilimani, and Sinza, which are divided into 397 ten-house cells. Sinza is strikingly different from the rest of Manzese. Although it grew in a similar pattern of unregulated housing, its residents are somewhat better off and the houses are of visibly better quality. In 1988 Manzese had approximately 6,655 CCM members (Table 3), or 11 percent of the population. It is ironic that even though the CCM had a proportionally stronger presence in Manzese than in Buguruni in the 1980s, by 1995 it was one of the

Table 3 Chama Cha Mapinduzi, Manzese, Dar es Salaam, 1988

Party Branch	Population	Number of Party members	Number of Ten-House Cells	Number of Households
Mnazi Mmoja	5,096	950	35	1,305
Mferejini	2,197	533	17	616
Muembeni	7,862	1,065	54	2,092
Midizini	4,698	739	28	1,113
Uzuri	8,698	700	63	2,231
Mwungano	4,803	500	38	1,255
Mvuleni	5,221	698	39	1,452
Kilimani	9,209	500	65	2,126
Sinza	11,816	970	58	2,205
Total	59,600	6,655	397	14,395

SOURCE: Bureau of Statistics 1989; records from Manzese and Buguruni CCM branches.

first wards to elect an opposition ward leader after Tanzania adopted multipartyism. In a June 1995 by-election Dr. Masumbuko Lamwai, who was the Dar es Salaam Chairman of the National Convention for Construction and Reform (NCCR-Mageuzi) party, won by a landslide, defeating the CCM and Civic United Front (CUF) candidates.[5]

The ward has two schools (Uzuri and Ukombozi primary schools), with a total enrollment of about 2,535 pupils (53 percent of whom are girls).[6] Manzese has several nursery schools, including one run by the YWCA in Uzuri and another started by parents in Muembeni. A nutrition center is located near the YWCA nursery. It was started by the City Council and Ministry of Agriculture in 1975 with World Bank funding to educate people about nutrition and providing farming inputs.

Although Manzese has a greater mix of ethnic groups than does Buguruni, it does have a concentration of Luguru: according to my survey, Luguru make up about 20 percent of its population. Manzese remains primarily Muslim, with eight mosques, at least four *madarasa*, and, like Buguruni, a strong Ahmaddiyah brotherhood. One Koranic school alone has 250 children. In addition, Manzese has a Catholic church (800 members), a Lutheran church, and Pentecostal Church Hall.

People from all over Dar es Salaam flock to Manzese's thriving market, especially on Sundays. The market was established in 1967 by the Mzizima District Council. Its 107 sellers are organized into the Nguvu Moja

Cooperative Society.[7] The market, a hub of activity, is surrounded by a major commercial area. Morogoro Road passes through the market, and buses from upcountry stop on their way downtown. In the mid-1980s the Manzese market became so congested that the authorities were finally forced to move some of the sellers to Tandale market in an adjacent ward. Both markets are famous for having been centers of the unofficial whole-sale trade in Dar es Salaam.

Most Manzese residents, like those in Buguruni, obtain their water from a nearby tap or purchase it from someone who has a private tap. Many also buy water from *mkokoteni* (pull-cart) vendors. A few, like store keepers, have electricity.

Manzese has a reputation throughout Dar es Salaam, especially among people who do not live there, as a place bustling with activity, especially il-licit activities (see the description in Ishumi 1984, 80). Parts of Manzese, like Mwungano, are known throughout the city for prostitution and bars. People who simply pass through along Morogoro Road see the myriad stalls selling jewelry and *mitumba* (secondhand clothing); the boys selling bread to passengers on buses that have stopped temporarily; the milling machines; the shoe-repair shops; the wood for sale; carpentry sheds; brick-making factories; food stalls; stores selling colorful wrap-around cloths called *khanga* and *kitenge*; and cassette-tape music stores. Outsiders often fear Manzese because it is said that most of the criminals in the city live there. Nonresidents also talk about "Radio Manzese" as the rumor mill of the city. Yet there is little to distinguish Manzese from Buguruni, Temeke, or any other part of Dar es Salaam. To its inhabitants, Manzese is an area of mostly hard-working and respectable citizens. Civil servants and workers return from work at 3 or 4 P.M. to concentrate on their income-generating projects. One finds more activity after hours and on the week-ends in Manzese than downtown, for example.

THE CHANGING URBAN HOUSEHOLD ECONOMY

Decline in Real Wages

The steady decline in wages among employed people is probably the most significant change affecting urban dwellers since the mid-1970s. The drop in real wages reflects the difficult position of the Tanzanian economy as a whole. The government had come to control the bulk of the nation's wages (wage bill) and wage employment after the 1967 Arusha Declaration, be-cause the declaration paved the way for the nationalization of key indus-tries and banks and an increase in the number of parastatals (companies in which the state owns at least 51 percent of the shares). This placed the wage crisis squarely on the government's shoulders. By 1968, government control of the country's wage employment stood at 53 percent of the total, while the wage bill was up to 57 percent. Eight years later, government control had reached 65 percent of wage employment and 70 percent of the wage bill.

Subsequently, the government took steps to lessen the fast-growing gap between urban and rural incomes and to reduce the difference between the highest- and lowest-paid employees. After 1967, the Standing Committee on Parastatal Organizations (SCOPO) was established to control wages and salaries of state companies, and the Permanent Labour Tribunal was formed to regulate wages in the private sector. As a result of these measures, the differential between urban and rural average incomes dropped from 2.45 in 1969 to 1.39 in 1980; the ratio of lowest to highest public-sector wages fell from 1:20 in 1967 to 1:5 in 1985. But around 1974 the downward spiral of real wages began, falling by 24 percent between 1974 and 1975. Even with continuing pay increases, real wages fell by 83 percent from 1974 to 1988. Under structural adjustment policies, incomes continued to worsen. By August 1995 the minimum wage was still only $31.50 a month under conditions of 28 percent inflation in which, according to the Organization of Tanzania Trade Unions (OTTU), the bare minimum wage should be $200 a month in order to survive (International Labour Organisation 1982, 267; Mtatifikolo 1988, 35; Valentine 1983, 52).[8]

As real wages dropped, non-agricultural incomes, generally in the informal sector, began to climb (International Labour Organisation 1982, 264; Sarris and van den Brink 1993, 158). According to official statistics, which can be used only as rough indicators, not precise measures, in 1976–1977 wages constituted 53 percent of the total urban household income, and other private incomes accounted for 25 percent of the total household income (Sarris and van den Brink 1993, 68). According to the Bureau of Statistics (1977), in instances where the head of household was a wage earner, wage earnings accounted for as much as 77 percent of the total household income, and private incomes accounted for only 8 percent of the total household income. In contrast, by 1988, according to my survey, informal incomes constituted approximately 90 percent of the household cash income, with wage earnings making up the remainder.

One way to gauge these changes is to examine the amount spent on food. In 1976–1977 food expenditure roughly equaled income in low-income groups (Bureau of Statistics 1977, Table 3C2). Nearly a decade later, according to my 1987–1988 survey, the average amount of money spent on food per day by the typical household of four, both with and without employed members, was TSh 325. This means that low-income household expenditure on food exceeded the minimum monthly salary eightfold. There is little doubt that informal sources of income made up the difference between wage earnings and food expenditure.

In low-income households the percentage of expenditure on food rose from roughly 52 percent of all household expenditures in 1940 to 85 percent in 1980 (Bryceson 1987, 174).[9] If we take Bryceson's estimate that food expenditure was 85 percent of all household expenditures, then informal incomes were contributing roughly nine times more than were formal incomes in households in which only one household member was an employed worker; that is, in 42 percent of all households surveyed.[10]

The actual income derived from self-employment correlates much more accurately with the household expenditure figures than do wage rates. According to my survey, the mean income from an income-generating project in Manzese or Buguruni was about TSh 15,500 a month. The median was TSh 6,000 per month, or four times the monthly minimum wage. The median was skewed by the low informal incomes of women, whose average monthly income from their projects was TSh 5,346 a month, whereas for men it was TSh 29,064 a month (23 times the minimum wage). One of the reasons for this large discrepancy between women's and men's projects was the fact that the self-employed men had been in business longer and were established in more economically rewarding enterprises, like carpentry and tailoring.

Only one-third of full-time self-employed interviewees had spouses who were self-employed, whereas more than two-thirds of those who were employed had self-employed spouses or had a sideline project. This suggests once again that self-employment was a more viable means of obtaining a livable income than was employment. Those who were self-employed clearly had less need for a second income in the household than those who were employed.

This shift in workers' households from depending mostly on wages to depending mostly on income obtained through self-employment had a number of repercussions. Some workers, finding that their official jobs could not sustain them, had to leave employment altogether in order to involve themselves full-time in informal income-generating projects or in agricultural production. Increasing numbers of employed workers sought sideline projects. Larger numbers of women, children, and the elderly

Table 4 Years in Which Dar es Salaam Residents Left
Formal Employment (in Percentages)

Year	Women	Men	Total
1950–1959	0	1	1
1960–1969	0	7	5
1970–1979	33	30	31
1980–1987	67	62	63

N = 93

SOURCE: Survey data I collected in Manzese and Buguruni in
1987–1988. For the methodology used, see Appendix A.

became involved in small, income-generating projects and farming, making their contribution to the household economy in monetary terms far
greater than in the past.

Flight from Wage Employment

Dramatic changes took place in the 1980s as large numbers of workers left
their jobs. According to the 1978 population census (Bureau of Statistics
1982, 51), 50 percent of the urban working population was employed. Of
the men, 66 percent were employed; and of the women, 22 percent were
employed. In Dar es Salaam, 84 percent of the men were employed, 39 percent of the women were employed, and 72 percent overall were employed
(Bureau of Statistics 1982, 52). Thirteen years later, according to the
1990–1991 labor force survey, only 36 percent of the urban working population was employed, which represents a 28 percent reduction in the employed labor force. Of the men, 45 percent were employed in 1991; and of
the women, 23 percent were employed.

My survey findings bear these patterns out. Of all the people I surveyed, 26 percent had left their wage jobs. One-third of this group that
had left their jobs had done so in the 1970s; 63 percent left after 1980.
Forty percent left between 1984 and 1987 (Table 4). About 45 percent ter-
minated employment because of low pay, and 17 percent left because of
layoffs due to plant cutbacks or closures. Other reasons of lesser importance included health problems, retirement, pregnancy, differences with
employers, and being fired.

According to my survey, of those who left employment for reasons
other than retirement, 87 percent had gone into self-employment and

40 percent into urban farming. (The numbers do not total 100 percent because most people engage in two or more activities simultaneously.) Of the 21 percent who remained employed, 38 percent planned to leave their jobs to engage in small enterprises, farming, or both. One-quarter were undecided, and the remainder said they would continue with their jobs and sideline enterprises or find a better sideline activity.

Those who left their jobs had been employed for an average of nine years, which indicates that those who were leaving were part of a stable workforce that had once sought employment with the intention of working their entire lives. Among the fifty-to-fifty-five-year-olds, the group of workers who had been longest employed, the average number of years employed at one job was fifteen.

One woman I interviewed who was running a successful soda kiosk had worked at the Kibo Match factory in the northern town of Moshi from 1970 until 1982. She said that many women worked there but were paid less than men, making between TSh 1,200 and 1,500 a month at a time when it cost TSh 350 to buy food each day for her family. When asked how her life had changed since leaving her job, she explained: "When I worked at Kibo Match I didn't have enough to eat, and I worked from 7 A.M. to 3 P.M. without food. I had to give priority to the children when it came to food. Since I quit my job and started my own business I have put on weight. I used to weigh 67 kilograms. Now I have gained up to 100 kilograms and the doctor has told me to lose weight before I can have another child."[11]

In another fairly typical case, a man who had worked for twenty years at a clothing factory found that he could no longer sustain his family and left his job in 1980 to start a laundering business with his wife, son, and younger brother. As he put it, "I have children and a wife. If I had stayed with my job I would have gone down further. I would have been destroyed. The cents that I get now help more than my earnings when I was employed."[12] His household of eight earned about TSh 425 a day and spent TSh 300 a day on food.

The problem was the same even for better-educated, higher-income employees, often resulting in a serious brain drain. The University of Dar es Salaam saw the departure of more than 100 faculty and staff members from 1977 to the mid-1980s, in pursuit of alternative sources of income either in Tanzania or abroad (Lugalla 1993, 205). In Manzese I interviewed one university-trained television engineer who had studied in the former Soviet Union for six years and had worked for ten years with the government-run television station in Zanzibar. With two children and a wife to support, he left his job in 1987 to go into business with his father running a bar. He explained his predicament: "There is no benefit in working. I liked my job and would return to it if I could, but I can't feed my family on those wages. Even though I have studied a lot, there is no benefit. My monthly earnings of 2,790 shillings lasted only five days of the month." [13] Even education and a high-status job are no longer a guarantee of financial security.

Although it is understandable that people need to find sources of income they can live on, some are perturbed by the effect of these departures on the quality of public institutions like schools and hospitals. As one primary-school teacher, Melania John, pointed out, "Although such problems [of people leaving their jobs to run businesses] are happening, I would like to ask that the ministries which are responsible find ways to help these workers see the importance of doing their job. If all these people are going away, can you tell me who is going to teach these classes? Who is going to provide service in the hospitals? Now let us look for a plan, so that those workers will stay in their positions and provide services to society." [14]

Combining Employment and Self-Employment

Although the gap between real wages and the cost of living was greater than ever before in the 1980s, militant resistance on the part of workers was less than in the past. Labor quiescence could be accounted for, in part, by the state's attempts to undermine the autonomy of the labor movement. But even if one takes into account the fact that the labor movement was largely under party control, the pressure to raise wages was still relatively small. Workers had little confidence that the government, which accounts for the majority of the country's wage bill, could improve their situation.

The average worker's salary was sufficient to pay for roughly three days of his or her household's monthly food budget in the late 1980s. Because the government is the largest employer, it would not be outrageous to suggest that workers were being charitable to the state by remaining on the job. Certainly one would be hard-pressed to find such loyal workers in the United States if one paid them one-tenth of what it costs to put food in their mouths. Thus a central issue for labor in Tanzania, as in other parts of Africa today, has to do not with issues concerning the job itself but, rather, with how to make a living outside one's workplace in order to keep up with the dramatic decline in real income.

It has long been recognized that Africa's urban dwellers rarely have depended solely on one source of income, either as individuals or as a household. Even in Britain, the classic example of an industrializing country, few families depended only on their weekly wages at the turn of the century. Most families derived income also from projects of women and children, similar to the ones found in urban Tanzania today.[15] Because informal sources of income and subsistence are the main means of survival for most Tanzanian urban dwellers, one may ask why people bother to work as wage employees when they could potentially make more if they went into managing their projects full-time. Instead, many work on both their jobs and their projects, keeping their options open in both the formal and the informal spheres of the economy.

Some argue that it is the security of the formal income rather than the size of the income that keeps workers on the job (Berry 1978; Peil, 1972; Pfefferman 1968). As Keith Hart explained (1973, 78):

> This preference for diversity of income streams has its roots in the traditional risk-aversion of peasants under conditions of extreme uncertainty, and is justified by the insecurity of urban workers today. The most salient characteristic of wage-employment in the eyes of the sub-proletariat is not the absolute amount of income receipts but its reliability. For informal employment, even of the legitimate variety, is risky and expected rewards highly variable. Thus, for subsistence purposes alone, regular wage employment, however badly paid, has some solid advantages; and hence men who derive substantial incomes from informal activities may still retain or desire formal employment.

This risk aversion is evident in the reasons Dar es Salaam's workers gave for remaining employed while pursuing more lucrative income-generating projects.

Some workers had not been in business long enough to be certain that they could succeed with their projects. This was the case with a young man in his twenties who, with a friend, had obtained a market stall and started selling fans, baskets to cover food, and *kamali* gambling boards they painted themselves. At night he worked as an embassy guard; during the day he worked on his project. From his painting project he earned about TSh 100 a day, which was 2.5 times his income as a guard. Lack of capital prevented him from expanding, and he believed that the business was still too risky to engage in on a full-time basis.

The same was true for one industrial machine operator at a textile mill. He had been employed for fifteen years but in 1988 was still making just

TSh 1,475 a month, only a little more than the minimum wage. He and his wife, who worked at the same textile mill and earned the same income as he did, had been unable to support themselves and their child until he decided in 1985 to start taking in laundry as a sideline business. After purchasing an iron, a table, and a cloth to cover the table, he went into business with his neighbor. By 1988 he was making about TSh 9,000 a month, six times his monthly salary. He saw no reason to leave his job and forfeit the additional income.

In another instance, two groups of neighbor men shared the same sewing machines. While one group worked the night shift at a nearby textile mill, the other group used the sewing machines in their sideline projects. Then, when the second group was at work during the day, the first group used the machines. None of them could afford to purchase a machine of their own and go into business full-time.

For many, jobs provided dependable sources of backup capital when business was in a slump. In one typical family that operated a food stall, the project was primarily the wife's responsibility. But the husband, a textile worker, went to the wholesale market downtown to buy fresh produce. His wife sold the fruit, vegetables, and fried cassava snacks from a stall in front of their home. When he came from work or when the children came from school they took over running the stall while the mother did housework. They planned to use the husband's small wage as capital to start up again if the business came to a temporary halt.

Some found that the prices of inputs were rising too fast, the sources of inputs were not secure, or their markets were not stable enough. This was the case for one worker at a suitcase factory, who, with his wife, started sewing mattress, pillow, and sofa covers as a sideline business because he was having a difficult time supporting his eight children. He bought thirty kilograms of scraps each week from the Urafiki and Sungura textile mills and made fifty to sixty mattress covers a week. He and his wife could make around TSh 30,000 a month, twenty-one times his wage earnings. But if inputs were not available and clients few and far between, at least there was always the wage at the end of the month to tide the family over.

Others saw no point in leaving their jobs because their spouse had a project that they thought was adequate to support the family. Of all married employees I surveyed, 54 percent had spouses engaged in projects. Wives were commonly found making and selling buns, fried fish, porridge, beans, tea, soup, retail charcoal, firewood, kerosene, or flour. Often the husband's only contribution to the project was to provide the starting capital. In one typical family, the husband, who was a welder, gave his wife

TSh 3,000, with which she started a project making and selling *mbege,* an alcoholic beverage made of bananas. With the starting capital she bought cups, pans, and a barrel, in addition to bananas and millet for fermenting. Less than one year after she began the project she was making about TSh 1,130 a day (twenty-six times her husband's wage) selling *mbege* to neighborhood residents.

In another household, a messenger and his wife built a restaurant with capital obtained from sales of cotton from their farm in Tanga. The wife supported their seven children and the husband's parents from what she made selling porridge, meat, beans, bread, and tea at their restaurant. The restaurant was primarily the responsibility of the wife, who made TSh 20,000 a month from her work in the project. The husband's job brought in only TSh 1,070 a month, which after deductions (such as taxes and insurance) amounted to only TSh 900 take-home pay. Although she had been in business since 1972 and considered the restaurant a fairly stable source of income, the messenger saw no reason to leave his job as long as his wife could manage the business, especially because unanticipated problems sometimes arose. For example, once a health officer closed down her restaurant for six months on the grounds that it was not sanitary because the walls were not painted, the building was too small, and the toilet not up to standard. Unable to afford the so-called requirements for the restaurant, the messenger finally gave the officer what he really wanted—a bribe. In the meantime, while their restaurant was closed, the husband's wages helped tide them over until they found another source of income.

Some workers remained at their job and merely hired employees to carry out projects. This pattern was more common among professionals, but such arrangements could be found even among workers. One thirty-five-year-old technician, who managed to purchase two sewing machines from his savings, hired two tailors to work for him. Other workers found their jobs necessary to obtain resources used in their projects. One man employed at the harbors brought home plastic bands used to wrap imported bales of secondhand clothing. After work he and his wife sat on their veranda each day and wove the bands into colorful baskets, which he sold at stores downtown. Workers sometimes obtained resources from their jobs illicitly and resold them. One worker at a printing company siphoned off paint, which was difficult to come by, and resold it on the outside to local sign writers and painters.

For professionals, jobs sometimes were sources of housing or access to parastatal automobiles or telephones, which came in handy in their projects. One primary-school teacher I interviewed had four projects, including a farm of 1.2 hectares and raising livestock and poultry. Her brother, who worked as a statistician, had access to an automobile from his research center, which he used to transport her oranges to the market and bring feed for the eighteen pigs and chickens she was raising.

For middle- and upper-income employees the workplace often was a source of contacts, a place where one could exchange resources, information, and favors useful in operating projects. It also was a source of status. The status may not have been reflected in monetary terms but could be important enough to one's self-esteem to make it worth holding on to the job while one obtained one's real income from a kiosk, piggery, chicken farm, or hairdressing salon. In addition to status, a number of professionals and semiprofessionals mentioned that they stayed on their jobs simply because they enjoyed them. One nurse made TSh 80,000 a month raising chickens. When asked why she did not leave her job, she responded emphatically that she would never leave her job as a nurse because she enjoyed it so much.

Other workers used their jobs as a source of clients for their project. One machine operator at a cigarette factory learned how to fix radios from his friend. Since 1983 he had had a sideline business of repairing radios. Because he did not have a license he felt he could not advertise openly. For this reason his clients came mainly through contacts at work.

Workers could be creative when it came to using their jobs as sources of clients. When I went to a government-run store to purchase a map of the city, the salesman told me that there were none available and that they had not had any in print for years. He added that he could sell me a print of the map he had made himself in his own private replicating service. In the course of what became a rather lengthy discussion, the salesman told me that he had worked there six years and still only made the minimum wage. By reproducing and selling these maps he made every two days the same income as his monthly wage. "This way I can help myself and the government too," he said, because the store had not been able to provide this service.[16]

Income-Generating Projects

Most of those I surveyed who had started small-scale projects had done so between 1980 and 1987; only 15 percent had started their enterprises in the previous five years. Of those who were employed and had projects of their own, 76 percent had started between 1980 and 1987; only 15 percent had begun within the previous decade (Table 5).

Table 5 Years in Which Dar es Salaam Residents First
Became Self-Employed (in Percentages)

Year	Women	Men	Total
1940–1949	1	2	2
1950–1959	0	4	2
1960–1969	3	7	5
1970–1979	10	21	15
1980–1987	86	66	76

N = 190

SOURCE: Survey data I collected in Manzese and Buguruni in 1987–1988.

A 1991 survey of 7,000 households found that most informal-sector operators in Dar es Salaam obtained starting capital from relatives and friends (51 percent) or financed their own small businesses (45 percent); none indicated obtaining assistance from a formal financial institution, like a bank (Planning Commission and Ministry of Labour and Youth Development 1991, 2–6). In Dar es Salaam, lack of capital and problems of marketing were overwhelmingly identified as the key constraints in establishing and operating an enterprise in the 1991 survey, followed by finding premises from which to operate, lack of equipment and spare parts, and government regulations. My own survey showed lack of markets to be almost four times greater a problem than even capital, and expense and availability of inputs as the second and third major problem entrepreneurs identified.

Determinants of Income-Generating Projects

People engaged in a great variety of enterprises, ranging from food vending to frame making, tailoring, shoemaking, carpentry, masonry, beer brewing, laundering, hairbraiding, and market sales to running small restaurants and kiosks (see Appendix C). The largest number of self-employed people were found in the areas of vending fuel, processed food, and other goods like water, newspapers, vegetables, and fruit. Of those involved in the manufacturing sector, tailors made up the majority; in the area of services, launderers predominated.

Women and men, however, engaged in different kinds of enterprises. Women were mainly involved in the making and selling of pastries, fried fish, porridge, beans, tea, soup, charcoal, firewood, kerosene, and flour. Men, on the other hand, tended to be tailors, carpenters, masons, launderers, mechanics, and shoemakers.

Lack of capital was a key constraint that kept especially youth and women locked in certain low-income-generating projects and prevented them from branching out into more lucrative ventures. This constraint, in turn, was reflected in the low incomes derived from their projects. Men, for example, reported four times higher starting capital than did women and had 5.4 times higher returns from their businesses. However, in general, the majority (54 percent) had low starting-capital requirements of less than TSh 1,000, and 30 percent had starting-capital requirements of 1,000 to TSh 5,000.

Ethnicity had some impact on the kinds of activities people engaged in, because many of the activities were organized along kinship lines, making it relatively easier for those with such connections to gain the necessary training, information, and contacts to start similar businesses. For example, according to my survey, one-third of those selling vegetable goods in Manzese (at the market, in stalls, on porches, or through street vending) were Luguru, for they were the ones with connections to traders of these goods in the Morogoro area. Similarly, W. Mashisa (1978) found that 71 percent of the market sellers in Manzese were Luguru. The Chagga were prominent in making local beers (especially *mbege*); the Pare, as store owners; and the Zaramo, as charcoal and wood traders.

The determinants of the kinds of projects that yielded middle and upper incomes were much different. It was not only starting capital but also contacts at work and relatives studying or working abroad who could provide resources necessary to run projects like raising chickens, tending cows (for milk) and pigs, and running hair salons.

Historically, lack of education was one factor that kept those involved in informal-sector activities out of employment and forced them to resort to self-employment. It has also been argued that lack of education adversely affects the types of goods produced and the ability to absorb technical information, while keeping managerial skills limited (Aboagye 1985, 22–23). However, given today's situation, in which even the middle- and upper-income salaries have fallen below subsistence levels, people of all income groups with all levels of education were involved in self-employment. In fact, I found little difference in the educational backgrounds of those with and without projects. Education and employment in and of themselves were no longer guarantees of economic well-being even in the higher-income brackets. Jobs that required more education, however, usually were important sources of contacts with whom one could trade resources and information that would advance sideline projects and affect incomes.

Income Differentiation and the Informal Economy

One of the consequences of the growth of the informal economy was the widening of income differentials. The gap is not discernible by looking simply at official statistics on incomes, but it is pronounced if one considers informal incomes, which by definition are not reported or taxed and are therefore not enumerated. The Tanzanian government's policy has been consistently to narrow official wage gaps, pulling up the minimum-wage earner's income while keeping the top salaries relatively constant. Through salary increments of the lowest wages and increased taxation of higher-income brackets, the ratio of the lowest to highest public-sector wages was lowered two and a half times between 1967 and 1985 (Mtatifikolo 1988, 35). These figures, however, tell only a small part of the story. The disparities between informal incomes were far greater. In the snowball survey I made of households in the middle- and upper-income brackets (earning between TSh 3,000 and 7,000 a month), women made an average income of TSh 51,130 a month from their projects. Because women were primarily involved in the family sideline projects of this income group, they became the focal point of the survey. These women were making almost ten times what the low-income women made from their small businesses and on the average ten times their own formal salaries as professionals or semiprofessionals. In terms of official incomes, however, these same middle- to upper-income women brought home only twice or at the most three times what the average woman worker made.

The differential between middle- and upper-income households and the majority of poorer households was even greater if one considers that usually those at the upper end of the income spectrum had numerous *marupurupu* (job-related fringe benefits). They often had housing provided for them at nominal rents and access to company vehicles. They also found it easier to use their positions (through both licit and illicit means) to gain access to resources necessary for their projects. Most of the Manzese and Buguruni residents complained of having to pay illegally hiked prices for necessities and inputs for their projects. Middle-income households more frequently reported having contacts who helped them purchase inputs for their projects at official prices, which were much lower.

The position of professionals and semiprofessionals gave them the prerogative to take time off from work more freely to check up on their projects or carry out business related to their projects, whereas those who worked in factories did not have this option. As one woman who worked at the Ministry of Education said, "If you have a job in the government, you have security, even if it is only small. You know your job will be there. The top people have to worry but other middle-level civil servants have little to worry about. If you are in a private company you have no time to do your own thing. The government is more tolerant about time. You can just go in and leave your handbag on the desk and then go about your own business. Or you leave your jacket draped on a chair if you are a man."[17]

Rural-Urban Linkages

Another development in the 1980s was the strengthening of rural-urban ties. These ties have always been strong, but the economic crisis bound the futures of urban dwellers inseparably to those of their rural kin. In the 1960s there was reason to believe that migrants had come to the urban areas to stay. A study done by Michaela Von Freyhold in the late 1960s in Dar es Salaam, for example, suggested that workers were unlikely to leave their urban jobs to return temporarily or permanently to farming (Von Freyhold 1972, cited in Stren 1982, 73–74). Another 1965 survey of 3,308 Dar es Salaam residents found that half planned to remain in the city (Market Research, Ltd. 1965a).[18]

By the 1970s the picture had begun to change. A 1974 study of migrants found that 54 percent did not plan to stay in town and that 27 percent said they did intend to (Sabot 1974, 53). A 1981 survey of 5,500 urban residents throughout Tanzania found that two-thirds planned to return to the countryside. Eighty percent owned land in rural areas. But even of those without land, close to half said they planned to leave the city eventually (Stren 1982, 73–74). By the end of the 1980s, large numbers of urban dwellers not only planned to retire in the countryside but were leaving their jobs and returning to the rural areas to farm.

Migration to the cities contributed to an 8 percent growth in urban population between 1967 and 1978. This slowed down considerably after 1978, according to my survey. Forty-five percent of those I interviewed had come to Dar es Salaam between 1968 and 1977, whereas only 27 percent had come between 1978 and 1987. This is corroborated by the 1988 census, which shows that between 1978 and 1988 the city's growth rate slowed to 4.8 percent (Bureau of Statistics 1989). Thus, during this decade, Dar es Salaam's 3 percent annual birthrate accounted for most of the increase in the city's growth rate rather than migration, which had been the main cause of city growth between 1968 and 1977.

The majority of those who did migrate found their way into self-employment. In the 1960s and 1970s those in younger age brackets were the most active in rural-urban migration. These trends are reflected in the fact that the largest number of those who said they migrated to the city were between the ages of thirty and thirty-nine. By the late 1980s, however, the majority (57 percent) of the fifteen-to-nineteen age group were born in Dar es Salaam, unlike youth of ten or twenty years earlier. Although more comprehensive studies are needed to further substantiate these trends, it was clear from my interviews that, for numerous households, life in the cities had simply become too costly, while the rural setting was beginning to hold more promise.

Although circumstances in the 1980s may have led to greater urban-rural emigration, it is worth noting that the rural-urban door has long been a revolving one, especially for those from villages in the Coast Region. This fact is often lost in migration studies. Apart from those with secure employment or self-employment, people would come to the city, stay a while, and go back to their villages either permanently or on a temporary basis, sometimes on a seasonal basis in order to plant and harvest crops.

Rural-urban ties were strengthened in numerous ways in addition to migration-emigration. As pointed out earlier, key social functions were still carried out in the countryside. Most of the city's fruit came from surrounding areas; green vegetables and potatoes came from the Uluguru and Usambara mountain areas (L. Swantz 1969; Van Donge 1992). In addition, many, especially those with better incomes, would send remittances to their rural relatives on a regular basis (Von Freyhold 1972, cited in Hyden 1980, 162).

Urban Farming

I have already shown how the drop in living standards forced many urban dwellers to return permanently to their home areas to farm. Others visited these home areas throughout the country simply for the planting and harvesting seasons. Most urban dwellers, however, farmed in the surrounding periurban areas of Dar es Salaam. For many, these areas were, in fact, their place of birth, where they continued to maintain close contact with their rural kin.

The new increase in urban farming in the 1980s is evident when compared with studies of previous decades. Historically, most of the food produced on plots around the city was for home consumption, and only a small portion entered the market. In the 1930s it appeared that workers in Dar es Salaam depended on the food parcels a wife or visiting relative brought from farms in their home areas. Basic foodstuffs were obtained from cultivation; wages were used to purchase luxuries (Bryceson 1987, 165).

A 1950 Survey of African Labourers in Dar es Salaam found that 14 percent had farms on the outskirts of the city, growing primarily rice. Leslie's study at the end of the 1950s showed that only 7 percent of household heads had plots for farming. Apparently there was a decline in urban farming in the 1960s, suggesting that urban economic conditions were improving and wages adequately covered food expenses. One 1965 study in Dar es Salaam found that only 1 percent of wage earners reported making a living from agriculture (Marco, Ltd. 1965). The government's 1968 master plan for the city found that only 2.2 percent of the city's wage earners farmed, and another 1968 survey did not find any residents farming (Hoad 1968, cited in Bryceson 1987, 189). A survey conducted in the Department of Sociology at the University of Dar es Salaam in 1970 found that 8 percent of the wives cultivated (Westergaard 1970, 8). Yet another study of civil servants in Dar es Salaam in the early 1970s found that 3 percent of the wives engaged in farming (Lindberg 1974, quoted in M.-L. Swantz 1985, 129). Once again, the reliability of all of these statistics can be questioned, but a general trend is apparent: in the 1960s and 1970s relatively few urban wage earners farmed, and those who did farm were primarily women.

What probably did not change throughout these years was the practice of having small vegetable and fruit gardens near one's home. A detailed study of Manzese in December 1974 by the World Bank–sponsored National Sites and Service Programme found that 70 percent of home owners had vegetable gardens and half had fruit trees. Only a handful of these gardens were larger than 10 by 15 paces. The majority of the plots (32 percent) were 5 by 5 paces or less. The main vegetables grown in these plots were peas, cassava, spinach, and pumpkins, while the most common fruits were pawpaws, bananas, pineapples, oranges, mangoes, guavas, limes, and grapes. The 1974 study found the majority of residents at that time wanted to expand their gardens in size but lacked the nearby space to do so (Pilot Nutrition Study 1975).

An initial boost for urban agriculture came with the 1974–1975 *Kilimo Cha Kufa na Kupona* (Agriculture for Life or Death) campaign, in which government offices, factories, and other workplaces were issued land outside the city for cultivation (Bryceson 1987). The number of people who

Table 6 Years in Which Dar es Salaam Residents
First Became Farmers

Year	Percentage
1948–1967	8
1968–1972	9
1973–1977	21
1978–1982	13
1983–1987	49

N = 160

SOURCE: Survey data I collected in Manzese and Buguruni in 1987–1988. For the methodology used, see Appendix A.

began to farm in the period after 1973 noticeably increased, so that the
1978 census registered farming as the primary occupation of 12 percent of
Dar es Salaam's women and 4 percent of the city's men.

My own study indicates that 21 percent of those residents who farmed
started doing so between 1973 and 1977, compared with the 9 percent who
had started in the previous five years (see Table 6). The number who began
to farm between 1978 and 1982 dropped to 13 percent and then picked
up rapidly in the five years between 1983 and 1987, when the majority
(49 percent) reported that they started farming. These figures can only be
taken as rough indicators, because the age of the respondents is not factored in. Nevertheless, these figures suggest some general trends.

The increase after 1983 reflects in part the expansion of urban farming
after the 1980 urban food crisis. A 1980 survey found 44 percent of low-
income wage earners with farms (Mganza and Bantje 1980, cited in Bryceson 1987, 190). By the late 1980s, my survey suggests, at least half of
all workers were farming, and 59 percent of all residents had farms in
1987–1988. Of the residents, 72 percent of the women cultivated, whereas
only 39 percent of the men did so (see Table 1). Another survey of urban
dwellers in the city in 1987 found that, of workers who were household
heads, 70 percent engaged in farming or raising livestock (Maliyamkono
and Bagachwa 1990, 126).

Around the 1980s, with the declining living standards in the city, many
began to believe that agriculture and village life held more promise than
did city life. One street cleaner who grew maize, millet, cassava, and fruit

on a 1.6-hectare plot put it this way: "Living in the village has more advantages than life here in the city. There I get everything: pawpaws, bananas, pineapple, and cassava. There is no need to buy them. Here in the city everything requires money. This morning I drank tea but now I am hungry. I had only one bun. In the countryside I could have eaten boiled bananas for breakfast. I would not have been hungry at this time of the day." [19]

The importance of farming to the survival of the urban household was underscored by a woman who said, "I farm and I harvest. If you have food you eat. I can't remain in the town and die of hunger. If I were to get some capital I could do something else, but I would never leave farming." [20] This woman was originally from Bukoba and had been farming since 1985 in her husband's home area of Mikese, Morogoro, where she lived with his parents during her three-month visits twice a year. Her husband, who had worked as a security guard for fourteen years, assisted her, but the farming was primarily her responsibility. They had 1.62 hectares of maize and millet and 0.2 hectares of *kisukari* (very sweet bananas). They consumed most of what they grew, but they sold about five bags of millet and the bananas each season.

For many workers, the goals were to acquire enough capital and move permanently to a rural setting. One secretary I interviewed was in the process of making the shift from the city to the countryside in a systematic way. She had bought a 0.4-hectare farm in the Kibaha periurban area, where she worked at a regional court. She started farming in 1987, growing oranges, bananas, and cassava. A single mother, she spent holidays and weekends farming with her children. When necessary she would rent a tractor at the standard 1987 rate of TSh 1,000 per 0.4 hectare. Her plans were to build a house near her farm and move there permanently. She had asked for a transfer in her job to work nearer her farm. Her plans were to expand the farm and eventually to go into agriculture full-time. In order to save, she was involved in several small, income-generating projects, including the sales of fried buns at work. She saved her money in two *upato* rotating-credit associations of women. One involved eight women at her workplace, each of whom pooled TSh 300 a month. The second association was of four people, who contributed TSh 400 a month. This meant that she was regularly saving TSh 700 a month (or 23 percent of her monthly wage earnings) in these societies. She also had money saved in a postal bank and in a credit union.

Urban farming after the 1970s was markedly different from the small garden plots that had characterized much of urban agriculture in the city until that time. The new farms were substantially larger than the small 5-by-5-pace gardens held by the majority of urban farmers in the 1974 Nutrition Survey of Manzese. Instead, I found Manzese and Buguruni farmers cultivating farms that averaged 1.2 hectares on the outskirts of the city. Large numbers of people began to farm not only in the areas near their homes but also, and mainly, in periurban areas surrounding the city itself. In the 1974 Pilot Nutrition Project (1975) survey, most who cultivated were home owners who farmed their own land around their house. Few renters, who made up 54 percent of the population in Manzese, had access to land surrounding the houses for cultivation because of well-established customary rights regarding landownership and use. By the 1980s, however, it appeared that even renters were farming in greater numbers, but they were cultivating land on the outskirts of the city. In contrast to the 1974 survey of Manzese, which found virtually no renters farming, my survey of the same part of Dar es Salaam thirteen years later found 38 percent of renters farming.

By the late 1980s the large majority (83 percent) of Manzese residents had acquired plots in the Dar es Salaam area or on the city's outskirts. Close to half farmed in their home areas, which for two-thirds was in Dar es Salaam and its vicinity. One textile worker and his wife, for example, farmed in the periurban area of Bunju, some forty-eight kilometers outside the city. The husband earned TSh 3,741 a month as an instructor at the mill, but he started farming with his wife in 1984 because they needed to find another means of supporting themselves—food costs for his family had risen to more than twice his monthly salary. The husband's parents were from Bunju and had a farm there. They gave him land, and in return he helped them farm. He paid for laborers when necessary, especially during the weeding season. They grew cassava, bananas, and oranges. The husband would stay there to farm on weekends, paying a TSh 60 round-trip bus fare, while the wife would farm for one or two weeks at a time.

Although the majority of people I surveyed were given land by relatives or friends (36 percent), others purchased it (23 percent), inherited it (15 percent), or simply claimed it in their home area at a time when land was still available (23 percent). The purchase of land had become commonplace by the 1980s, in violation of laws prohibiting its sale. Land speculation was rampant. Because land could not be bought or sold officially, people evaded this stipulation by claiming to buy the coconut, pawpaw, mango, or other trees on the land, which could legally be purchased. In areas surrounding Dar es Salaam, fallow land sold for around TSh 2,000 per 0.4 hectare in 1988, whereas closer to the city, cultivated land could sell for as high as TSh 100,000 per 0.4 hectare. The price of land was determined by its proximity to the center of Dar es Salaam, by whether the land had been tilled, and by the number of fruit and coconut trees on it.

As in the rural areas, urban women were more likely to be involved in farming than were men. Of the households surveyed, two-thirds of those who cultivated were women, and one-third were men. Of the 84 percent of the married couples who farmed, both the husband and wife said they cultivated, although the wife was likely to spend considerably more time in the field. In the households that farmed, approximately half of the household members were active in agricultural production. Children were also active in farming, although the extent of their involvement varied with their age. Frequently, younger children would sit in little huts, charged with scaring away pigs, rabbits, monkeys, and birds from ravaging the crops.

Urban dwellers with means would hire what were called *vibarua* or laborers to assist in planting and harvesting and to watch over the fields in their absence. Frequently living in close proximity to the farm, the laborers guarded the farms from animals, birds, and thieves who would help themselves to produce around harvest time. Of those farmers surveyed, 13 percent reported hiring laborers. The average amount paid to a laborer was TSh 820 per season.

Urban dwellers most commonly reported growing cassava, rice, maize, bananas, coconut, and millet. They grew fruits like bananas, oranges, and pineapples, which were most popular, and also guavas, breadfruit, pawpaws, and mangoes. They mentioned vegetables like potatoes, beans, spinach, and tomatoes most frequently, while cashew nuts, coffee, cotton, cloves, and groundnuts were the most popular cash crops. One-half said they sold their produce, but, with the exception of those who produced cash crops, they usually sold small quantities because the main purpose of cultivation was consumption.

CONCLUSIONS

The drop in real wages since the mid-1970s was one of the most important changes that set the stage for the developments described in this book. It resulted in the dramatic increase in the pursuit of income-generating activities by workers and members of their households. Some workers or their family members were involved in sideline occupations, which usually provided greater compensation than did their formal jobs. Others left formal employment altogether because their jobs simply could not sustain them. In all, reliance on the government, which had been the largest employer, diminished as people increasingly sought private and informal economic strategies. The drop in real wages resulted in a slowing down of migration to the cities, strengthened rural-urban linkages, and increased urban farming. Income differentials also expanded significantly as a result of greater reliance on informal incomes. Access to the informal economy was determined largely by access to capital, with the most lucrative projects requiring the largest amounts of starting capital. All of these developments had an impact on the way in which people defended their right to subsist. They found themselves challenged not only by the adverse economic conditions in which they found themselves but also by a state whose policies made it ever more difficult to pursue productive economic activities.

3 Shifting Boundaries of State Control

The informal sector is filling gaps where the government has failed.
We have failed to meet the needs of people. The people are planning
for us.

Dar es Salaam urban planner, City Council

Although there is a consensus that in Eastern Europe and countries like India, China, and the former Soviet Union the impetus for economic restructuring has come almost entirely from internal pressures, it is at the same time commonly believed that economic reform in Africa and Latin America has been externally induced, both by developments within the world economy and by institutions like the IMF and the World Bank (Nelson 1989).

My study of the informal economy in Tanzania suggests that the scenario may not be so simple in Africa. The IMF, the World Bank, and foreign donors no doubt played a major role in inducing such change, but external pressures do not entirely explain the mechanisms of change and cannot account for the internal conditions that permitted these policies to be carried out. Moreover, many reforms were not tied to donor conditionality. Many of them had to do with legalizing aspects of the informal economy and adopting small measures in the direction of creating an atmosphere more conducive to micro- and small-scale entrepreneurs.

Part of the explanation for the mechanisms of change will be dealt with in chapter 4, which discusses the role of intra-elite conflicts in changing the direction of the country's policies. But first it is necessary to explain in broader strokes why a strongly interventionist state like the one in Tanzania began to pull back the boundaries of its control in regulating the economy and social relations. Given the leadership's ideological leanings toward state-centered development and given the large group of bureaucrats who had vested interests in protecting state monopolies, how did this state move toward privatization, liberalization, and legalization of various economic activities that had previously been considered illegal?

It is clear that the more the Tanzanian state tried to pursue an interventionist stance, the less capacity it had to redistribute resources and affect social relations. Robert Bates's argument that economic inefficiencies could be tolerated as long as they served political rationalities applied to Tanzania until the mid-1980s. According to Bates (1981), state intervention in markets created economic inefficiencies, but these interests also generated resources by which to govern and help establish loyal constituencies. At some point, however—and Tanzania clearly reached this point around the mid-1980s—the cost of economic inefficiencies and distortions outweighed the political gains. It eventually became politically inexpedient to carry out economic policies that undermined key strata of the population, especially the rural sector.

The need to address some of these economic irrationalities resulted in a coalescence of external and internal pressures for change. To explain the linkages between these pressures in affecting the new direction in Tanzania's policy making, it is necessary to show how and why the borders of state control over the economy and society were expanded in the first place. In Tanzania, as in other parts of the Third World, much of the state's role in society was a consequence of the central role it had played during the colonial era. When African nations were becoming independent, developments in the West influenced the new African leaders' thinking about the state. In particular, they were influenced by the market failures of the 1930s and the reconstruction policies of the 1940s and 1950s. The views of development economists, who saw an even greater need for state intervention in the economies of developing countries, were fused with those of nationalist Third World leaders. In Africa, these nationalists frequently looked to the state as a means of exerting domestic interests over foreign interests (Brett 1987, 31; Wilson 1988, 25). Moreover, at independence, there was only a small African entrepreneur class, which meant that the state sought to fulfill functions that might otherwise have been undertaken by the private sector.

Centralization in Tanzania, as in other parts of Africa, took the form of highly concentrated administrative powers in the central government, with diminishing revenue, personnel, and authority allocated to the localities. Local authorities tended to become simply functionaries of central government, at times holding limited powers to collect revenue and carry out hiring. Bureaucratic programs emanated from national plans or directives that all too often were implemented with little regard for local conditions. Nongovernmental bases for organization were systematically eliminated, competing parties were banned, and independent voluntary associations were kept under surveillance and harassed. Judiciaries and legislatures lost their independence in varying degrees to the executive (Wunsch and Olowu 1991).

In Tanzania the emphasis on the centrality of the state was not only a holdover from the colonial structures but also a legacy of British Fabian socialist influences, which saw the state as the great equalizer of incomes and provider of social services, governing the commanding heights of the economy and owning key sectors of the economy (Coulson 1982, 327).

In the 1960s Tanzania embarked on a path of non-Marxist socialism, which saw the emergence of a highly centralized state that placed itself at the center of the development agenda. The state's increased interventionism was directly related to the expansion of the party's role and its gradual assertion of dominance over the government. State involvement in the economy grew dramatically after the party's 1967 Arusha Declaration, which resulted in the nationalization of major financial, commercial, and manufacturing institutions. The parastatal sector grew at an unprecedented rate: parastatal companies numbered around 450 by the 1980s. The government took over the purchasing and marketing of crops through large, state-run crop authorities. It regulated prices, wages, interest rates, internal and external trade, and investment. By 1976 the government controlled 65 percent of wage employment and 70 percent of the country's wage bill (International Labour Organisation 1982, 267). From 1972 to 1975 the government also carried out a massive campaign to resettle rural people into villages; it launched a Universal Primary Education campaign in 1976; and it expanded health and water services in the 1970s.

As Tanzania was hit by a series of especially hard external shocks in the late 1970s, the economy simply could not sustain this kind of government expansion; and as a consequence Tanzania became even more dependent on foreign aid and loans (Boesen et al. 1986). Tanzania fell into economic crisis and stagnation in the late 1970s. This crisis manifested itself in various ways, including a balance-of-payments crisis; poor performance in the agricultural and industrial sectors; government budget and trade deficits; and declining standards of living for most ordinary citizens. The GDP per capita annual growth rate declined from 5 percent in the 1960s to -0.8 percent in 1984, hitting an all-time low of -4.4 percent in 1981 (United Republic of Tanzania, Economic Survey 1984).

In the 1960s Tanzania had the highest rate of increase in food production for all of Africa in the 1960s and was exporting food to neighboring countries. By the mid-1970s the country was importing food, and by the mid-1980s food accounted for 20 percent of all imports. By the end of 1984 Tanzania's debt was $3.3 billion. Moreover, the country's debt-service ratio had risen to 70 percent (Lofchie 1988, 144, 147).

Although industry suffered considerably, falling to a −11.2 percent annual growth rate in 1981, the crisis was primarily an agricultural one in a country where 85 percent of the population was involved in the agricultural sector. Agriculture suffered setbacks from the unavailability of foreign and domestic inputs, adequate transportation facilities, and fuel, which in turn led to difficulties in the collection of crops and to crop wastage. In 1981 an already troubled economy took a turn for the worse, with the output of commercial agriculture and cash-crop exports declining to half of what they had been in the 1970s. Real agricultural output declined by 8.7 percent in 1982 alone (Lipumba 1984, 24).

The heavy state centralization of the 1960s and 1970s gave way in the 1980s to economic reform and liberalization as the boundaries of state control were pulled back. In this chapter I explore the background to this process, first by looking at external causes of crisis and the role of state interventionism in the economic crisis. Then I show how the state, as part of its policy of interventionism, expanded its control over independent social organizations. The state never could completely dominate the domain of voluntary associations. Eventually it was forced to accept the activities of many of these organizations, which had become crucial in sustaining society throughout the years of hardship. I conclude the chapter with a brief explanation of state responses to the crisis in the form of various economic-recovery programs and the role of external pressures in directing some of these reforms.

EXTERNAL CAUSES OF CRISIS

Tanzania's position in the world economy as an exporter of agricultural crops and other primary products set the initial parameters of state capacity. Agricultural commodities, which have generally suffered from depressed price levels, accounted for 80 percent of Tanzania's total export earnings. Moreover, Tanzania's large-scale industry was heavily dependent on imports. Tanzania's dependent position in the world economy was especially evident in its vulnerability to external shocks like the rise in import prices, notably oil prices. The first oil-price shock, in 1973, had a severe effect on Tanzania's economy, but the second increase, in 1979, and the subsequent world recession had a crippling effect on Tanzania's economic performance. Expenditures for oil imports rose from 7–8 percent to 23 percent of total imports between 1980 and 1982 alone (Svendsen 1986, 62).

One of the most important causes of the balance-of-payments crisis in Tanzania was the declining terms of trade between 1973 and 1980, dropping 1.7 percent a year during this period. Tanzania's largest export commodity, coffee, was especially hard hit when world market prices dropped by 36 percent between 1977 and 1978. The fall in terms of trade between 1977 and 1987 was steeper than in the previous decade. Nevertheless, in both decades Tanzania's purchasing power declined dramatically, due to the declining volume of exports (Lele 1984; Lofchie 1988, 152; Ndulu 1988, 11; Sharpley 1985).

The 1978–1979 war with Uganda, another external shock, cost approximately $500 million. It compounded Tanzania's economic troubles and caused major disruptions in production (Lipumba 1984, 27). It also had a major impact on the government's budget deficit, which jumped from 10 percent of the GDP in 1976–1977 to 20 percent in 1978–1979 (Svendsen 1986, 67). After the war, however, military expenditure continued to increase, in part due to Tanzania's support of Mozambique in its battle against the South African–backed RENAMO guerrilla forces.

Recurring droughts also took their toll on agricultural production, especially those of 1973–1974 and 1984. Moreover, the break with the East African Community in 1977 put an additional burden on Tanzania's failing economy. Tanzania lost out in the breakup, having to use its limited foreign-exchange reserves to replace railroad engines and cars, airplanes, and other formerly joint properties.

STATE INTERVENTIONISM AND ECONOMIC CRISIS

These external pressures exacerbated the internal causes of the crisis that culminated in the early 1980s. One of the most significant manifestations of the crisis was the foreign-exchange shortage. The shortage became especially severe in the late 1970s, affecting not only the trade deficit but also development projects, social services, and the maintenance of the infrastructure.

Drops in agricultural production and exports were the most important factors in explaining the foreign-exchange crisis. The volume of exports was reduced by half from 1970 to 1980, even when commodity terms of trade improved. Therefore, even without the drop in coffee prices in

1977/1978 Tanzania would have experienced a balance-of-payments crisis because of the decline in production.

Reasons for the decline in production are varied. The food harvest failures of 1973–1975 had thrown the Tanzanian economy into the most serious crisis it had experienced since independence. With oil prices rising and foreign-exchange reserves depleted because of the need to buy grain on the international market, the government increased the prices of domestic crops after 1975, while export-crop prices deteriorated.

The decline in the production of cash crops in favor of food crops in the 1970s was also caused by the growing gap between world market prices and the prices paid to agricultural producers by state-run-crop authorities. From 1970 to 1980 agricultural producer prices for fourteen key crops declined on an average of 31 percent, while their sales prices on the world market increased in real terms by 12 percent. This means that there was a continuous decline in producer share of crop sales, from 66 percent in 1970 to 42 percent in 1980. Half of the transferred revenue went directly to the central government through taxation of exports, and the other half went to the running of crop-marketing authorities, in particular the National Milling Corporation, that were running at a loss (Ellis 1983). Frank Ellis concluded that the transfer of resources was so crucial that the survival of the state itself became contingent on the transfer of financial resources from agricultural producers. Overvaluation of Tanzania's currency also contributed significantly to declining production of export crops by reducing the real prices accruing to smallholder producers. By 1985, for example, it was estimated that the shilling was overvalued by about 1,000 percent (Lofchie 1988, 156).

Apart from shifting to the production of food crops, agricultural smallholders also responded by selling their export crops on parallel markets to neighboring countries. Others shifted to small-scale manufacturing to obtain necessary cash or migrated to cities to enter the urban informal sector.

But even with the shift from export crops to food crops, Tanzania registered a decline in net food-crop production. Part of this probably was not a real decline but a function of the fact that food was increasingly making its way through parallel markets. However, overvaluation of the currency contributed to the decrease in food production by lowering the producer prices on food staples by the same amount that export-crop prices were lowered because of the country's pricing structures. It encouraged the importation of relatively cheap foods and kept the costs of agricultural services, transport, and inputs high (Lofchie 1988, 156).

Another major cause of the crisis that culminated in the early 1980s was the focus on industrial programs at the expense of agriculture in a country where the majority of the population are rural smallholder producers and where agricultural commodities are the main source of domestic revenue, the base that sustains other sectors. The investment structure favored expansion of an already underutilized industry, with few results in increased production. Industrial production declined despite massive capital inflows at a rate of 20 percent a year from 1978 to 1982 in monetary GDP (Boesen et al. 1986, 19). Concomitantly, investment in agriculture was neglected. Although agriculture continued to be the main sector contributing to real output and the key generator of foreign exchange, investment in agriculture declined from 1976 to 1981 by 37 percent (Ndulu and Hyuha 1984, 53).

Moreover, agricultural producers were subject to a number of policies that had adverse effects on production. These included the low prices paid to them for export crops; the villagization program of 1972–1975; the 1976 abolition of cooperative unions, which were replaced by cumbersome, inefficient crop authorities; and the funneling of scarce resources into costly state farms.

The impact of the decline in agricultural production on the economy was dramatic. The trade balance, which had been in surplus in the 1960s, experienced a rapidly increasing deficit of more than 60 percent from 1970 to 1980. Tanzania thus found itself in a severe and chronic foreign-exchange crisis that persisted throughout the 1980s.

Other factors also contributed to the balance-of-payments crisis. Tanzania had several minor balance-of-payments crises in the early 1970s, but the problem did not become serious until 1977. In fact, at a crucial juncture in 1977 the IMF and the World Bank advised Tanzania that its accumulation of external reserves was too high and that it should not hoard its reserves but spend them to develop more rapidly. Thus, following the advice of the Fund and the Bank, Tanzania "deconfined" its imports from control by six parastatal organizations under the Board of Internal Trade; that is, it liberalized imports, allowing importers to purchase goods outside government control. As it turned out, the government was unable to control the kinds of goods that were being brought into the country, and a substantial proportion of the money was spent on luxury goods instead of badly needed industrial inputs that the liberalization policy had intended to bring in. The upshot of these policies, in particular the liberalization of imports, was the depletion of foreign reserves (Payer 1982, 10–11). Imports increased by 54 percent from 1977 to 1978, while foreign reserves declined from $300 million to $30 million in the same period (Svendsen 1986, 67).

In addition to the balance-of-payments crisis, there were inflationary pressures on the economy related to the continuing expansion of money supply without a simultaneous increase in real output. Between 1970 and 1977 the money supply grew at an annual rate of 20 percent, while real monetary GDP during the same years was around 4 to 5 percent. Expansion of the money supply helped finance government spending, which increased by 47.4 percent between 1978 and 1980, while revenue increased by only 27.6 percent. By 1979–1980, what had been a net surplus position quickly became a net deficit, while the ratio of overall budget deficit to GNP rose from 10.6 percent in 1977–1978 to 20.4 percent in 1979–1980 (Ndulu 1988, 11).

The deficit was financed primarily by external donors and borrowing from domestic banks. The public sector became the largest debtor to the National Bank of Tanzania, with the marketing authorities and public corporations owing the most. The crop authorities, which were supposed to be money-making enterprises, were responsible for an overdraft of Tsh 6 billion at the end of 1982—an overdraft of 200 percent of the value of the crops purchased. The National Milling Corporation's overdraft alone was 715 percent of the value of the crops purchased; the Tanzania Cotton Authorities had an overdraft of 324 percent of the crops purchased (Lipumba 1984, 30).

The government continued to invest heavily in programs that had political imperatives but little in the way of economic return. One of these programs was the transfer of the capital from Dar es Salaam to Dodoma, located in the heart of the country. The transfer, planned in 1975, has been exceedingly costly, for it has involved the maintenance of two capitals. Although some government buildings were constructed in Dodoma, no foreign embassies moved, and new embassies continued to be built in Dar es Salaam throughout the 1980s. The prospects that the transfer would actually take place looked dim twenty years after the initial plans were drawn up.

EXPANDING BOUNDARIES OF STATE CONTROL IN SOCIETY

The expansion of government and party control of the economy in Tanzania was accompanied by the equally interventionist role of government and party in society and in relation to social organizations. As in many African states, Tanzania's ruling party in the years after independence absorbed or coopted key organizations like trade unions and cooperatives. The government, likewise, eliminated or curtailed the activities of other independent organizations. In the 1980s these same organizations increased in importance as Tanzania plunged more deeply into economic crisis. Similarly, people formed new organizations and revitalized old ones to cope with the growing economic and other uncertainties of life.

Tanzania has a rich history of voluntary associations, mutual-aid societies, and various kinds of self-help organizations and networks. As in other parts of Africa, voluntary associations and social networks, rather than individuals (as in electoral politics) or broader social constellations (such as class or ethnicity) form the basis of social, economic, and political activity. People joined voluntary associations to further their social, economic, and political interests, to enhance their personal status, or simply to cope with a changing social environment (Chazan 1982, 185; Chazan et al. 1988, 72–73).

During the colonial period, urban voluntary associations in Africa grew to serve a number of purposes. Some of the first organizations (burial societies, for example) emerged to provide new migrants with social services that in rural areas had been taken care of by relatives (Wallerstein 1964, 320). Other forms of organization in this period included football clubs, dance societies, credit associations, occupational groups, cooperatives, trade unions, and Christian religious organizations, which provided most of the health and education services prior to independence.

Voluntary associations continued to proliferate in the postindependence years. Religious organizations, both Christian and Muslim, continued to be among the most vital institutions in the country. Professional associations of teachers, nurses, and lawyers flourished, as did welfare associations. The majority of groups—mutual-aid societies, harvesting groups, and cultivating teams, for instance—remained community based, informally organized, and usually not registered.

As in other parts of Africa, in Tanzania the role of local nonformal organizations increased as avenues for participation in formal associations were cut off (Chazan 1982, 170). Moreover, where the state's attempts to exert monopolistic control over society and the economy exceeded its capacity to regulate social relations and allocate resources effectively, people's own organizational structures often emerged to fulfill a variety of societal needs. The state's growing inability to guarantee adequate police protection, to ensure that wages bore some relation to the cost of living, and to provide basic social and public services has led people in recent years to form their own organizations to cope with some of the difficulties they face.

POLITICAL PARTICIPATION

Unlike most African states, Tanzania from the outset adopted an approach that saw the political participation of people as vital to the success of the nation's development plans (Tripp 1992). The party, however, served as the main vehicle for this participation. By 1988 the CCM had a membership of 2,529,362 members, or 11 percent of the population. Participation was not intended to take the form of local, autonomous organization or grassroots initiatives outside the party sphere. The party was hierarchically structured, so that at the ground level every ten or so houses had a party cell representative through whom directives from the upper echelons filtered down. Little input, however, filtered up through these same channels, although this was one of the aims of creating the cells. The curtailment of independent initiative within the party led numerous political scientists to conclude that real citizen participation in formal institutions was limited (Samoff 1974, 45).

Local practices, forms of organization, and ways of thinking were rarely taken into account or used as a basis for policy development by the government or the party. The lack of input at the local level prompted one party branch leader, a textile worker, to remark in an interview: "Party leaders treat people like small children and tell you, 'Don't cry, I'll give you sweets.' In the past the party was secure, and the life of the people was considered. People even came to cell meetings at that time. Today they come only if we press hard for them to come. At that time it was something to be a party leader. Now if you come around they don't want to be troubled by you."[1]

In the early 1970s the party bureaucracy was strengthened from the regional level down to the ward level, leaving salaried party bureaucrats with more power than elected officials of comparable rank. At the same time, the government eliminated potential channels for participation when it launched a decentralization program and abolished local governments in 1972. Local government in Tanzania had been patterned along the lines of the British system, which had responsibility for managing schools, dispensaries, refuse disposal, and all key public services. The Dar es Salaam Municipality was established in 1945 as the first local government. At independence in 1961 it became an urban council. With the 1965 establishment of the one-party state, local governments came under greater party control but remained under the central-government ministry in charge of local governments (Kulaba 1989, 217–19).

Theoretically, the 1972 "decentralization" should have meant more opportunities for genuine participation, better comprehension of local conditions, faster implementation of policies, and a shift of resources and decision making from central to local government. Decentralization was described in the press as a move toward greater democratization to encourage local participation in decision making and planning. However, the adopted decentralization plan, drawn up by a private consulting firm, the McKinsey Company, shifted power to the field administration away from the regions (Kleemeier 1984, 188). Decentralization proved in practice to be a move toward greater centralization. Local governments were replaced by an extension of the central civil service at the regional and district levels under the direction of the prime minister's office, making the bureaucracy accountable not to the people but to central government, which controlled funds and personnel (Coulson 1982, 254).

Like colonial authorities who feared that voluntary associations would serve as "unconscious nurseries of democratic life," as David Kimble put it (Kimble 1953, 28), the new leaders saw the unbridled expansion of voluntary associations as a threat to the dominance of their states (Liebenow 1986, 234; Wallerstein 1964, 333). Tanzania was no exception, as the independent government and party set out to coopt or eliminate existing organizations and form new ones under the party's aegis.

Throughout the early 1970s local political and economic organizations were systematically undermined. In urban areas the trade-union movement was significantly curtailed; in rural areas the cooperatives were replaced by crop authorities in 1976, bringing them more under direct state control. Like local governments, they had been relatively accountable to the local communities prior to their removal (Kleemeier 1984, 187). Genuine grassroots initiatives in the countryside were also crushed in this period. The Ruvuma Development Association was a case in point. It succeeded in organizing communal production and providing social services to its members. Its autonomy and emphasis on democracy and self-reliance were perceived as a threat by regional authorities, who disbanded the association in 1969. As Joel Samoff wrote (1974, 69), "In Tanzania, Party policy frowns on the formation of interest groups in general, and economic interest groups in particular. . . . It is assumed that the political functions performed by interest groups in other polities—especially interest aggregation, articulation and communication—are performed by

TANU and its auxiliaries and that interest groups, which could be used to form competing centers of power, are both unnecessary and dangerous." By the early 1980s the ruling party had five affiliate organizations under its wing: the Union of Tanzanian Women, the Youth Organization, the Union of Tanzanian Workers, the Union of Cooperative Societies, and the Tanzanian Parents Association.

The suppression of independent organizations was disastrous for both the state and society. As Gus Liebenow has pointed out, it represented a loss of creativity and different perspectives regarding alternative courses of development. Given the party's limited scope and revenues, it could ill afford to assume the services and functions of such organizations even if it wanted to. As a consequence, the party had to bear the burden of failure in times of crisis, contributing to the demise of its legitimacy (Liebenow 1986, 234).

THE CASE OF ORGANIZED LABOR

The state felt especially threatened by organized labor, so the autonomy of the trade-union movement was usurped soon after independence. The party's stance toward labor in the urban setting is indicative of its general posture toward voluntary associations and for this reason is worth exploring briefly. Tanzania had a history of militant strike action, but such confrontations were surprisingly few by the 1980s, considering the large incongruence between wages and the cost of living. In the past, when wages fell behind inflation, workers organized and initiated strikes.

The first trade unions were formed by Asians in the 1930s, including the union of shop assistants of Tanganyika and the Asiatic labor union of Sikh carpenters (Iliffe 1979, 346). Domestic servants formed the largest occupational group in Dar es Salaam, and the first registered African trade union was the Cooks, Washermen and House Servants Association, started in 1939. Other unions were soon to follow, including the African Teachers Association, established in 1944, and the Railway African Association, which by the end of 1945 was the most powerful workers' organization in the territory (Iliffe 1979, 396–97).

Because the docks were originally the largest employer of laborers, they were also the scene of the earliest militant labor action. Dockworkers walked off their jobs in 1939, 1943, and 1947 in efforts to keep wages abreast with wartime inflation (Iliffe 1970). The 1947 victory by dockworkers, in particular, made them the best paid and most formidable labor force in the country, according to historian John Iliffe. Later that year dockworkers organized the Dockworkers and Stevedores Union (Iliffe 1970, 134).

The labor movement that emerged in the 1950s was vital to the success of TANU's drive for independence. The Tanganyika Federation of Labour (TFL) emerged as the leading organizer of workers in 1955, launching a union drive that is said to be unequaled in Africa's history. By 1961, 42 percent of Tanzania's workers were unionized, compared with 12 percent in Uganda and 8 percent in Kenya in the same period. The union movement had grown from 1 registered union with 381 members in 1951 to a powerful movement of 35 registered unions in 1961 representing 203,000 members (Iliffe 1979, 539). Although the colonial government had forbidden cooperation between the TFL and TANU, the two groups jointly mobilized successful boycotts during the 1957 bus strike and the 1958 brewery workers' strike (Coulson 1982, 116–17). TFL's cooperation with TANU proved to be decisive for the independence movement.

The autonomy the labor movement had exhibited in the 1940s and 1950s was sharply curtailed after independence in 1961, even though much of the leadership of the new nation came from the organized labor movement. The government, fearing instability, effectively limited the right to strike in its 1962 Trade Disputes (Settlement) Act and prevented civil servants from joining unions. In the course of the 1964 army mutiny, all of the trade-union leaders in Dar es Salaam who were suspected of being antigovernment were detained, and only one trade union, the National Union of Tanganyika Workers (NUTA), was allowed. NUTA was affiliated with the party, and its general secretary was appointed by the country's president. Membership in the union was made compulsory for workers (Coulson 1982, 137, 140).

Thus after 1964 most labor opposition necessarily took place outside the union. With the exception of a wave of strikes in the early 1970s, the state had, for all intents and purposes, succeeded in subduing the labor movement. The unusual outbreak of resistance occurred in 1971, when the party issued guidelines called *Mwongozo*, which had clauses stipulating that Tanzanian leaders could not be "arrogant, extravagant, contemptuous and oppressive." Seizing on the *Mwongozo* guidelines as a charter, workers initiated thirty-one strikes against management over a period of two years. By July 1973 the government had crushed the wave of strikes. Elected workers who had led the labor action during this period were fired, and from then on all forms of mass action required party approval. In 1977 NUTA was replaced by a workers' mass organization, the Trade Union of

Tanzanian Workers (JUWATA), affiliated with the ruling party (Coulson 1982, 284, 289; Jackson 1979).

The JUWATA Association of Tanzanian Workers had virtually no independence from the ruling party, and management and workers were fused into this one organization. When I interviewed a worker who had been at a textile factory for twenty years, he expressed a common viewpoint regarding the workers' association: "JUWATA does not help much because it is linked to the management. So it does not represent the workers' interests. The same person can be a manager and JUWATA representative. What good is that?"[2]

In the few instances of independent labor action, the outcomes were unusually violent in a country that enjoyed relative stability compared with most African countries. For example, in 1986 three workers were killed, seventeen injured, and thirteen arrested in a riot that broke out at the Kilombero II Sugar Company in Morogoro. Five hundred sugarcane cutters were protesting low wages and, in particular, the fact that a customary bonus had been left out of their monthly paychecks. They blocked the gate of the factory, preventing other workers from entering or leaving, and were shot at in a confrontation with the Field Force Unit policemen.[3]

Only after the party severed its formal ties with JUWATA in 1991 did labor begin to exert its independence once again. Workers began to strike in 1994, mainly over wage issues. The new trade-union umbrella organization, OTTU, initially found it difficult to shake the legacy of two decades of party control, as individual trade unions (such as the teachers' union) sought to gain independence from the body, openly questioning the extent of its autonomy from the CCM.

RESPONSES TO THE CRISIS: RETREATING STATE BOUNDARIES

Attempts to suppress independent organizations were only partially successful. As the crisis deepened, local informal organizations (such as rotating-credit associations, local-defense teams, and informal agricultural and fishing cooperatives) flourished and helped people manage their difficulties. These organizations helped take the heat off the state: functions that once were the prerogative of the state were now more frequently assumed by other groups and individuals. Thus demands that would have otherwise been placed on the state were diverted, possibly averting a more serious legitimacy crisis. When people made demands, they called on the state to lift its numerous and often tedious restrictions in order to make it easier to cope with the economic difficulties they were facing. The kinds of demands people did make on organs of the state had to do, as I try to show in chapter 6, with easing licensing restrictions on the poor, ending militia harassment of vendors, and abolishing party restrictions on members with two incomes. The focus of popular demands was not on extracting goods from the state but, rather, on getting the state to extricate itself from society.

And indeed, the government and the party began to extricate themselves from their domination both of social institutions (as I show in the final chapter) and the economy. The crisis limited the government's options significantly and forced it to initiate a series of economic-recovery programs. Declining revenue from taxation of the export sector was threatening the state's very existence because agricultural producers channeled most of their commodities through parallel markets. The state's ability to regulate social relations was rapidly deteriorating as the informal economy and other evasions of state control flourished. Moreover, the economic hardships the people experienced had led to a serious legitimacy crisis for CCM and government leaders.

These domestic pressures were reinforced by mounting pressures from the donor community for Tanzania to adopt an IMF program with increasingly rigorous austerity measures. In fact, without such forceful external pressures, it is unlikely that the reforms would have been as extensive as they were. Indeed, the first two reform programs that were initiated prior to the 1986 IMF agreement were largely unsuccessful and not as drastic as the kinds of measures implemented in the recovery programs of 1986 and 1989. Those in the government who pressed for greater reform were bolstered by the impact of the IMF agreement and the positions of donors. Even though they were critical of various IMF conditions, their political futures had became tied to the success or failure of the new economic strategy and the amount of donor support Tanzania could attain.

After an unsuccessful attempt to obtain IMF support in 1980, differences between the IMF and the Tanzanian government effectively kept Tanzania from signing an agreement with the fund until 1986. Meanwhile, Tanzania adopted its own National Economic Stabilization Program in 1981, which was poorly designed and did not run its course. In 1982 a more far-reaching, three-year Structural Adjustment Program was implemented in the hope that it would lead to an agreement with the IMF and the World Bank. It aimed to strengthen the government's control of financial flows. In particular, it sought measures to restore output, reduce the budget deficit, reduce money-supply growth, and restore the external balance through expansion of exports. The program involved modest currency devaluations and shifting of resources from capital to recurrent uses, but ultimately it did little to reverse the deterioration of the economy until 1984. At that point measures to restructure incentives occurred through a liberalized "own-funds import scheme" and price deregulation to encourage a movement from illegal to legal importation of goods (Ndulu and Mwega 1994, 119).

Finally, in 1986 a three-year Economic Recovery Programme (ERP) was launched. Some of the ERP measures included exchange-rate adjustments, raising official producer prices, lifting price controls, increasing foreign-exchange allocations, and efforts to raise the level of domestic savings in order to improve the infrastructure and to launch major rehabilitation projects.

The initiation of the ERP, however, could not solve Tanzania's foreign-exchange crisis. As foreign-exchange supplies dried up, Tanzania had little choice but to return to the negotiating table with the IMF. An agreement with the IMF was reached in July 1986, as a result of which the IMF provided a Structural Adjustment Facility (1987–1990). Had Tanzania failed to reach this agreement, it would have faced drastic cuts in aid from the Nordic countries and other Western donors, which made their continued support contingent on the signing of an agreement with the IMF. In addition, Tanzania would not have been able to reschedule its previous loan payments.

The IMF agreed to a standby arrangement subject to various criteria, which included substantial devaluations, restrictions on the amount of credit that could be transferred from the banking system to government institutions, limits on the accumulation of new debt, and controls on new external borrowing and on the overall budget deficit. Even though Tanzania and the IMF came to an agreement, ending a six-year impasse, differences persisted. In signing an agreement with the IMF, Tanzania also came under considerable pressure to adopt various measures opposed by the country's leaders. These included the fast pace of currency devaluation, constraints on wage increases, and cuts in public services.

The government launched a second three-year Economic and Social Action Program in 1989–1991 along the same lines as the first, which included initiatives to begin reversing the deterioration of social services that had occurred during the previous decade of reforms. Similarly, the IMF continued to support the government's economic program through a three-year Enhanced Structural Adjustment Facility starting in 1991, but no drawings on these funds were permitted after December 1992 because the country fell short of meeting set macroeconomic targets (*Country Profile* 1994–1995, 11).

The results of the economic restructuring programs were mixed. One of the main consequences was the rise in growth rates, with the real GDP increasing from a 1.8 percent average rate of increase in the 1977–1986 period to a 4.4 percent average rate of increase between 1987 and 1994. The year 1994 saw the beginnings of a downturn in the economy's growth, declining from a 4.1 percent annual growth rate in 1993 to a 3 percent annual growth rate in 1994. Yet, in spite of its improved economic growth rates, Tanzania remained one of the poorest countries in the world in the mid-1990s.

Agricultural production registered a 4.9 percent anverage growth rate from 1986 to 1993. Although still below peak production levels, crops like coffee, tea, cashew nuts, tobacco, and sisal made a recovery and did, in fact, respond to price incentives. Manufacturing was growing at an average rate of 6 percent annually from 1987 to 1991, reversing the downward trend so evident between 1976 and 1986, when real value added by manufacturing fell by 30 percent (*Country Profile* 1994–1995, 21). Industrial production, however, continued to be constrained by erratic power supply and poor infrastructure and had begun to slow down significantly after 1992 (*Country Profile* 1994–1995, 13).[4] It dropped from 70 percent capacity in 1989 to about 30 percent in 1994.[5] Mining reached a 45.5 percent real growth level in 1991 largely due to the Bank of Tanzania's policy of purchasing gold directly from miners at prices above the official exchange rate in order to undercut the black marketeers. Prospects for an even higher rate were expected as new investments in this sector grew.[6]

After 1985 both exports and imports grew, but the total import bill was almost four times greater than export receipts by 1993. The current-account deficit widened from $435 million in 1986–1987 to an estimated $1,103 million in 1993. In this same period, Tanzania's external debt jumped from $3.5 billion in 1986 to $7.6 billion in 1993, at which point its debt had risen to almost four times its GNP and seven times its export earnings, which is high compared with the rest of Africa (World Bank 1995, 658–59). By 1995 Tanzania's external debt was $6.9 billion, and the country was borrowing up to $1.2 billion annually from donors. Tanzania's dependence on donors increased dramatically, to the point where by the mid-1990s it expected foreign assistance to finance 82 percent of the development budget (Bagachwa 1993, 42). This dependence was especially problematic, given the shrinking of donor development budgets for Africa and bilateral donors' own domestic pressures to cut foreign assistance. Donors were also worried about the lack of improvement in the accounts deficit and about corruption. Tanzania's key donors suspended aid at the end of 1994 to protest corruption and illegal use of tax exemptions, which, according to a World Bank investigation, had cost the national treasury as much as $120 million.[7]

Thus even though Tanzania's economy showed signs of improvement, the external-payments position remained vulnerable to declines in commodity prices, rising import prices, and growing debt-service obligations. According to a November 1995 Bank of Tanzania monthly report, Tanzania was spending more than three-quarters of its annual loans in debt servicing and repayment in 1995. Equally troublesome have been the social costs of these adjustments. Suppressed wages and large cuts in social services continued to adversely affect the livelihood of Tanzania's people. Cost sharing in education and health services put additional burdens on the poor. For example, enrollment rates in schools fell from 92 percent in 1977 to 40 percent in 1994, and teachers left the profession in large numbers. Teachers were making only $40 a month, whereas some casual laborers had a monthly income of $50 in 1994.[8] Another indicator of the decline in public services was the worsening of urban dwellers' access to safe water. In 1969, 90 percent of urban dwellers had access to safe water, but by 1993 only 56 percent did. For rural dwellers the deterioration of these services was less dramatic: 22 percent had access to safe water in 1993, down by 4 percent from 1976 (Ferreira and Goodhart 1995). Although these drops in the standard of living can be, in part, attributed to the economic crisis that preceded structural adjustment, it is also clear that adjustment did little to reverse the general direction of decline in these social and public services.

At the same time, inflationary pressures and declining real wages in the formal sector slowed down under economic reform. Per capita expenditures (in nominal terms) increased by 12 percent between 1991 and 1993 if one accounts for an inflation rate of 26.5 percent during this period. For rural dwellers, the average annual growth rate of per capita expenditures (with inflation factored in) was around 9.6 percent during this period, whereas for Dar es Salaam residents it was 27 percent (Ferreira and Goodhart 1995, 8). The critical explanation for these increases in expenditures lies with the increasing importance of the informal economy, which continued to expand while formal incomes continued to stagnate.

CONCLUSIONS

The party has used the government in its bid to expand its control, first by declaring supremacy over the National Assembly in 1975 and over the government in 1977 and then by increasing the government's role in directing development to an even greater extent than before. What emerged was a highly interventionist state, which, in spite of its professed goals of self-reliance and popular participation in development, intervened in the economy and in regulating social relations in a manner unacceptable to large numbers of Tanzanians. At its worst, the state was coercive, as seen in its attempts to forcibly remove people from their homes during the massive Operation Vijijini campaign to resettle the rural population in villages in the early 1970s. Its more benign manifestations involved the paternalism that leaders expressed in their interactions with local people.

Party and government efforts to crush independent organizations were not entirely successful. Many independent associations persisted, and some, such as informal, community voluntary associations, even proliferated during the years of crisis. Moreover, people found ways to work around government and party restrictions that interfered with their ability to obtain a living income. Selling crops on parallel markets and many other such strategies, which I explore in detail in chapter 6, undermined the capacity of the state and began to seriously threaten its viability. External shocks to the economy exacerbated these internal conflicts. These factors, coupled with mounting pressures from external donors, left the government with little alternative but to retreat from the kind of interventionist policies it had maintained throughout the 1970s. How this crucial transition from state expansion to state retreat was engineered is explained in greater detail in the following chapter.

4 The Informal Economy and the Politics of Economic Reform

When Tanzania went to the Washington-based institution after years of resisting, the International Monetary Fund (IMF) said like Shylock to Antonio 'Ah, at last you have come.' As it turned out, Antonio could not repay the loan. Shylock then demanded his pound of flesh. . . . Of course, sometimes we cannot repay the debt and, of course, the IMF demands its pound of flesh. . . . The IMF is now a tool to control the Governments of the Third World.

    Daily News, 10 June 1988, quoting Party Chairman Julius Nyerere

The pound of flesh usually demanded by Shylock [IMF] will be taken without shedding a drop of blood.

    Daily News, 29 July 1986, quoting President Ali Hassan Mwinyi

By the mid-1980s two broad coalitions had emerged in Tanzania, one led by those favoring economic reform and the other led by those who wanted to see more modest changes at a slower pace. The reformists, who had coalesced around the government, prevailed over opponents of reform, who had aligned themselves more closely with the party.[1]

However, when Tanzania embarked on its path of economic reforms, neither supporters nor detractors of these new policies had accounted for one crucial factor that would explain why the austerity measures of the reform program were met with so little resistance among the sectors of society they affected the most: workers and civil servants. What they had not accounted for were the survival strategies within the informal economy. These strategies emerged with the crisis in the late 1970s and continued to sustain people through the reform period, which began in earnest in the mid-1980s (see chapter 2).

Neither coalition had sufficiently considered how the crisis would force people to devise their own means of coping through income-generating projects. Julius Nyerere, who was party chairman at the time, explained why he did not want an agreement with the IMF, saying in 1985 that the price of such an agreement "would be riots in the streets of Dar es

79

Salaam!"[2] In contrast, President Ali Hassan Mwinyi and those pushing for an IMF agreement believed that the government's refusal to come to an agreement would result in a similar crisis of confidence. When Mwinyi finally concluded the agreement with the IMF in 1986, the riots in the streets never materialized. The government's meager wage increases at a time of soaring inflation made little difference to Tanzania's urban dwellers because by the late 1980s wages accounted for little more than 10 percent of household income in the poorest families. The prospects that the government would increase wages to keep up with the cost of living were so slim that workers had long since given up on their demands for wage increases. Until the 1960s Tanzania had a vibrant labor movement which fought vigorously and successfully to raise wages and keep them in line with the cost of living. The ruling party's elimination of this independent labor movement since the 1960s, coupled with the state's inability to guarantee adequate wages, had made fighting for meaningful wage raises almost pointless. Workers had realized that even if they were to resist openly, little would come of it. Were the government to cut the pie up in a different way, workers would not necessarily receive any more than they already had. The cupboard marked "state resources" had been bare for quite some time. By the 1980s workers' energies were devoted to increasing their incomes off the job rather than mobilizing for pay increases on the job. Wages merely supplemented their informal businesses.

The fact that workers and civil servants were relying not on their official wages but on their income-generating activities was an important factor in facilitating the ascendancy of the economic reformers and their policies. Those pushing for economic restructuring were bolstered by the popularity of the 1984 import-liberalization measure and by the 1986 agreement with the IMF that brought with it an infusion of foreign exchange. Tanzania's economic situation was so severe at that point that the government had little choice but to conclude an agreement with the IMF. But government leaders were also able to go through with their reforms because the urban population, which had the most to lose from government policies, did not pose any serious opposition. Meanwhile, the government had become more responsive to popular pressures to loosen restrictions on small businesses (see chapter 6). Although this loosening was carried out slowly and reluctantly, it bought government leaders sufficient time to implement what otherwise were unpopular restructuring policies and austerity measures. This coalescence of external and internal factors created the conditions for the liberalization measures to be initiated and sustained.

In this chapter I look at the emergence of divisions within the leadership over the direction and pace of economic reform. I explain how alliances were consolidated; how various sectors of society lined up behind the two coalitions; and, finally, the political implications of the intra-elite conflicts.

EMERGING DIFFERENCES: 1980–1985

The initial liberalizing measures aimed at coping with the crisis were not effective, but they opened the door to more sweeping reforms. By the end of the 1980s Nyerere had begun to respond to some of the pressures for economic reform by initiating two relatively unsuccessful programs: the National Economic Stabilization Programme in 1980 and the Stabilization and Adjustment Programme in 1982. He downgraded the crop authorities to marketing boards and reinstated cooperatives in 1982 in an attempt to diffuse the monopolistic power of the crop authorities.[3] He also initiated trade liberalization in 1984 as a temporary measure to relieve the crisis in the shortages of consumer and capital goods. In May 1985 Tanzania began to sell twelve sisal estates run by the Tanzania Sisal Authority and began to talk about privatizing large commercial farms, which had experienced difficulties allegedly due to management problems.[4]

Some have explained Nyerere's shift toward economic liberalization two years before his retirement as president as an attempt to influence the course of reform because he realized that reform was inevitable. It was known that all three presidential candidates under consideration prior to 1985 had gained popularity from endorsing liberalizing measures. If selected, they would undoubtedly pursue this course with greater vigor. The late Premier Edward Sokoine liberalized the importation of pickup trucks; Salim Ahmed Salim announced the liberalization of secondhand-clothes imports; and Ali Hassan Mwinyi, then president of Zanzibar, had energized the island's ailing economy by liberalizing all imports (Maliyamkono and Bagachwa 1990, 115).

This new direction in policy making was not a concession on any ideological front or an attempt to transform the socialist orientation of the country. Nyerere was under pressure from forces advocating aggressive liberalization measures by the time he stepped down from the presidency. Moreover, foreign donors had made their continued support contingent on the conclusion of an agreement with the IMF. Reformist leaders realized that Tanzania had little choice but to submit to external pressures or face the collapse of the entire formal economy.

Mwinyi's choice as presidential successor to Nyerere in 1985 sheds some light on the lines that were being drawn within the leadership. Mwinyi represented a compromise between contending forces that were increasingly becoming polarized between the leadership of the government and of the party. Mwinyi was favored over the more reformist-minded Prime Minister Salim Ahmed Salim and the staunchly antireformist party Secretary General Rashidi Kawawa. It was suggested at the time that the selection of either Salim or Kawawa for the presidential seat might have led to a split in the party. Kawawa represented the senior party members closely tied to the state bureaucracy, whereas Salim represented those seeking greater involvement of market forces in the economy (Addison 1986). Pressures from the military played a part in eliminating Kawawa as a possible candidate. Salim, though popular among Tanzanians, did not have the same ties to the old-guard party leadership who had built strong allegiances during their years at Pugu, Minaki, and Tabora secondary schools or at Makerere University.[5] Although these were contributing factors, they could not have been decisive in eliminating Salim as a candidate; Mwinyi, who was ultimately chosen, was also not affiliated with the "old-boys' network." It is likely that the conflict between the islands of Zanzibar and Pemba (to the north of Zanzibar) and the constitutional necessity of having a Zanzibari represented in the top leadership either as president or vice president eliminated Salim, who was born in Pemba. Mwinyi, on the other hand, was from Zanzibar. He was perceived at the time as a moderate, a unifier of contending forces, yet one who had a record of successfully initiating various economic reforms on Zanzibar while president.

A similar conflict was played out over who was to be nominated as president of Zanzibar. One group supported Seif Sharif Hamad, who had been Zanzibar's chief minister since 1984 (Hamad later became vice chairman of the Civic United Front Party). Hamad, along with Mwinyi, Zanzibar's president since 1982, had encouraged foreign investment in Zanzibar, had liberalized trade, and had started to retreat from state interventionism in the economy a few years before the mainland did. Hamad's supporters included leaders like Salim A. Salim, Col. Adam Mwakanjuki, Machano Khamis, Hamad Rashidi Mohamed, Soud Mgeni, Suleiman Hamad, Shaaban Mloo, and Ali Pandu.

The other group, which was linked to antireformist forces on the mainland, backed Idris Abdul Wakil. Wakil claimed the nomination for presidency in 1985 but won the election by a close margin. Whatever popularity Wakil could claim in Zanzibar at that time he soon lost after the election. The Zanzibari leaders who backed Wakil came to represent a forceful bloc within the party's Central Committee. They included Brig. Abdallah Said Natepe, Ali Mzee Ali, Hassan Nassor Moyo, and Salmin Amour. These men were especially suspicious of Hamad and Salim, who had a strong political base in Pemba, which had always maintained close informal economic and cultural links with the Middle East. They argued that these men would bring Arab sheikhs from the Persian Gulf to Zanzibar and reintroduce capitalism. In 1988 they engineered the ouster of Seif Sharif Hamad and five others on charges of sabotaging the party and destabilizing the Tanzania-Zanzibar union.[6]

DEEPENING RIFTS: 1985–1990

Not until Mwinyi took over as president of Tanzania in 1985 did the real conflicts over the direction and speed of economic reform heat up. Mwinyi endorsed the 1986 Economic Recovery Program (ERP), which attempted to revive output, lower the trade and budget deficits, and reduce inflation. The ERP was used as a basis for negotiations with the IMF later that year. The agreement with the IMF, in particular, exacerbated the conflicts between the two coalitions, becoming a major point of contention, as I will show later in this chapter.

It was significant that Nyerere retained his post as chief of the ruling party after he left the presidency, even though on earlier occasions he had argued that the separation of the presidency of the nation and the party chairmanship could only lead to disunity. The joint position of party chairman and the president of the republic had been one way of ensuring party supremacy, which was enshrined in the constitution in a 1975 amendment subordinating the National Assembly (parliament) to its leadership. Party supremacy was reinforced by the party's 1977 constitution, which stated that "All activity of the organs of the state of the United Republic shall be conducted under the auspices of the Party." The National Assembly was also subordinated to the party's largest ruling body, the National Executive Committee (NEC), where all major policy decisions were made (Mlimuka and Kabudi 1985, 64; Pratt 1979, 221).

Nyerere's nomination and reelection as party chairman in 1987 bewildered many Tanzanians, who had expected him to step down, as he had earlier indicated he would. His reelection further exacerbated the political differences between the party and government. Nyerere's bid for reelection as party chief can be accounted for by a number of different pressures coming especially from the party old guard, who believed that their own political careers would be threatened by Nyerere's departure. Many within the NEC owed personal allegiance to him. Some of them were skeptical of the economic policies advocated by what they called capitalist roaders and felt that Nyerere was needed to act as a counterweight to these new forces for change. Among those pressuring Nyerere to remain party chairman were a group of influential regional party chairmen from Arusha and Mwanza. Sections of the military also exerted pressure on Nyerere to stay. Finally, Nyerere himself may have been concerned about the impact of his departure from the political scene on the union between Tanzania and Zanzibar, which had been showing increasing signs of strain.

At the NEC meeting that followed the 1987 party congress, the old guard asserted itself again by dropping two reform-minded Central Committee members, Finance Minister Cleopa Msuya and Zanzibar's chief minister, Seif Sharif Hamad. The removal of Hamad was an especially transparent power play because at the 1982 congress the Zanzibari chief minister was automatically guaranteed a position on the Central Committee. Mwinyi responded by removing three antireformist party leaders from the Cabinet, beginning with Minister of Local Government and Cooperatives Kingunge Ngombale-Mwiru, who took over the party's Ideology and Education Section. This was followed by the move of Gertrude Mongella from minister of lands, natural resources and tourism to minister without portfolio. Daudi Mwakawago was relieved of his position as minister of industry and trade to be in charge of the party's propaganda and mass-mobilization department. These three leaders, in particular, were believed to have tried to obstruct Mwinyi's liberalization policies and block reforms that were tied to negotiations with the IMF.

Thus, as the party Central Committee eliminated reform-minded leaders from the Central Committee, the president reshuffled his Cabinet so that by March 1990 almost all those who were opposing reform measures had been ousted. Whereas in the past there was considerable overlap between the Central Committee and the Cabinet, by 1990 only Mwinyi and Prime Minister Warioba were represented in both bodies. Moreover, by this time the only reformist within the Central Committee, apart from the moderates Mwinyi and Warioba, was Salim Salim. Clearly, the way in which the membership of these two bodies was skewed reflected attempts to counterbalance the strength of various coalitions against each other.

The conflict between the party and the government was mediated by a military also divided over the issue of reform. In fact, prior to the signing of the agreement with the IMF, political commissars of the Tanzania People's Defense Forces (TPDF) and national service warned the government not to accept IMF conditions because this "would bring about political and economic turmoil, disrupt unity, peace and tranquility in the country."[7] The Central Committee member in charge of defense, Col. Andrew Shija, presided over the meeting that made this declaration. Similarly, as I mentioned earlier, various generals were influential in persuading Nyerere to remain party chair in 1987, another indication of opposition to the reformist wing of the government.

Nyerere's close relationship with various groups within the armed forces had been carefully cultivated over the years. He had created a loyal network of officers in the army, field forces, police, prisons, and secret intelligence organizations. By promoting close associates within the army, he gained access to it and could freely visit the barracks without arousing suspicions.[8] He also promoted the armed forces to full and permanent representation in the National Executive Committee (NEC) of the party in 1987, giving them regional status like the other twenty-five administrative regions in the country.[9] The predominance of the army representatives in the armed forces seats in the NEC over the other sections of the armed forces (police, intelligence, prisons, national service) was also an indication of his need to make special concessions to this key component of Tanzania's power configuration.

But Nyerere's loyal supporters were not the only faction within the army. Mwinyi, mindful of the potential consequences of a divided military with one faction not entirely consolidated behind him, abolished the position of defense minister and took over the defense portfolio himself in September 1989, when the previous defense minister, Salim A. Salim, became secretary general of the Organization of African Unity. Salim's own popularity among the armed forces was an indication of the support for the reformists within the military. When former Prime Minister Edward Sokoine died in 1984, army officials were said to have pressured Nyerere not to appoint his closest ally, party Secretary General Kawawa, as prime minister and instead persuaded him to appoint Foreign Minister Salim A. Salim to the post.

IDEOLOGICAL POLARIZATION

Many different interests underlay these competing groups, some ideological and some rooted in the different societal interests they represented. One side, for example, held that Tanzania's crisis was primarily the result of external factors, including drought, low commodity prices, rising prices of imports, and the war with Uganda. The reformists, in contrast, believed that external factors had exacerbated the internal causes of crisis. They blamed much of the country's crisis on domestic policies like the excessive growth of government expenditures. As Damas Mbogoro, a key negotiator for Tanzania in its talks with the IMF, said, "I wouldn't say that our predicament was necessarily externally induced. The worst thing that can happen to an economy is to allow it to get into a stage when you can't manage things on your own, and therefore have to go to the Fund. Had we been putting certain macroeconomic policies in place all along, we would not be in this situation. That is the essence of the problem."[10]

As I mentioned earlier, the two sides were polarized over the IMF agreement. The party was hostile to the IMF because it feared that Tanzania's independence would be compromised by an agreement with the IMF and that it would have to submit to conditions that undermined the socialist orientation of the country. At one meeting of the NEC in February 1987, the IMF agreement was strongly condemned, and the finance minister was called in to defend his support of the IMF deal. The reformists saw the pursuit of external funding through the IMF as necessary to stave off a more serious economic crisis, but they differed with the IMF on many key issues. They opposed the speed with which the IMF had sought a devaluation of the Tanzanian currency and rejected IMF efforts to freeze wages, suppress government expenditure on social services, and cut back on the numbers of public institutions. They saw some, but not all, of the adopted reforms as responses to IMF pressures. To them, the process of economic reform was necessary for the economic survival of the country. As Prime Minister Warioba explained, "Measures such as reducing Government expenditure would have been taken because of the country's serious economic situation even in the absence of an agreement with the IMF."[11] Even Nyerere, who was most critical of the IMF's infringement on national sovereignty, defended his lifting of maize subsidies in 1984 by saying that it was not in any way influenced by the IMF and that it had been dictated purely by the current economic difficulties.[12]

Trade liberalization has been one of the most controversial policies. Initially it was implemented in 1984 as a temporary measure to relieve a commodity-starved population. A decade later there were few signs that it was about to be repealed. Those in favor of trade liberalization argued that it had compelled local industries to improve the quality of their produce and become more competitive. It had pushed the trading companies to become more consumer oriented. Likewise, they argued, it spurred higher agricultural production and enhanced political stability in the country, relieving the Board of Internal Trade of a public outcry over serious shortages, which had been endemic prior to 1984. Trade liberalization was said to have brought stability in price levels because goods were no longer so scarce. It opened up new avenues for revenue collection from import duties, sales taxes, and income taxes arising from imports under trade liberalization. Moreover, those supporting trade liberalization argued that it enabled the government to channel its precious foreign-exchange supplies to priority sectors, while private traders imported consumer and capital goods.[13]

Those opposed to trade liberalization said that it had increased the smuggling of livestock, hides, and precious stones in order to gain foreign exchange with which to import goods into Tanzania (Shivji 1992, 52). They expressed doubts over how private importers could sustain a constant flow of imports when they were selling their goods in local, nonconvertible currency.[14] They also argued that trade liberalization had hurt local industry, particularly the textile industry, which could not compete with cheap imports because of shortages of foreign exchange and subsequent shortages of inputs.

Nevertheless, once trade liberalization took affect the voices of those political leaders who were opposed to it were rarely heard. As one commentator observed, "Many Party and Government officials do not speak against liberalization for fear of losing popularity! Perhaps the only anti-liberalization voice has now and then been heard from the Party Chairman Mwalimu Nyerere and a few heads of parastatal organizations whose survival hinge on total monopoly."[15]

The role of the private sector was also intensely debated in Tanzania, a debate that went back at least as far as the 1967 Arusha Declaration (see chapter 7). Some top leaders accepted the private sector as a reality. These leaders felt strongly that the country would not progress unless individual initiative was unleashed in the form of the private sector, given the harsh economic conditions. Economic redistribution would be carried out through taxation of private initiatives. To be serious about self-reliance, they argued, meant that the private sector should be supported. Other leaders straddled the fence, pretending that these businesses did not exist. Holding on to past policies and ideological commitments, they hoped that the issues would go away. Yet a third group of leaders wanted to suppress the new growth of businesses, seeing them as the beginnings of capitalism that needed to be nipped in the bud. Nyerere, one of the most outspoken opponents of the policy of encouraging the private sector, had argued that giving greater leeway to market forces would lead to greater exploitation and inequality in Tanzania. He had always held that development could not be equated with economic growth but, rather, ought to occur through the promotion of equality and justice. Only the state, not private interests, could lead development in a way that enhanced equality.

EFFECTS OF THE GOVERNMENT–PARTY RIFT
ON POLICY MAKING

Despite the attempts by Tanzania's leaders to portray a unified front to the nation and to the world, their differences had serious consequences for policy making. One of the main effects of the widening gap between the party and the government was the inability to move forward with one unified set of policies. Mixed signals made it difficult for the private sector, foreign companies, and even the informal sector to progress with complete confidence that policies, once adopted, would not be reversed. In 1986 the government started encouraging the private sector, but it kept vacillating as a result of internal conflicts over concrete measures due to party vetoes of various policies adopted. The government had aimed to privatize numerous parastatals that were not making a profit and did, in fact, close some down, but then it balked and did not sell them. In 1988 private investors were permitted to build five breweries, but the decision was later rescinded.[16]

Such reversals in policy as a result of party pressures were commonplace in a number of different areas, leading to considerable unpredictability. For example, Mwinyi, under pressure from the IMF, raised the price for maize flour in March 1987. Soon afterward, Nyerere forced the prices down again.[17] In another instance, the party refused to allow the removal of the National Milling Corporation's (NMC) monopoly of the grain market. The government finally went through with the demonopolization of the NMC, but the party's opposition dragged the process out. Similarly, the party opposed the further relaxation of price controls and further devaluation in 1988, slowing down the implementation of these measures.[18] Thus the party was often able to slow down the pace of reforms.

The competition between the party and the government took an important turn in 1990, when Nyerere introduced the possibility of moving into a multiparty era. He had unsuccessfully tried to stall the introduction of the National Investment (Promotion and Protection) Act, which was passed in February 1990. This effectively reversed a key Arusha Declaration tenet that promoted public-sector investment at the expense of private-sector investment and discouraged foreign investment. The 1990 act offered safeguards against nationalization without compensation, a package of investment incentives, including customs-duty exemptions, and it established an Investment Promotion Center (Bagachwa 1992b, 210). Nyerere lost his bid to veto the investment code when the code was brought to the CCM Central Committee for approval (Baregu 1993, 111). The so-called pragmatists in control of the government had now clearly gained the upper hand in the party. Nyerere resigned his chairmanship of the party and began to pursue a new strategy to reinvigorate the CCM, to inject greater accountability into the political leadership of the country, and to fight corruption in the government, which had reached unprecedented proportions under Mwinyi. In an unexpected turn of events, Nyerere, who had been considered an ideologue, suddenly became a champion of multipartyism and of greater political reform. Mwinyi and the pragmatists resisted these political reforms initially, and when they finally succumbed to them, they did so reluctantly and in a way that would ensure CCM dominance.

WINNERS AND LOSERS

Given this intense conflict over the direction of economic reform in Tanzania, the question remains, how did the government come to prevail in its liberalizing endeavors? To answer this question, it is necessary to examine how the government responded to different sectoral interests. In other words, it is important to identify who gained and who lost from various policy measures adopted. By examining these sectoral interests, it becomes clear how the informal economy facilitated many of the measures by taking pressures off the state and allowing people alternative sources of income, especially in the case of labor and civil servants.

Those attempting to preserve the status quo were part of a distinct patronage network that linked the party to state companies. Some were older party leaders who owed their political careers to Nyerere and had strong allegiances to one another, often having gone to secondary school and university together. Known as *watoto wa chama waliolewa na chama* (children of the party raised by the party), they had become involved together in the early years of CCM's predecessor, the Tanganyika African National Union (TANU). The proponents of economic reform, in contrast, were a disparate group, representing the major cash-crop-producing regions. Located primarily in the government, their power base was their rural constituencies, to whom they were accountable and on whom, in the case of members of parliament, they depended for their votes. Unlike the old guard, many of these leaders had been envoys abroad (Salim had been

Tanzania's ambassador to the United Nations; Diria was ambassador to West Germany), which had not only widened their perspectives but had made it more difficult to establish and maintain patronage links back home. Those from Pemba and Zanzibar were undoubtedly linked to fellow islanders who wanted to expand the historic trade with the Middle East and to encourage foreign investment from Europe and the Middle East in the islands.

SECTORAL INTERESTS IN ECONOMIC REFORM

Public-Sector Managers

Public-sector managers and employees were threatened by the elimination of a system in which the government protected their corporations' monopoly status through regulation and subsidies (Bagachwa 1992a, 39). Moreover, the raising of producer prices and the liberalization of internal trade undercut parastatals and government institutions like the NMC. Large parallel-market traders had collaborated with parastatal directors, taking advantage of the shortages to extract high rents. Official pricing and government rationing of foods that evolved to deal with the shortages had the opposite result of pushing even more commodities into the parallel market (Boesen et al. 1986, 27). The complicity between these directors and traders explains in part why their patrons in the party were so anxious to protect the monopoly status of the parastatals and stave off liberalization of internal trade, fearing competition from other quarters. As Tanzanian economist Nguyuru Lipumba (1984, 37) pointed out, "The combination of acute shortages and official controls has given very lucrative money making positions for all those who have the responsibility for distributing the scarce goods. There is usually a partnership between these officials and private businessmen who sell the scarce goods in the black market."

Often the crops would be sold at low, controlled prices to well-connected officials and businessmen with ties to official supply lines. They, in turn, sold the crops on parallel markets at hiked prices. Most urban dwellers had to buy their maize in parallel markets at five to eight times the official price. In fact, when Nyerere abolished food subsidies in 1984, most urban dwellers were already paying exorbitant prices for the maize they purchased in parallel markets. They barely noticed the removal of the subsidies that some had predicted would be accompanied by unrest. Scarcity premiums earned by retailers ranged from 60 to 300 percent. Thus the removal of price controls penalized the black-market traders and benefited the majority of consumers, because the prices of key open-market goods dropped (Lipumba 1984, 43; Ndulu 1988, 9; Ndulu et al. 1988, 11, 17).

Corruption permeated parastatals, as goods worth millions of shillings also disappeared from warehouses. Coupled with inefficient management, corruption was so extensive that by 1995 the Parastatal Sector Reform Commission admitted that only a few parastatals had been productive and profitable but that most had been "economically inefficiently, incurred heavy financial losses, and took more than their fair share of domestic credit." [19]

Since coming to office Mwinyi, under pressure from donors, had demanded that state corporations reduce the number of employees and increase accountability and efficiency, thus irritating public managers. His administration cut subsidies to the parastatal sector and pushed for privatization schemes by openly describing these as efforts to curb political interference in production. Some parastatals were completely eliminated: the first to go, in 1986, was the large General Agricultural Export Product Corporation (GAPEX). GAPEX had suffered a loss of $3 million through deliberate underpricing and underinvoicing of crops. Later schemes involved joint ventures between the private and public sectors (Tanzania Breweries, Williamson Diamonds, Kisarawe Bricks), outright sales (Tanzania Shoe Company), and the leasing of companies like Tanzania Hotels Investments (TAHI) hotels. In some cases employees and management bought shares in their enterprise while continuing to work for it, as was the case with Tanzania Publishing House. In other cases the buyers were individuals, companies, or institutional investors who bid on a parastatal through what was called a unit trust.[20] But in general, in spite of pressure from donors, divestiture was extremely slow and had almost ground to a halt by 1994, partly as a result of bureaucratic infighting between the Loans and Advances Realization Trust (LART) and the Parastatal Sector Reform Commission (PSRC), both of which were government agencies formed to facilitate privatization.

Private-Sector Manufacturers

Private manufacturers, who accounted for half of all value added in manufacturing in the late 1980s, were ambivalent about the liberalizing measures, which many felt were long overdue.[21] Several policies in the 1990s were aimed at promoting the financing and investment of large-scale manufacturers, including the Investment Promotion and Protection Act (1990), the Banking and Financial Institutions Act (1991), which was to encourage the growth of private banks, and the Capital Market and Securities Act (1994), aimed at assisting the development of a Tanzanian stock exchange.

In spite of these efforts to improve the business environment, the large-scale manufacturing sector still experienced enormous constraints and believed that the government was dragging its feet in creating conditions that would promote private-sector investment. In the mid-1990s investors complained about the inefficiency of the government agency, the Investment Promotion Center, that was to process investment proposals. Other obstacles included limited sources of local capital and an inefficient banking system. Local industries suffered from the corporate tax system, which levied taxes across the board with no differentiation made on the basis of firm size, level of capital, or technological basis. Moreover, unpredictable changes in tax and exchange rates made planning on a yearly basis difficult. Tanzanian manufacturers continued to contend with a weak infrastructure (an unreliable supply of electricity, inefficient telecommunications, and poor roads, railways, and air transport). Legal institutions remained weak, and the process of obtaining title deeds, business licenses, company registrations, industrial licenses, and other necessary legal documents to conduct business were cumbersome. According to Iddi Simba, chairman of the Confederation of Tanzanian Industries (CTI), these legal-documentation-clearance processes had been created "in order to satisfy a myriad of rules most of which are arguably less safeguard measures than corruption pit-stops."[22]

Because industry was operating at such low capacity (20–30 percent), production costs (per unit) were high, making locally produced commodities even less competitive. Moreover, the taxation system discriminated against local industrialists because of the high sales tax and customs duty on imported raw materials and inputs needed by local industries. This made imported goods more attractive to buyers.

The policy of trade liberalization was also controversial. It had been especially harmful in the areas of textile production, which suffered from the importation of cheap secondhand clothes and better-quality material, with which local industries could not always compete. In fact, the private-sector and the public-sector manufacturers of textiles joined to form a lobby to press for greater restrictions on importation and for greater controls over abuses of the trade guidelines.

Although trade liberalization put particular pressures on the manufacturing sector, the general atmosphere of encouraging private-sector activity, in sharp contrast to the pre-1986 period, helped give rise to a fledgling

African business sector, as seen in the emergence of African-owned companies like Industrial Projects Promotion, Ltd. (better known by its acronym, IPP). In addition, in the mid-1980s women for the first time began to set up private flour mills, textile factories, bakeries, and other such small industries. By 1990 a group of middle-class and big businesswomen had formed a national Association of Businesswomen in Tanzania to assist in dealing with some of the problems women faced going into business, such as lack of capital and neglect by financial institutions. Because it was no longer possible to make a decent living in government service, many highly educated younger Tanzanians were opting to go into the private sector. Others who had retired from civil service, knowing their pensions were insufficient, used their savings or took out mortgages on their houses and went into business.

Private-Sector Importers and Exporters

Guests at a dinner given in Nyerere's honor in October 1986 by the predominantly Asian Dar es Salaam Merchant's Chamber congratulated Nyerere for permitting the return to Tanzania of foreign-held funds as part of the country's liberalization policy. To their dismay, Nyerere responded that he did not like the practice and reminded them that it was only a temporary measure.[23] Until 1984 the government had controlled all imports. In 1984, with the introduction of an own-funded import scheme, importers were allowed to use their own foreign exchange (no questions asked about how they obtained it) to import commodities. The scheme was enormously popular among importers, and by 1989 own-funded imports accounted for at least one-third of all imports. In 1988 the government began to make foreign exchange available to private traders for selected high-priority import categories (such as spare parts, raw materials, intermediate goods, drugs, and pharmaceuticals), through an Open License System (OLS). Both policies served to relax trade restrictions, thus discouraging the evasion of official channels that had been commonplace.

Importers and exporters alike benefited from trade liberalization and the export retention scheme, which allowed exporters to keep a portion of their foreign-exchange earnings in the country and a portion abroad. The fastest-growing sector of exports was the nontraditional category (birds, spices, flowers, and seafoods, for example).

Not all traders benefited from liberalization through legal means, however. Importers frequently skirted customs regulations with the complicity of customs officials, bringing in unapproved commodities in containers with false labels. Government officials had been known to cover for traders who brought in goods like paint, condensed milk, or even medicines that had passed their expiration date. Such goods were obtained abroad at little or no cost and sold in Tanzania at exorbitantly high prices. Traders who wanted to conduct an honest business found that not only did they face fierce competition from those resorting to illegal practices, they also had to operate within prohibitive government restrictions on trade.

Although exporters found the export-retention scheme beneficial compared with past policies, many still felt it was too restrictive. The money kept in Tanzania was controlled by the Board of Trade (BoT) and could not be used without board approval. They found it difficult to gain access to their foreign-exchange earnings. One way they worked around these restrictions, according to one exporter of spices, cocoa, seafoods, and vegetables, was by underreporting their foreign-exchange earnings. But, the exporter quickly added: "This is an indirect form of smuggling and if you get caught at my age you are in trouble. If I spoil my name today I spoil the name of my children."[24]

Race and the Changing Business Community

Because such a large section of Tanzania's larger businesspeople are of Asian descent, the gains made by import-export traders, wholesalers, and retailers after the 1984 liberalization brought to the surface old hostilities that had been suppressed with various measures adopted after the 1967 Arusha Declaration. The Asian community had always been well represented among the large plantation and estate owners, large wholesalers and produce merchants, professionals, highly paid civil servants, managers, and executives, as well as among the self-employed in areas like retailing, tailoring, shoemaking, and carpentry. Areas like wholesale and retail trade had been dominated by Asians and Arabs since colonial times. In 1960–1961, for example, not a single wholesale license was issued to an African, and only 12 percent of the retail licenses were in the hands of Africans (Sporrek 1985, 100).

Many of the measures that followed the Arusha Declaration, though not adopted with an overt intent to target a specific racial group, certainly had this effect. Even prior to the Arusha Declaration, Africanization of the civil service had occurred, affecting British and Asian professional civil servants, most of whom emigrated because they did not intend to take Tanzanian citizenship. The establishment of the wholesale Cooperative Supply Association of Tanganyika in 1962 was also an attempt to curtail the position of Asian wholesalers (Shivji 1976, 69–74). The Arusha Declaration represented an attempt to exert state control not only over banks and private manufacturers but also over the export-import trade, whole-sale trade, and light industries, in which large numbers of Asians were represented. The declaration affected primarily the upper classes of the Asian community, who, instead of saving, accumulating, and investing capital, began instead to export it. The process of Africanization continued with the 1971 nationalization of houses in urban areas, which had a large impact on the Asian community, particularly Asian shop owners. Similarly, a short-lived 1976 campaign to put all shops under government control, Operation Maduka, also had its heaviest impact on Asian and Arab shop owners, because at the time only about 30 percent of Dar es Salaam's shops were owned by Africans (Sporrek 1985, 101).

With the reversal of so many of the older policies that had had the effect of Africanizing economic activity in Tanzania, new tensions began to manifest themselves between a small but growing group of African and Asian businesspeople involved in manufacturing and trade. African businesspeople and others were openly challenging the loyalties of the Asian business community in what was referred to as the indigenization debate. Joining in the attacks on Asian businesspeople were not only religious extremists like Rev. Mtikila, but also church leaders and political leaders like Augustine Mrema, leader of the opposition NCCR-Mageuzi party and one-time CCM leader. Some of the attacks were so inflammatory that President Mwinyi was forced to intervene at various junctures, threatening to deal ruthlessly with people who extended business rivalries into "racial or tribal tensions."[25]

Many of the new African manufacturers whom I interviewed and who had emerged since the mid-1980s said they might have gone into the private sector much earlier had it not been for the political and economic environment that discouraged such activities. They believe that the Arusha Declaration delayed the emergence of an African private sector. After the declaration Asian businesspeople continued to predominate in the private sector and found ways to work around the restrictions, linking up with the necessary "godfather" patrons within the government and the party to protect them and help them through the bureaucratic red tape. With the more encouraging atmosphere for the private sector after the mid-1980s, greater numbers of African businesspeople also became involved. As one African director of a company said, "The Government failed to allow us to invest. There was overcontrol, most people could not do things. . . . Liberalization gave us greater confidence."[26]

In interviews with me, African directors of various private companies appeared to feel disadvantaged compared with their Asian counterparts, who owned the majority of private companies in Tanzania. Likewise, most of private-capital-stock formation was in the hands of Asians, some of whom owned family businesses that had been in existence for a hundred years. One of the largest, Karimjee Jivanjee, Ltd., had been established in 1895. Even the Asian-dominated Dar es Salaam Chamber of Merchants, with 4,000 members, was the more powerful body compared with the primarily African Dar es Salaam Chamber of Commerce, which had a membership of only 150 in 1988. Moreover, foreign companies were more likely to deal with Asians, who had been established for a long time in business, when given a choice between an African-owned company and an Asian-owned company with similar products or commodities for sale.

These differences created distrust between the African and Asian business communities. As one former director of a large multinational corporation said to me: "There was never complete trust on both sides. Partnerships between Africans and Asians were necessary for Africans to get started in business. Africans needed them for capital and they needed Africans for the 'science of who you know'—your contacts."[27]

Historically, the main problem keeping Africans out of business has been lack of access to capital. As in the case of the manufacturing sector, the biggest change for importers and exporters was the increased role of new African traders, who were especially involved in the export of nontraditional goods. One of the largest exporters in Tanzania believed that the African export sector was "competing very well with the Indians" because Africans had begun to find niches in this nontraditional export category, which proportionately fewer Asian exporters had entered.[28] Part of this trade had previously been carried out illegally but was legalized with the export retention scheme. African exporters whom I interviewed said that they could use their extended family and other networks to find the best prices. They believed that it was easier for them than for Asians to convince local farmers and fishermen to sell to them and give them better prices.

Women also entered the trade sector in the mid-1980s on a scale not seen earlier in the decade. They were involved in such businesses as importing chicks from Zambia, exporting prawns to Botswana, and exporting Makonde carvings and other crafts to the West.

Agricultural Producers

Agricultural producers theoretically had the most to gain from the policies of devaluation, increasing producer prices, and lifting restrictions on internal trade. Indeed, production of crops like coffee, tea, cashew nuts, tobacco, and sisal grew at a rate of 4 percent from 1986 to 1989. The production of cotton more than doubled between 1986 and 1989, and similar patterns were evident with other crops. Similarly, production of domestic crops like maize and rice increased with the liberalization of internal trade, in which cooperative unions and primary societies were free to sell crops to anyone and restrictions on internal movement of crops were lifted. Overall, the agricultural sector registered an average annual growth rate of 5 percent between 1986 and 1991, compared with an average annual growth rate of less than 3 percent from 1981 to 1985.

Some of these changes can be attributed to changes in pricing policy, but others argue that improved weather conditions after 1984 and the incentives provided by the new availability of consumer goods may have played a larger role in facilitating increases in agricultural output. A careful disaggregation of the beneficiaries of adjustment policies shows that agricultural producers experienced only a 30 percent increase in terms of trade in 1985, while the marketing boards and cooperative unions experienced a 100 percent improvement in terms of trade. One of the reasons for this was the inability of the prices to keep up with changes in the exchange rate. Similarly, although inputs became more accessible, it was primarily middle and large farmers who benefited from these policies at the expense of smallholders (Havnevik 1993, 298, 304–5, 307). Other studies yield more ambiguous findings. Some argue that rural incomes have increased substantially since reform policies were implemented: Luisa Ferreira and Lucy Goodhart note a 14.6 percent increase in rural income between 1983 and 1991. However, others have pointed out that some of this increase in rural incomes can be explained by poor accounting of rural producers' nonagricultural sources of income (wood sales, fishing, crafts, and so forth) in the prereform period (Ferreira and Goodhart 1995, 7; Havnevik 1993, 311–12).

Urban Workers and Self-Employed Workers

Why the trade and agricultural sectors supported many aspects of the government's reform policies is clear. The real puzzle was the reaction of urban dwellers, the group that had the most to lose from austerity measures and from devaluation.

In 1986 a delegation of the Trade Union of Tanzanian Workers (JUWATA) went to the president to thank him for a fair budget after he had launched the Economic Recovery Program, which included various austerity measures.[29] On another occasion, JUWATA Secretary General Joseph Rwegasira had announced that his organization supported the agreement with the IMF because if the present economic situation continued, the nation's political, ideological, and social life would be threatened. The government's rejection of the wage freeze the IMF was proposing helped make the IMF agreement palatable to JUWATA. The organization expressed concern, however, over the rate of devaluation and the raising of interest rates.[30]

In 1991, when JUWATA became independent of the party and was renamed the Organization of Tanzania Trade Unions (OTTU), the newly constituted umbrella body became slightly more aggressive in its defense of workers' rights. Unlike JUWATA, OTTU rejected the argument that the civil service had been cut for efficiency. OTTU argued that the wage bill claimed only a small percentage of public expenditure, most of it going to vehicle maintenance. It rejected a proposal to treat fringe benefits given to workers as part of the salary to be taxed. In spite of its more critical stance toward the government regarding economic reform, OTTU met with opposition from other labor unions, which felt that it had not severed itself sufficiently from the legacy of being a party association. The Tanzania Professional Teachers' Association (CHAKIWATA), formed in 1985 with a nationwide membership of 56,982, became independent of OTTU in June 1992, in spite of protests from OTTU that this was illegal and that CHAKIWATA was not complying with the laws of the land. CHAKI-WATA leaders said that by becoming independent, their trade union would be in better position to develop teachers professionally and to fight for improved working conditions.[31]

But apart from these few murmurings and splits within the worker's movement over OTTU's reluctance to vigorously fight for the interests of workers, labor's lack of response seemed incongruous. After all, workers and civil servants continued to suffer from severe drops in real wages throughout the 1980s; workers faced plant closings due to industry's low levels of operating capacity; and major layoffs of civil servants occurred in 1985 and 1992. In other words, the austerity measures hit urban dwellers harder than any other sector of society. The lack of riots, demonstrations, and other forms of opposition to the measures suggests a certain level of acquiescence to the new direction that had been adopted. For example, virtually no critical letters to the editor appeared, although a few supported liberalization. Nevertheless, there were few open signs of support for the reform measures and certainly no open support for the IMF agreement.

Some have suggested that the absence of public debate about the issues may have been engendered by the authorities themselves for fear of creating opposition to these measures (Kiondo 1992, 35–36). There is no question that the public was not informed about many of the economic reforms that had been adopted. However, when in my 1987–1988 survey I asked workers and self-employed people about how their lives had changed over the past five years, from the previous administration to Mwinyi's administration (which marked the beginning of the more far-reaching economic reforms), only 22 percent responded that they were worse off, whereas 44 percent said that their own financial situation was the same and 34 percent said that it was better. Those who said that their financial situation was better attributed the improvement to their own involvement in income-generating projects. Another survey, of 866 urban workers, rural households, traders, and transporters cited by Maliyamkono and Bagachwa, revealed similar results: 92 percent of urban dwellers of all occupational levels indicated support for economic liberalization (1990, 117). Surprisingly, they found that only 60 percent of rural agricultural workers supported economic liberalization, even though they had potentially the most to gain by it.

This anomalous situation of city dwellers can be accounted for in a number of ways. To begin with, people were busy surviving and making ends meet in their informal occupations, leaving little energy for mobilization around such issues. Second, as is evident in the challenges from the teachers' union, the trade-union movement, which was the only organized structure capable of mounting significant opposition to the measures, was too weak to do so. Moreover, decades of interference by the party had weakened its capacity for independent leadership, even as the movement was granted autonomy from the party. Third, although public and private manufacturers were hurt by trade liberalization because they had difficulty competing with cheaper, imported products, the informal economy ironically benefited considerably from the new availability of nets for fishermen, cloth and sewing notions for tailors, and tools for carpenters, in spite of the high cost of these products. The alternative, as they had experienced in the years prior to trade liberalization, was the complete unavailability of these inputs. Moreover, the fact that there were goods on the shelves gave added impetus to people to find ways of earning extra income.

People I interviewed who were laid off because of cutbacks in industry and the civil service, though unhappy about forfeiting this extra source of income, simply continued full-time with their informal businesses or found one if they did not have one already. Monthly salaries were frequently seen as hedges against the unpredictability of informal businesses but ultimately supplemented the larger income obtained from businesses. Had formal jobs been the primary sources of livelihood, the response of labor and civil servants would probably not have been quite so complacent.

To place the issue in sharper focus, it should be noted that by the mid-1980s many people were leaving their formal jobs of their own accord to become self-employed because they simply could not make ends meet through formal employment.

Expectations of the government regarding employment were quite low by the mid-1980s. This was evident from workers' responses to our survey question (roughly translated from Swahili), "What should your monthly salary be in order for you to get by?" Invariably, the initial response was an amount only slightly higher than what they were already making and far below their stated daily food expenditure. So ludicrous was this question that interviewees balked when pressed further on this issue. Even the second answer was considerably below their stated daily expenses. For instance, one messenger and his wife supported a household of ten on about TSh 20,000 ($200 at 1988 exchange rates) a month, which they obtained mostly from a restaurant operated by the wife. Initially the husband responded that "2,260 shillings [$22.60] would be a good sum" for his monthly wage. When asked why, he answered: "The government would never give me more." [32]

Although it may appear from these observations that labor and civil servants did not oppose the authorities, such an assessment is not entirely correct. Opposition was, in fact, fierce, but it was mounted, as I show in chapter 6, against policies that encroached on people's ability to pursue income-generating activities outside their formal jobs. Their resistance contributed to the greater legitimization and legalization of informal-sector activity and created a better environment for the pursuit of such small-scale private enterprises.

Lack of resistance to economic reforms on the part of labor and civil servants was also a consequence of a series of other government policies and nonpolicies (turning a blind eye to various activities) to accommodate these sectors. However slow and imperfect, these measures were an indication of the beginnings of some long overdue readjustments in state-society relations that would make the state more responsive to societal needs and preferences. Where fundamental shifts in policy were not possible without relinquishing the ideological principles on which the state had based its claims to legitimacy, tacit compromises were often worked out. In these instances, the parameters of societal action and initiative were drawn much more broadly than official policy allowed. People perceived the quiet and not-so-quiet acquiescence of the leadership, or various sections of the leadership, as an attempt to come to terms with hardships brought on by the crisis.

This kind of silent negotiation between state and society could be considered part of a process of governance as formulated by Goran Hyden (1989), in which he stresses the role of individuals in overcoming the inertia of institutional and systemic structures through their own initiatives. Individuals or collectives, he argues, can bring about changes that move toward greater legitimacy, new reciprocities, trust, and accountability between state and society.

CONCLUSION

By the mid-1980s two contending coalitions had emerged, one coalescing around the government and the other around the CCM. The split was manifest in the widely diverging composition of the Cabinet (proreform) and the party Central Committee (antireform). In the struggle that ensued, after two decades of trying to assert its centrality in Tanzania's political life, the party began to relinquish considerable control to the government by the end of the 1980s and to take steps toward a multiparty system that would effectively undermine its own monopoly of control. Proreformers were backed by sections of the private sector, importers and exporters, while the CCM, which was trying to slow down the pace of reform, gained support from those tied into patronage systems that were dependent on government monopoly of the economy and CCM monopoly of the political system.

Some of the reforms opened old wounds and created new conflicts between an incipient African entrepreneurial class and the more established Asian business community. At the same time, new possibilities for legal business activities heightened tensions between the entrepreneurs operating outside the illegal patronage networks tied to the government, on the one hand, and those who were using their government positions to enrich themselves or their connections with the government to give them market advantage, on the other hand.

Finally, the lack of opposition from labor, the one group that one would have expected to oppose the measures, was a consequence of years of CCM control, which had weakened its independence even as the party withdrew its formal links with the movement. Moreover, workers were simply too preoccupied with survival through informal means to protest. They believed that the government would have little to offer them in the way of higher wages and saw any move to make such demands as pointless. They reasoned that the only way to survive was through their own endeavors; hence their involvement in the informal economy and the absence of greater demands on the state.

5 Informal Strategies for Survival

I went to the legal counselor at our party branch to try to get out of paying the license. I told him I have an old mother and father to support. My husband is blind. I have my own children to support, and my sister died so I am taking care of her children. I have to support them from my pastry sales. All the counselor said to me was, "Tough. That is not my problem. That is your problem." I left his office and thought to myself, what can I do? All I have left to do is swallow stones!

                                                    Woman pastry maker, Manzese

With the deepening economic crisis in the 1980s, urban dwellers were forced to seek alternatives to the state's diminishing resource base. In chapter 3 I showed how the state's attempts to exert control over society and the economy increasingly exceeded its capacity to regulate social relations and allocate resources effectively. The state's growing inability to ensure livable incomes, to provide a modicum of social and public services, and even to guarantee adequate police protection led people to find their own solutions to cope with some of the growing uncertainties of life.

Victor Azarya and Naomi Chazan suggest, in the case of Ghana, that "because the informal economy grew in direct relationship to outcomes induced by Government policies (low producer prices, high costs, unrealistic foreign exchange rates and regulation), most Government employees, unemployed, commercial groups, and farmers gradually became involved in this strategy. . . . The degree of internal organization in the informal economy reflected the degree of disarray in the formal system (1987, 127)." Azarya and Chazan argue that nonformal strategies can represent a form of disengagement from the state. This disengagement was visible in Tanzania in the late 1980s, leading to a situation markedly different from that which had prevailed only a decade earlier. For example, in the early 1980s Goran Hyden observed that peasants and patrons made demands on the state for more schools, dispensaries, water, and roads but were unwilling to cooperate when it came to official policy demands on them (1980, 31–32): "What had been a state with limited access was now turned open to a flood of popular demands. As most politicians had ridden to power in support of these demands, they had great difficulty in resisting them (1983, 19)."

More common during and after the 1980s, however, was the frequent absence of demands on the state and the reliance on group or individual self-help solutions to meet various societal needs. Members of Parliament with whom I spoke sometimes even complained of a lack of pressure from their constituencies for access to resources. The reasons for the absence of demands varied in the postindependence period. Initially this phenomenon could be explained by the lack of independent vehicles through which to assert such demands because opposition parties, independent labor and agricultural associations, along with ethnically and in some cases religiously based organizations, had been suppressed until the 1990s. Parliamentary assertions of local interests could be rejected on grounds that they were expressions of particularistic ethnic interests even though ethnic and local interests often overlapped due to the demographics of a particular constituency. By the 1980s the state was clearly unable to fulfill many of its promises, making efforts to demand more resources increasingly futile. During the crisis of the 1980s the state's increasing inability to live up to the many obligations for which it took responsibility made it necessary for individuals, households, networks, and local organizations to fill some of these needs.

Where people made demands, they called on the state to lift its numerous and often tedious restrictions in order to make it easier for them to cope with the economic difficulties they were facing. As I will show in the next chapter, the kinds of demands people did make on organs of the state centered around, for example, easing licensing restrictions on the poor, ending the harassment of vendors by the militia, and privatizing medicine.

With political liberalization in the 1990s, many of the political demands centered around pushing back unnecessarily interventionist state policies in much the same way that people had made economic demands. Lawyers, academics, and journalists supported recommendations regarding the removal of forty oppressive laws, as they came to be known after they were publicized by the presidentially appointed Nyalali commission that investigated popular views on political liberalization. They pushed for the repeal of these laws, which limited freedom of organization and freedom of the press, including the Societies Ordinance, the Newspapers Act, and, most importantly, the Preventive Detention Act of 1962. Similarly, journalists resisted efforts by the Ministry of Information to control the press through a Media Professions Regulation Act. Since the emergence of a vibrant, independent press in the early 1990s, journalists, editors, and publishers have been detained arbitrarily and at times charged with sedition. Thus much of the economic and political engagement of the state has had less to do with extracting resources from the state and more to do with extracting the state from strangling the expansion of societal resources and institutions.

AGENCY AND SOCIAL CHANGE

To account for the many changes in Tanzanian state-society relations it is necessary to engage a theory of agency that incorporates the role of autonomous social actors. Agency in this context is the means of exerting power and influence to bring about change, whether at the level of individuals, the household, or larger collectivities, like networks and groups. Agency has to do with sources of influence and directions of power (Strathern 1987, 23).

My inquiry begins with the following questions: How do people view their constraints and options? What strategies do people employ, and what decisions do they make? How do they explain their decisions and choices? What mechanisms do people have at their disposal in influencing others and in shaping the contours of the everyday world around them? Even more important, what are their capabilities to affect their world and the actions of others? Agency is concerned with power and control, which implies, as Anthony Giddens puts it, the "capability that some actors, groups or types of actors have of influencing the circumstances of others" (1979, 283). Although much scholarship has been devoted to power in the context of asymmetrical or conflictual social relations (such as the Marxist view that social change comes about through class struggle), it is necessary also to see agency and change in relations of cooperation, reciprocity, and solidarity (Ortner 1984, 157). This is especially significant in the context of the household and local communities, which I will explore in this chapter, where some aspects of a relationship may be asymmetrical and others may be characterized by reciprocity.

Finally, it is necessary to explore the terrain of agency. The domestic domain is often perceived as the basis of systemic conservatism because action is thought to take place in the form of highly patterned and routinized behavior with little reflection (Ortner 1984, 150). The separation of domestic and public spheres in Western thought, especially in the study of politics and economics, tends to deny agency in the domestic realm. Since the 1970s feminist scholars have argued that dichotomizing the public and the private "is misleading and that it operates in a way that reifies and thus legitimizes the gendered structure of society. It immunizes a significant sphere of human life (and especially of women's lives) from the scrutiny to which the political is subjected" (Okin 1979, 16). On one hand, public spheres, characterized by rationality, are frequently associated with male spheres of activities like government, production, and economic exchange. Private spheres, on the other hand, are characterized by emotionalism. They are seen as female spheres, including the activities of the family and reproduction (Howard 1987, 283). Feminist social scientists challenge such characterizations, arguing that these two spheres are inseparable. In urban Tanzania today, a majority of men, women, and children, as well as those employed in the formal economy, obtain most of their livelihood from self-employment and working on projects located in the home. To compartmentalize and marginalize the domestic realm under such circumstances would be to overlook some of the most important dynamics in society at this time. Changes at the household level—that is, within the domestic sphere—were altering the entire societal landscape, including relations between society and the state.

These changes radically undermined the direction of existing dependency relationships and ties of obligation. At the societal level the former household dependence on wage earners was reversed, making the wage earners dependent on the informal incomes of other household members. Similarly, the dependence of urban women on men, of children on their parents, and of parents on their adult children was altered radically as resources began to flow in the opposite direction because of the way in which the crisis undermined wage incomes.

The late historian Fernand Braudel was attuned to the importance of the household economy. In reflecting on the great expanse of Western economic history he observed that, by looking only at the workings of the market economy and capitalism, scholars have failed to see one of the main aspects of economic life—what he calls material life or the socially necessary activities that ensure social reproduction at the household level. The market economy is well recorded and therefore draws the most attention. However, it is only a "fragment of the vast whole" that until the nineteenth century was "merely a layer—more or less thick and resilient, but at times very thin—between the ocean of daily life that lay stretched out beneath it and the capitalist mechanism that more than once manipulated it from above. . . . One must keep looking down into the well, into the deepest water, down into material life. . . . So any economic history that is not written on two levels—that of the well's rim and that of the depths—runs the risk of being appallingly incomplete" (Braudel 1977, 40–43).

Changes at the household level, therefore, need to be accounted for, not only by looking at structural constraints but also by looking at the actors themselves and their perceptions. People are actively seeking solutions in their daily struggle to survive, creating spaces and autonomy for themselves, and remaking their everyday lives and relationships. As I will demonstrate in the next chapter, some efforts to create space have brought survival strategies into conflict with the state. Noncompliance with state policy then becomes an act of resistance, sometimes resulting in changes in state policy.

In this chapter I explore agency and the pursuit of autonomy within the context of the household economy by looking at the various survival strategies of women, children, and the elderly. I focus on their capacity to transcend the limitations imposed by the lack of resources, education, and capital in pursuing effective survival strategies of their own. These developments ultimately have had an impact on the latitude the government has had in adopting various measures and in shaping the direction these policies have taken.

WOMEN AND CHANGING HOUSEHOLD DEPENDENCIES

Urban women's social and economic isolation and dependence on men is a theme that is often repeated in the literature on African women (Little 1973, 29; Pellow 1977, 26). In Tanzania the evidence pointed in this direction until the 1980s (Sabot 1979, 92; M.-L. Swantz 1985, 130). With the deepening of the crisis and the increased economic role of women in the household, many scholars continued to emphasize the dependence of women and exhibited a tendency to overlook the measure of autonomy they had gained in the process. These authors argued correctly that for the urban poor these were difficult times that had placed new burdens on women to engage in small businesses. But they left the argument at that, describing women as simply caught between the dictates of a relentless economic situation and the demands of their husbands. Although it is true that women have borne more responsibility for feeding their families than they did in the past, their involvement in income-generating activities also has given them greater control and autonomy within the household. They have not been merely passive victims of the hardships wrought by the economic disintegration of the formal economy; they have been actively pursuing solutions to their individual difficulties—solutions that have had a collective impact at the societal level.[1]

Autonomy within the context of the household economy involves women's ability to decide freely whether to pursue an income-generating activity, to determine what kind of activity it should be, and to make all of the major decisions relating to the operation of the project. It involves a woman's prerogative to do as she pleases with her returns; that is, to decide whether her income should go toward the daily consumption of the household, for major family expenses like the building of a house, toward reinvestment in the business, or into savings. Although autonomy in one sphere does not necessarily replicate itself in other spheres of life, it is nevertheless important to recognize those areas in which women do exert a measure of control. Even in situations where real limitations constrain women, it is important to recognize the ways in which women assert their power. As Annette B. Weiner aptly put it (1976, 228–29):

> Whether women are publicly valued or privately secluded, whether they control politics, a range of economic commodities, or merely magic spells, they function within that society, not as objects but as individuals with some measure of control. We cannot begin to understand either in evolutionary terms or in current and historical situations why and how women in so many cases have been relegated to secondary status until we first reckon with the power women do have, even if this power appears limited and seems outside the political field.

Women generally sought revenue from projects that were considered within the sphere of female work: making and selling pastries, frying and selling fish, or braiding hair, for example. In a nationwide survey of informal-sector activity, women predominated as stall sellers, pottery workers, and street food vendors (Planning Commission and Ministry of Labour and Youth Development 1991, 1–77). For the most part, the production of these goods and services took place at home.[2] Goods could be marketed by children. Even if a woman did the selling herself, it usually involved only a brief excursion outside the home; that is, a woman who made *maandazi* pastries sold them for an hour or two in the morning to people on their way to work. If a woman kept her finances separate, her husband did not have to openly acknowledge the importance of her work to the financial well-being of the family. The projects often appeared benign to men, who might otherwise have been threatened by such real assertions of economic independence.

Women's Income-Generating Activities

Women's increased involvement in income-generating activities is by far one of the most significant changes in urban households in the 1980s. As far back as the 1940s and 1950s, when women first began to migrate to the cities, they had been involved in small, income-generating projects (Leslie 1963, 168–69, 226; Mbilinyi 1989, 116–22). Although it is difficult to gauge the prevalence of these activities in the past, the few quantitative studies available indicate that they never reached the proportions seen in the late 1980s. In his survey, R. H. Sabot found 66 percent of women in 1970–1971 with no source of income (1979, 92). A survey conducted by the Department of Sociology at the University of Dar es Salaam in 1970 found 4 percent of the wives in Dar es Salaam self-employed and 9 percent wage employed (Westergaard 1970, 7). Another 1974 survey showed 2 to 3 percent of the wives of low-income civil servants engaged in self-employment (Lindberg 1974). Anders Sporrek's 1976 survey of market sellers found that only 3 percent of 3,223 sellers were women (1985, 181).

The situation could not have been more different in the late 1980s, with the majority of women (69 percent) in Dar es Salaam self-employed and 9 percent wage employed, according to my survey (see Table 1). Half of the wives were self-employed; only 3 percent had wage employment. Similarly, another survey of 134 women conducted in Dar es Salaam in 1987 indicated that 70 percent of all women had projects and that only 5 percent were employed (Tibaijuka 1988). Women began their projects more recently than men, with 86 percent starting their businesses between 1980 and 1987, compared with only 66 percent of men in the same period (see Table 5). For most with small projects this was their first.

The paradox of the situation in the late 1980s was that women who might have once unsuccessfully sought employment and coveted a wage-earning job were now in a better position to increase their earning power outside the workplace. Whereas in the 1950s and 1960s one could talk about "unemployment" among women in the city, the 1980s saw a dramatic rise in women leaving the workforce to pursue projects on a full-time basis.

Wage earners in general made up 48 percent of the adult urban population in Dar es Salaam in 1984; women wage earners constituted only 9 percent of this same population (Bureau of Statistics 1986). One of the reasons for the disparity between the numbers of male and female workers has to do with the fact that women have been discriminated against in the workforce. They faced employers' rigid notions of what women could and could not do in industrial production. Employers' beliefs that women were not as productive as men due to childbearing and menstruation acted as another constraint on the hiring of women, as did the low educational levels of women in general. Furthermore, the problem of childcare and the lack of daycare facilities mitigated against women's participation in the workforce (Bryceson 1980, 20–21; Bryceson 1985, 142; M.-L. Swantz 1985, 150–51). From 1967 to 1978 women's wage employment declined from 44 percent to 24 percent, compared with a decline from 74 percent to 70 percent for men during the same period. In 1971 women had a 20 percent unemployment rate (in contrast to 6 percent unemployment for men) (Sabot 1974, 8). This had largely to do with increasing rates of rural-urban migration for women at that time.

In the late 1980s, however, with the decline in migration, the lack of wage employment among women could be directly attributed to individual decisions to leave the workplace. My survey, for example, showed that although few women left their jobs from 1953 to 1980, between 1980 and 1987 the numbers leaving employment more than doubled (see Table 4). As I mentioned earlier, the most common reason men and women gave for leaving their jobs was low pay.

The choice to leave employment, however, was mainly an option for married women, whose husbands generally remained at work. A woman who was employed and single, divorced, or widowed needed her job for the same reasons a husband tended to stay on the job if his wife had a project: wages often served as backup capital if one's project took a temporary downturn. Although employment may have been inadequate as a source of income, it nevertheless remained a source of status, of access to people, and of resources that could be useful in one's project.

Finding Niches in the Market

Because large numbers of women were starting income-generating projects much later than were men, they faced additional market constraints. In overcoming these they had to employ a number of innovative and imaginative strategies.

One strategy women employed was to find an uncaptured niche in the market. In the early 1980s a Haya woman became one of the first women sellers in one of Dar es Salaam's largest markets. She found her niche catering to the appetites of people from her home area of Bukoba by selling *matoke* cooking bananas. Another woman had been inspired to purify and whiten salt, which is usually gray in color. She then took the salt to the market to sell. Another made small paper bags from larger, discarded cement bags.

In order to open up new areas of entrepreneurship women often needed to create a demand for their products or services. One woman reported having been the first African to open up a hair salon in Dar es Salaam in 1984 that did permanent waves. Since then dozens of similar hair salons have sprung up throughout the city. In the past, African women had done each other's hair, and until recently hairdressing was noncommercialized. Because of this, the hairdresser initially encountered resistance to the idea. As she explained, "The Asian and European women who had salons told me that an African hair salon won't work because people won't pay to have their hair done. But now look at how well I have done."[3]

Most women preferred to enter businesses that in the past had been considered female enterprises. One of the most common income-generating activities among women was making buns and pastries known by their Swahili names as *maandazi*, *vitumbua* (rice cakes), *chapati*, *mkate wa ku-mimina* and *bagia*. Women also make confections like *visheti*, *vibata*, *vijo-goo*, and *kalimati*.

All of the sixty-one women we interviewed who made these pastries operated independently, but children frequently helped sell the goods. They would prepare the mixture at 9 P.M. before going to bed and would get up to fry the pastries from 3 A.M. to 6 P.M. They would then go out and sell them until around 10 A.M. Some sold near garages and factories or along the street near bus stops, hoping to catch workers on their way to work in the morning. Others would give a dish of pastries to a shopkeeper or the owner of a restaurant or teahouse to sell. A few simply placed them in a dish on a stool in front of their home, hoping to entice passersby. Still others sold near school grounds to children on their way to school or during breaks. Women were also found selling pastries at outdoor eating places that served food to workers on their lunch breaks.

On average, women pastry sellers had been in business for six years. Women making *maandazi* brought home a daily profit of around TSh 190 ($1.90 at 1988 exchange rates), whereas those making *chapati* took in TSh 144, and those making *vitumbua* earned only TSh 70. Nevertheless, they were still making considerably more than they would have if they had been employed. The average monthly income from making *maandazi* was still 4.5 times the minimum salary. The main difficulties they reported included shortages of flour, rice, and sugar, along with illegally hiked prices for these and other inputs.

The story of one pastry maker, Mama Hamza, is typical.[4] Mama Hamza came to Dar es Salaam in 1968, settling in the part of town called Keko. A few years before I met her, her husband had moved to Songea to be with his first wife in their polygynous marriage. Unable to depend on him, Mama Hamza started selling *chapati* and *maandazi*. She would wake up at 3:00 or 4:00 in the morning and make about fifty to eighty *chapati*. She took them to the Chang'ombe industrial area, where she sold them to workers at TSh 6 apiece. Her daily profit was between TSh 200 and 340. She would have liked to sell fried fish, but she needed more capital than she had to start such a project.

She said she was like other women she knew, most of whom had begun projects around 1982. When asked why it was only in recent years that women had become involved in these projects, she answered without hesitation: *"Jua kali!"* ("The hot sun!"). Life had become more difficult, and a woman could no longer depend on her husband's wages, she explained. She said she had used her earnings to build a four-room house near her farm on the outskirts of the city and to educate her youngest son, Hamza, one of four children.[5] She was visibly proud of Hamza, explaining how he had been a top student and was now in form 2 (ninth grade). She was sorry she was not educated, saying that she valued education more than anything. Mama Hamza observed, "You can tell that the country is progressing by the fact that my children can learn to speak foreign languages and can speak to foreigners." In order to save money, she participated in two rotating-credit associations.

Although the majority of women like Mama Hamza engaged in low-income projects such as making pastries, women were also entering more profitable businesses, even those that were considered male occupations. In the 1980s women were increasingly finding their way into tailoring, a business that men had dominated until recently.[6] Mboya Bagachwa and Benno Ndulu (1989) found in their survey of the Dar es Salaam informal sector that 23 percent of the city's tailors were women. Lack of capital to buy equipment and inputs was perhaps the main reason women had found it difficult in the past to enter more lucrative trades like tailoring. They also had fewer opportunities for training, for social mores did not permit women to work with men as apprentices in such close collaboration. The women we interviewed had all learned to sew either from vocational schools, which were difficult to get into, or from other women seamstresses, who were few in number. Some had been taught by their husbands. Today, because women have more money in their hands from other projects, capital is less of an impediment to entering such trades as tailoring.

We found some of the most ambitious projects among the few women seamstresses we came across. One woman in Manzese, who had hired two women in their twenties to work for her, already had up to six clients a day one month after opening. The outside walls of her sewing shop were painted in bold, striking colors and designs. Inside, the shop was immaculate, with a long, wooden counter behind which the women sewed. On the counter were Butterick and Vogue pattern catalogs, from which clients were to select dress designs that the seamstress would replicate.[7] In another Manzese family two women and their daughter ran the business while the women's husband (whom they shared in a polygynous marriage) worked in a larger sewing cooperative that made school uniforms.[8]

Sewing was also popular among wives of middle-income families. In one household, the wife had left her job as a technical-college instructor of mathematics and physics in order to support the family through her sewing business, which she had started while employed. Her husband, having been sent by his employer to study in Germany, was able to bring back two sewing machines. They had obtained several accounts from shops. This meant that when their orders were in, she would sew seven days a week from early morning until late into the night, aided by her husband when he arrived home from work.[9]

Another seamstress worked with three hired women and, on occasion, her artist boyfriend and her twelve-year-old daughter. Not only was she known throughout the city for her talent in making wedding gowns, she had even contracted out her services to various international organizations to organize shows exhibiting African fashions. Her business was on an upswing, she said, because the fear of AIDS had prompted a flurry of weddings. She started sewing in 1984 for friends and friends-of-friends but decided to get a license for the first time in 1987 in order to obtain larger accounts. She said that, even though she turned a tidy profit, what pleased her most about her work was making people happy. "I do it for the enjoyment, not the money," she commented.[10] A decade later her business was still booming.

Many women in the higher-income brackets were involved in some of the most lucrative projects in which private citizens could engage. Having started out with small, informal projects, they had succeeded in branching out into larger and more formal private-sector businesses like setting up shipping and receiving companies, secretarial-service companies, private schools, textile factories, bakeries, flour mills, dry-cleaning businesses, prawn-exporting companies, and chick-importing businesses. One of the most successful businesswomen in Tanzania in the 1990s was a forty-two-year-old mother of six, Ester Mkwizu. She was the managing director of Magole, a company exporting horticultural products to the United Kingdom, Sweden, Germany, and the Middle East. In 1993 she won the Euromarket award for her business performance. She was also director of Plan Group consulting engineers and owned a travel-consultant company that made travel arrangements for individuals, companies, or groups and organized meetings and seminars. At a 1994 seminar on women entrepreneurs she stated that women in enterprise were often quite aggressive and clearly determined to succeed but that they faced constraints, including societal attitudes that discouraged potential businesswomen. To do well in business, she argued, women needed a sufficient information base, financial backup, training, and exposure. Nothing could defeat a woman, and no business was too difficult for a woman to undertake.[11]

Stella T. was another businesswoman who made her mark in Dar es Salaam. Stella was thirty-four years old, had two children, but had never married. She was from the Moshi area and had gone to secondary school up through form 4 (eleventh grade). She had worked for ten years as a secretary at various companies, in government offices, and, most recently, at an international agency. While working at the agency she offered temporary secretarial services to law and accounting firms after hours. Stella also sold milk and eggs from her cows and chickens. With her savings from these projects and some help from friends and relatives, she was able to buy used typewriters, desks, a photocopying machine, and several duplicating machines. She left her job in 1983, and with this equipment she started a secretarial-services business. Facing little competition because only two other such businesses were operating in Dar es Salaam, she was so successful that by 1985 she was able to start a shipping and receiving business that handled large quantities of goods to be imported or exported. When asked why so many more women were involved in ambitious enterprises like herself, Stella observed, "Things have changed. Women are now getting the courage and realize that they can stand on their own. They are now members of parliament and have confidence. They feel they can now go into business."[12] In spite of her individual success, Stella found that the main constraint on women like herself was the lack of access to credit and loans, and she believed that lending institutions discriminated against women because of the conditions they placed on loans.

In the early 1980s it was virtually unheard of for women to be managing such ambitious private enterprises. Many of these women had left professional or semiprofessional jobs as secondary- or vocational-school instructors, nurses, accountants, or secretaries to become the main bread-winner in the family through their projects. Their husbands typically re-tained their formal jobs, along with the benefits (allowances, transport, housing) and status associated with these jobs.

Changing Attitudes

The implications of these changes in the household economy have not been lost on men—or on women, for that matter. Gender relations and perceptions are clearly in flux (Tripp 1989). This ambivalence was reflected by the fact that 44 percent of the women we surveyed with projects had re-ceived starting capital from their husbands. Yet these men would fre-quently downplay their wives' roles as important economic actors with in-dependent sources of income by saying that women "just make a few cents" with their projects. Refusing to acknowledge women's actual contri-bution to the household became a way of minimizing their activities and thereby making them appear less threatening. Other men, fearing that their wives would become too independent or leave them, were more openly hostile to women's income-generating projects. They might even refuse to let their wives become involved in projects or would restrict the kinds of projects they could engage in. One tailor said he would not give his wife capital to start a project because, as he put it, "She will do well and leave me."[13] Other men imposed other kinds of limitations on their spouses. A woman who had a hair-braiding business at home wanted to sell *maandazi* buns in the streets or open a kiosk, but her husband, a po-liceman, would not let her. She said she had a thriving hair-braiding busi-ness with up to fifteen clients a day and made four times more than her husband did in a month. She calculated that from her savings the family could start building a house in her hometown of Tanga within about two years. She described her situation thus: "My husband is jealous. He won't let me do business outside the home because he doesn't want me to draw the attention of other men. By braiding hair I meet women only. If he were not so jealous I could do something better. . . . At least I have the op-portunity of seeing other women and of exchanging ideas. I wouldn't have any other chance of meeting others if I hadn't started this business. . . . My life is sad."[14]

In Buguruni, one of the areas I studied, a Lutheran pastor told me that one of the new problems he encountered among members of his congrega-tion was husbands' coming to him complaining that they did not want their wives involved in projects because of how this would reflect on them

and on their ability to support the family.[15] Nevertheless, economic necessity had apparently convinced most men to encourage their wives' projects. One woman hairdresser explained it this way:

> Some women get money from their projects and it makes them less re-
> spectful of their husbands. They say, "I am free and can budget on my own,
> I can buy what I want. I don't have to ask my husband for money for
> everything." For them it may have caused more problems. But for most
> women these projects have meant solving the budgetary problems in their
> family. So they have made family life easier. . . . We would not have
> worked to have projects in the 1970s. Then you could live on the salary of
> the husband and it would have caused problems if the wife had a project.
> But today because of hiked prices and shortages, if it was only the husband
> working, most of us would go crazy.[16]

Another woman who had started a women's fishing cooperative on the
outskirts of Dar es Salaam explained how the twenty-one women in the
cooperative also had their own individual projects transporting and selling
coconuts to the city, growing and selling vegetables, making and selling
pastries, and frying fish for sale. She noted that since women had become
increasingly active in such activities, the men would have liked to object to
these projects "but they keep quiet. They know they can't support the
family and they need the woman's income. Some men are even getting
ambitious and are trying to find businesses for themselves."[17] Some men
had gone so far as to calculate the value of a woman as a wife by her ability to manage a successful project. One young man described half-jokingly
the kind of woman he wanted to marry: "I want an intelligent woman with
brains who will know how to find a project. She can take care of the project
better than I. I can't manage to look after a large amount of money because
I will end up drinking a lot. But if my wife is bright, she can take care of
the project and we will do well."[18] In general, women's involvement in
these projects profoundly challenged the views of men who otherwise
would have had women playing a less conspicuous economic role in the
household. More importantly, it changed women's own view of their role
in the household and in society.

When asked why so many women had started businesses in recent
years, a woman selling spinach with thirteen other market women said,
"We were late but we are progressing these days."[19] Another woman who
had started a hair salon was even more explicit in her assessment of the
role of women in the 1980s: "Today, most women are in business and are
no longer dependent on men. . . . Women are getting confidence that they
can stand on their own."[20] This hairdresser's new-found confidence was

also reflected in the remarks of a woman sewer who said, "In fact, there is no business that can be done without a woman behind it. Take my own husband. He started a project, but it collapsed. Now he wonders how I can continue to progress until now."[21] This seamstress was making ten times more income from her sewing project than her husband was earning as a teacher at a business school.

These changing attitudes are felt in other parts of Tanzania as well. In Mbeya one Tanzanian researcher found that it was not unusual to encounter husbands of middle-income women traders staying home and taking care of household matters while their wives traveled around the country to conduct business.[22]

A twenty-one-year-old woman who grew seaweed as a cash crop in Zanzibar reported that before starting seaweed production she owned only cooking utensils. "Since I began seaweed farming six months ago, I have managed to purchase a radio and seven pairs of shoes and fifteen dresses. I named my second child Mtumwa [slave], to remember the old days when farming in the coral area only gave two bags of rice a year."[23] In Zanzibar an estimated 10,000 women have become involved in seaweed production as a cash crop since the late 1980s. Many of them have done extremely well for themselves through the sale of seaweed to foreign companies. Seaweed exports are fast replacing cloves as Zanzibar's major foreign-exchange earner and are sold to countries like Japan for use in the production of pharmaceuticals, textiles, adhesives, food, and rubber.

Another woman, a potter in the northern town of Usangi in Kilimanjaro region came to the following realization at a seminar of women entrepreneurs. I quote it at length because it conveys beautifully not only how women are struggling to change gender relations in this new economic situation but also how they want to affect national trends through these localized changes:

> Making plans is the responsibility of both the mother and father. When we decide that today we are going to cultivate, men shouldn't say, "Why does she tell me such a thing? She will delay me in my plans." I think it would be a happy family in which the father would contribute and advise without avoiding work as a leader of the family.
>
> We would also like people to understand the importance of women's service [to the household]. The father may earn 10,000 shillings per month salary. . . . When he comes home he sits in a clean chair, gets food, takes a shower and changes into clothes that have been washed. Think if you were single and you had a worker at home who washed your clothes for you and did everything. You would find that you would have to give a portion of your wages to the servant. If fathers could respect women and consider that

what women are doing at home is worth a lot they would help women at home with great love so women can better engage in their business activities.[24]

Control over Earnings

It is clear from the examples above that women showed considerable initiative and independence in the projects they chose and in their decisions to remain on the job or to leave work to engage in projects on a full-time basis. They operated within the constraints of low capital and of their lack of education and skills and, often, within the limitations imposed by their husbands. Nevertheless, through their enterprises women found room to maneuver around many of these constraints and took control of their lives in other ways.

The independence women gained from the projects was reflected in their ability to do as they pleased with their earnings. Many, for example, chose to save their money through a number of arrangements. Although quite a few men saved a portion of their incomes, women appeared to be much more organized and consistent about it. Many women saved their income by participating in rotating-credit societies. The proliferation of these organizations in recent years reflects the fact that women were significantly more involved in income-generating projects and had more cash at their disposal. Half of all self-employed women we interviewed in Manzese and Buguruni admitted that they participated in such societies, referred to as *upato* games.

The number of members in these societies ranged from five to fifty-seven. Women pooled an average of TSh 900 each month; that is, close to one-third of the monthly income from their small businesses. The majority put money into the kitty every five days, thus making contributions six times a month. Each woman had her designated turn to draw from the pooled money. Women liked to put money in the kitty frequently, because if it stayed around the house too long, it was likely to be spent. One-fifth of those who participated in these *upato* societies were involved in second societies as well. One person, called secretary-treasurer or *kijumbe* (literally, go-between or special secret messenger) was paid a small sum in exchange for collecting the pooled money and distributing it. However, she herself could not belong to the society. In some of the larger societies participants provided the name of the next of kin who was responsible for making her installment should she fail to contribute. This person could also claim the kitty were the member to die before it was her turn to claim it.

In the past, women participated in such societies, but rather than pooling money, they pooled *khanga* (cloths) and food. One woman, also a cell leader, said that she had been in such a society since 1972, when clothes and shoes were put into the kitty. At that time she belonged to a group of twenty women friends who started pooling things. In recent years they had adopted what she called a new style of *upato* involving money.[25]

The aims of poorer and higher-income women converged somewhat in the area of savings. Women said they saved to clothe their children (more of a priority among poorer women) and to pay for their education; that is, school fees, uniforms, and school supplies. Women also saved to build houses.[26] We found in our survey that women owned roughly 13 percent of the houses in Manzese and Buguruni. Two-thirds reportedly built them using earnings from their small businesses; one-third inherited their houses. Even if the husband and wife jointly decided to build a house, usually the wife made the plans, saved the money, and saw to it that the construction was completed. Many a family moved into an uncompleted house, gradually finishing other parts of it as they accumulated enough money to pay for it. Women also saved for themselves, although this was after they felt they had taken care of their family's needs. One spinach seller we interviewed at a market said that she and her friends spent their extra money on clothing and having their hair done: "These days women want to buy *khanga* from Mombasa and China. Women want *rasta* [hairpieces woven into the hair to make longer braids] and wigs. It costs to have these and have your hair relaxed or curled."[27]

Other studies, not just in Tanzania but in East Africa as a whole, substantiate the claim that women's involvement in small projects have enhanced their decision-making power with respect to household finances (Obbo 1980, 153). In a 1956 study of Dar es Salaam, J. A. K. Leslie observed that neither husbands nor wives disclosed their earnings to each other (1963, 14, 226). Another 1974 study of self-employed women in Dar es Salaam found that 70 percent controlled their own earnings, 8 percent decided how to spend their earnings jointly with their husbands, and the remainder gave their earnings to their husbands or brothers (M.-L. Swantz 1985, 141). These patterns of financial control continued into the 1980s. In a series of studies of women's economic activities in three fishing villages (Mbweni, Pande, and Mlingotini) in the Dar es Salaam vicinity, women reported controlling their own incomes from their projects (Bashemererwa 1986, 84; Masaiganah 1986, 92; Tungaraza 1986, 96). One Pande wife of a trader was quoted as saying of her husband: "I don't ask what his income is and he doesn't ask for mine." To ensure that her earnings were not disclosed she chose not to deposit her money in a bank. In another village, Bunju, in the Dar es Salaam vicinity, a woman owned some coconut trees, and her husband paid her to tap *tembo* palm wine from the trees (M.-L. Swantz 1986, 55–56).

As I mentioned earlier, often a clear division of labor was established in the household in which women would have their own projects, while men had theirs. Where these distinctions were made, husbands and wives kept their earnings separate. Sometimes projects were claimed by one spouse or the other but were in reality joint household projects. In these cases the couple worked out their budgets together. The businesses that involved this kind of mutual cooperation included *magenge* (vegetable and fruit stalls), sewing businesses, local beer-brewing businesses, and small restaurants called *hoteli* or *mgahawa*.

Descriptions of urban Tanzanian women as isolated and financially dependent may have been accurate ten years ago, but in the 1980s women assumed a central role in the household economy. No longer do characterizations of inactivity hold true, for the majority of women are involved in self-employment or farming. The decline in the real earnings of workers, coupled with the rising cost of living, has forced women into greater economic activity, drawing them out of the home and into more contact with broader sections of society. It is also important to look at the areas in which women have challenged the constraints they find surrounding them and have begun to assert more independence within the household and within society overall. This new independence is found in the changing attitudes of both men and women toward women's new economic importance in the household. Women are making decisions about what to do with their earnings. They are creating new networks. In asserting their autonomy and power vis-à-vis their husbands, women have used noncompliant, nonconfrontational means. Only by looking at women's perceptions of their options and obstacles and how they go about making decisions in their lives can we begin to see women more as agents than as merely victims of change.

WOMEN'S ECONOMIC ACTIVITY AS EMBEDDED ACTIVITY

Women's increased involvement in the informal economy has not only changed household dependencies and enhanced women's autonomy. The way women invest and save capital, how they go about setting prices, how they select the kinds of activities they choose to engage in, how they establish clients and customers, how they form support networks, and how they contribute to the larger community all challenge notions of self-interest, decision making based on individual gain, competition, profit maximization, the separation of market and nonmarket activities, and so forth that are so prevalent in neoclassical economic thinking. Government and donor economic policies rarely have taken into consideration the particular ways in which women (also poor people more generally) engage in economic activity as producers of capital, as investors and savers, and as members of the labor force. Policies tend to be based on underlying assumptions that women's economic activities are discrete activities, separate from the rest of their responsibilities.

Women's entrepreneurial activities are heavily embedded in their daily lives and are part of a whole array of day-to-day activities. Women's involvement in the market takes place within the context of all of these life-sustaining activities and is not separate from the many other dimensions of life. These activities include childcare, family care, buying and cooking food, housecleaning, keeping the home and its surroundings tidy, physically building houses, clothing the children, fetching fuel wood and water, taking care of the health of the family, taking care of the disabled, elderly, and sick, cultivating, tending cows and goats, helping neighbors with needs, taking care of the poor in the community, organizing celebrations, helping raise funds for the community, helping with extended family needs, assisting other women in childbirth, assisting in funeral preparations, helping in the husband's business, and many other such activities. These alternative logics are revealed in a number of ways.

Building Trust

Women's economic activities revolved around activities predicated on high degrees of trust. One woman talked about how, when she first joined a savings club of close friends in 1972, the purpose of the club was *kutunzana,* an endearing way of saying "caring for or looking out for one another."[28] By the late 1980s she was involved with women who were not necessarily friends, and they had found ways to extend these ties of trust and mutuality beyond their friends. The one characteristic of these savings societies that women stressed time and again was the fact that they necessitated trust in order to function. As one woman who put TSh 300 into the kitty twice a month said, "Because we trust ourselves we can save on our own."[29] She was a seamstress who also made and sold fried *maandazi* buns. Another woman, who along with eighteen other women, put TSh 100 into a kitty every three days, said much the same thing: "*Upato* is like putting money in the bank, but you need trust."[30]

Flexible Funds

Women (94 percent) in my survey generally owned their own projects to a slightly greater extent than did male entrepreneurs surveyed, of whom 88 percent owned their own business. The decision to go into business on one's own instead of a partnership, cooperative, or employment stemmed in part from the need to keep control over decisions involving the use of money. Even though most women engaged extensively in collaborative arrangements with others, having complete ownership of the project allowed them the necessary flexibility to blend family concerns with business ones. In other words, financial resources could be moved freely from business to home based on one's day-to-day needs. If a child fell sick or some other life difficulty arose, there was no hesitation in using working capital, even if it meant a temporary halt to the business. At times like this it was more important to eat or care for a sick child than anything else. Because of the kinds of support systems that existed, one could almost always scrounge up enough capital from various friends and relatives to start up again.

Economic strategies evolved to enable women to care for their families. One of the many reasons why women saved money in *upato* rotating-savings-club arrangements rather than in a bank was so that they would not spend the money on themselves and could have it available when they needed it for larger family expenses or to invest in their business. Dorthe Von Bülow (1993, 7) found this to be the case in Kilimanjaro Region, where women believed that by putting money in a savings club they were more likely to save because of the public pressure to do so and also because of the knowledge that the money belonged to the whole group.

Flexible Work Strategies

The embeddedness of economic activity in other life activities is evident in the ease with which many women decided to leave formal employment to pursue self-employment. The decision was facilitated by the fact that it often solved two dilemmas at once: the need to bring in a livable income and the need for childcare. The solution is by no means peculiar to Tanzania. Esther Boserup observed that in most developing countries women tended to prefer working in home industries and avoided working in large-scale industries. She found that women enjoyed the flexible hours, the possibility of keeping an eye on one's children while at work, and the freedom to come and go and to interrupt work to carry out pressing domestic duties (Boserup 1970, 115).[31] As one seamstress explained, "I had worked as a nurse and sewed at the same time, but I wanted to take care of my children at home. I felt I was neglecting my children by leaving them with someone else. I especially didn't like night duty and didn't want to be away from home. Going full-time into my project, I could work and care for my children at the same time."[32] This woman had left her job as a nurse at the government hospital to sew. As a seamstress she earned almost twenty times more than she did from her wages and almost seven times more than her husband, a teacher in a vocational college, did.

Networking Strategies

Women's networking and collaborative strategies also reflected the embeddedness of part of their businesses in societal considerations. Although most women generally owned their own projects, most collaborated with others to one degree or another. Half worked with one or two others in a loose and rather informal arrangement. They generally worked with another family member, a distant relative, or a friend. One common arrangement was for a woman to prepare fried foods at home and for her children or a younger sister to sell them in the streets.

In larger projects that involved more skill, women would recruit younger relatives, providing them with training until they could establish themselves, usually with yet another younger relative. One woman accountant we interviewed who had a poultry sideline business explained that she had a cousin from upcountry come and live with her to help out with the chicken business. In return, she would let her cousin use her sewing machine and paid for her evening sewing classes. Having learned to sew, the cousin would go back upcountry, whereupon another cousin would come to live under a similar agreement. These kinds of arrangements were made to help the relative and not always out of considerations of business profitability.

Other kinds of arrangements existed. For example, two sisters had separate businesses: one cooked beans; the other, rice. They then sold together at the same bar. This arrangement enabled them to help each other out, buying inputs or preparing and selling the food. It also made them feel more secure when they returned from the bar late at night.

Companionship represented another important factor in explaining why women chose to work with a close friend or relative. The need for companionship was one reason women market sellers tended to sell in the same part of the market. Market sellers also sat together because they brought their small children with them, enabling them to share in childcare if necessary. Similarly, they tended each others' stalls if one had to go away temporarily.

Another reason for selling together had to do with evading the City Council militia that came around to check licenses. Many women, for example, sold maize and flour in rows outside the market because they could not afford the licenses and fees required to obtain a market stall. In addition, they felt the unpredictability of their businesses did not warrant procuring a license. Selling together gave them a sense of security and mutual support in the event that they were caught.

Although many women organized their projects, drawing from kin- and clan-support systems, others were breaking out of these older patterns of cooperation to establish new networks that were made possible in the urban setting. Because of the paramount importance of mutual trust, small businesses frequently included members of the same ethnic group or clan. However, with the large mixture of ethnic groups in the city and the inter-marriage among many different groups, these factors, which once might have inhibited such cooperation, were breaking down. For example, one hair-braiding salon was owned by a Zanzibari woman who had hired a group of women of different ethnic origin who had lived as neighbors for many years and had become close friends. They included a Chagga, a Makonde, a Maasai, a Zaramo, and a Hehe. Through such arrangements women were extending the responsibilities of kinship relations that emphasized mutual trust to new contacts.

Urban life also provided women with opportunities to come in contact with a broader circle of people who could provide them with information and ideas crucial to the expansion of their businesses. These kinds of networks were not possible in rural settings. Moreover, they were not always necessary, even in the urban setting, until large numbers of women became involved with projects. Women found hairdressing salons good places in which to socialize. Here women could share information about projects, sources of cheap inputs, and other relevant business information. "In the past you did not find women having discussions like this," one hair-salon owner remarked.[33]

A few women found it possible to network with male friends, business associates, and work partners, which suggests a movement toward relationships on a more equal footing between men and women in certain spheres. One woman was visibly embarrassed when she admitted that two of her best sources of advice and encouragement were in fact male friends. "When business goes down," she said, "sometimes you lose hope. But my friends give me courage. They tell me when to expand and when to save to take care of things if they don't go so well."[34]

Sharing information, providing contacts, assisting others in the same business, and selling the same product in the same location are distinctly noncompetitive. When we asked respondents whether a purchase from one market seller sparked jealousy in another seller of the same product, the answer typically was, "Why should it? Some days she may do well in sales; other days I might." Jealousy and competition were present among these women, as they would be anywhere. But other logics of business were also prevalent, and the view that cooperating with others and creating relations of mutual assistance are beneficial ways of conducting business was pervasive.

Finally, another characteristic of the new networking strategies has to do with the genuine desire on the part of better-off women to assist women of lesser means. Some did this through associations; others gave interest-free loans to poorer women or shared their skills and advice. Von Bülow, for example, found that in the Kilimanjaro Region wealthier businesswomen liked to help poorer women, believing that they did not lose anything themselves, that they gained personal satisfaction from such assistance, and that they obtained regular customers for themselves (1993, 10).

One of the few studies of women's economic activity in Tanzania that incorporates an analysis of women's rationales and motivations revealed many similarities between women traders in the northern part of the country and women entrepreneurs in Dar es Salaam. Päivi Mattila (1992, 53, 62), in her study of marketing networks in Moshi and Mwanga districts, found that women established networks with friends and acquaintances to solve specific business dilemmas, to share a mutual dependence, and to create a sense of togetherness and understanding. They considered themselves to be on an equal footing with these collaborators. Women formed marketing networks, for example, to make their businesses more profitable by assisting one another with transport, storage of goods, marketing, and household work. They also used networks to combine goods in order to gain a higher position in the market hierarchy, to pool resources to buy and sell products requiring larger amounts of capital, and to provide a safety net in case one's business temporarily failed.

Thrift

Another characteristic of women's economic activity that is pervasive in the informal economy is that of thrift. Everything conceivable is recycled:

bottles, paper, string, plastic containers. For example, I found women sewing baby pants using elastic their children had collected from discarded bicycle tires. Their children would go to bicycle repairmen to buy or search their garbage for these scraps. They sewed these pants out of plastic material purchased in downtown shops and secondhand nightgowns bought at the market.

I could not help but be amused once when I bought some fried potatoes and found that they were wrapped in a page of the 1986 World Bank report I had been trying to find in the library! A family of frame makers in Buguruni made their nails from scraps. Another family used aluminum scraps from a nearby factory to make flutes. Thrift is clearly integral to the logic of small-scale production.

The Right to Subsist

Many who appreciate that women are sustaining life through their activities do not see the sense of licensing small-scale women entrepreneurs, and, indeed, women reported not having licenses nine times more often than men. Young people and women were more likely to be involved in these unlicensed and often less stable enterprises. For this reason it was especially women and youth who found themselves the targets of harassment by City Council militia. The militia usually extracted bribes from them or confiscated their goods. This kind of harassment confounded most people, who could not see the logic of making the poorest members of society pay for the right to seek a living, especially poor women who were already supporting many family members from their business and were shouldering many expenses, including school fees, healthcare, and care for the elderly—all basic needs that the government could not come even close to covering. As one male resident of Manzese said to me regarding unlicensed women who face harassment by City Council militia, "I don't know why the government wants to license small businesses. Women do not have any capital. Some with small businesses have lost their husbands and have six or seven children and can't get employment. Others may be too old to work. They just want to make money to live. And then the government wants them to pay for a license. This question should be looked at again. Even the president has said that people should be left alone to do their small businesses. But it won't make a difference because the City Council won't stop their harassment."[35] A woman entrepreneur described this alternative logic eloquently in a seminar of small-scale businesswomen:

You may see that a mother is selling her cassava. When she sells her cassava she gets money. At that time you may see that that mother has borrowed some money from someone and bought cassava, carried it, carried firewood and roasted it, you may think that this is just a simple thing and say, "This mother is just roasting cassava." But this mother is feeding five kids, her husband, her mother-in-law, father-in-law, sisters-in-law, and children of her sisters-in-law. If that woman gets 200 shillings profit, she will buy a kilo of maize flour and some spinach, cook for the family that day, and be satisfied.[36]

You may think that being a mother is a simple thing, but this is why problems are occurring. Municipal officers, city council officers, and village officers do not see that these women are trying to be self-reliant by employing themselves, by raising the family. One thing that we may ask the guest of honor who is the minister is that he meet with his other fellow ministers and health minister and other district officers, some of whom them are here, and let us help each other open our eyes.[37]

You see someone roasting her cassava. Then you [the militia] come and tell her, "Take this away" and throw her business in the trash. They shouldn't discriminate against us because there isn't any compensation when you humiliate that poor person, when you break down her stall. She has brought firewood and wood for building the hut, she has hired a tractor or cart, she has hired a mason, and you just look at her and pass by there, and you tell her that she should pay 3,000 shillings per year. You receive the money and give her a receipt. Tomorrow you tell her to break it down. Things like this are a curse, a painful thing to that poor person.

That mother stays there crying. She has borrowed someone's money, and the family stays hungry. But you could have told her, "Mother, running such a business at this corner isn't permitted. You go to that corner, put your box there, and throw all your garbage there. Do not spread it everywhere." Then you would have educated her, and she would do her job peacefully. But our problem is that the big shots are having their meetings, and they don't invite women. We ask for these city officers to count the number of those [women] who are self-employed at the market, kiosks at the road, and those roasting cassava and maize. Women do a lot in the family and in the society. We want to make this clear to all village leaders, wards, districts, and everyone to open their eyes, and those who have been given the task of serving as city officials and health officers must do their jobs.

Some say, "What should we do? Should we start stealing?" That problem exists. I ask these big shots to know that these poor people have a big task of being self-reliant. They don't ask for your money. . . . They don't ask you for school fees. . . . They ask nothing of you because they are self-reliant. They should be encouraged, and the big shots should recognize their existence. Therefore we ask our guest of honor, because you know these problems are in all cities. . . . Remember that those who are facing such difficulties are mostly women who are trying to be self-reliant. Therefore, when we see women taking on challenges in various activities, we ask our leaders to help them and encourage them, and those who are responsible for the city council must be aware.

Women's Economy as a Moral Economy?

Although the economic rationales outlined above apply to poor micro-entrepreneurs in general, they are often more easily identified in women's approaches to economic activity. The rationale underlying this economy of reciprocity and mutuality is a sense of community: its participants share a common plight, in which survival is paramount, and everyone's survival is contingent on the survival of the others. The only way to ensure survival is to assist, share, and take care of one another through various networks and groups that in the urban setting emerge from the family, the neighborhood, the workplace, or other forms of selection. This is no pure moral economy, but the main characteristics of women's economic activity parallel many of the ideals, values, and underlying principles so familiar in the work of George Dalton (1961), Karl Polanyi (1957), Marshall Sahlins (1972), and James Scott (1976). As the moral-economy argument goes, community interests, not markets, define the values that shape economic activity. Conversely, in a highly developed market economy the self-regulating market rules society, the goals of the market are supreme, the economy is disembedded, and individuals and their activities are atomized (Booth 1994, 657, 660).

These distinctions are too sharp to reflect a real economy, especially one in flux like the Tanzanian economy or even women's activities within that economy. Just as advanced market societies are governed by societal institutions (laws, contracts, courts, police) that impose their own moral order on economic relations (Booth 1994, 661), so too, those who live with a worldview of embedded economies do not operate simply in a context of reciprocity, mutuality, altruism, or considerations of broader community imperatives. They can also be self-interested, profit maximizing, and competitive. They too may hire on merit rather than affective association, and they may price goods at fixed rates rather than according to the means of the buyer or one's relation to the buyer. Nevertheless, by identifying a women's way of sustaining life that adopts a moral-economy model rather than a market-economy model, one is better able to explain conflicting rationales that are at the root of the issues most fiercely contested between the actors in the informal economy and the state, as outlined in chapters 6 and 8. What is interesting is that even with increased market activity, the moral-economy rationales have not given way to more market-oriented ones, as predicted by such authors as Polanyi in *The Great Transformation.*

These alternative decision-making rationales are resilient, and people have transformed them to meet new needs.

CHILDREN AND YOUTH

Children and young people have always played an important role in the urban household economy, but in recent years their significance has increased to an even greater extent. This heightened economic activity among children and youth is related to the increased involvement of women in income-generating projects, for children are vital to these projects. In fact, 61 percent of women with projects reported relying on children to help them prepare the foods to be sold or, more commonly, to sell foods the mother made.

Like women's work, children's work is not separated into two spheres of household chores and income-generating work. For this reason, children's involvement in food vending is seen as an extension of what they do at home to help their mother in cooking, cleaning, and taking care of siblings.

The increase in children working has not gone unnoticed. One woman observed: "Since I have lived here in Manzese (fifteen years), mostly men did work. Because of changes in life, everyone has a business [today]. Even small children are doing business. Children work mainly for their parents, but a few work for themselves. Children forget about school and so may leave school completely. All they think about is money." [38] She had worked for fifteen years at a garment factory, waking up at 4 A.M. every day to make rice cakes. She sold some of the cakes at work, and her children sold the rest at school.

In another fairly typical family in Buguruni, the children went to the large wholesale market downtown at 8 A.M. to buy potatoes and peanuts. They fried the potatoes from 11 A.M. to 1 P.M. to sell to lunch customers and then went to school in the afternoon. (Schools are run in two shifts, morning and afternoon.) They gave the money they made to their mother. In the evening they packed peanuts in plastic bags to sell the following day. The mother, who was divorced, was a messenger at nearby Radio Tanzania. Because of her high blood pressure and other health problems, she said she could not do any other project. She believed she was helping her children by giving them a business because she did not believe her children would ever be able to obtain a wage-paying job.[39]

At the Ilala market we came across two boys, aged twelve and fourteen, who were intensely absorbed in a project for their father, a market seller. The boys were making *vibatari* lamps with scraps of metal obtained from several Dar es Salaam factories. They barely looked up from their work to speak to us because they were so preoccupied with molding the lamps with a makeshift welding rod heated in a charcoal stove. Visibly proud of their craftsmanship, they said their father had taught them. They made Tsh 50 to 100 a day and sold each lamp at TSh 7 wholesale or TSh 10 retail. In another common scene, every morning fifteen children, aged seven to eleven, sat in a row chattering in a lively manner across from the local party offices in Buguruni while selling pastries. Situated near some large garages, they would sell the food to mechanics on their way to work. The children disappeared by 10 A.M. to get ready to go to school in the afternoon. They sold *maandazi* buns, *vitumbua* rice cakes, and *mkate wa ku-mimina* confectionery breads made by their mothers.

Children have historically played an integral role in household work and income-generating projects. In fact, such child labor has been pervasive throughout Africa (Schildkrout 1982). Leslie (1963, 245–46) found in a small sample of fifty children at Mnazi Mmoja in the late 1950s that one was an apprentice carpenter, five were domestic servants, three were unskilled laborers, and five sold cakes and cashew nuts for their parents or other relatives. He noted that young people could be found selling newspapers, working as apprentice mechanics, being tennis boys, collecting scrap, or "selling oranges, nuts, fritters, coconut ice or sweet beer."

No literature indicates the status of children's work over time in urban Tanzania. What little evidence available is fragmentary. Sporrek, for example, found in his 1976 survey that 9 percent of all market and street sellers were children under the age of fifteen (1985, 165). One can only surmise that the universal primary education program, started in 1969, decreased children's participation in projects somewhat. By 1977, 80 percent of all school-age children were in school (Coulson 1982, 217).

Projects and School Attendance

School records, however, provide some clues for the 1980s. The decrease in attendance and enrollment in the areas we surveyed strongly suggests that children have increased their involvement in small businesses. In Buguruni there was a 30 percent drop in primary-school enrollment from 1985 to 1988 for standards 4 through 7 (fourth through seventh grades). In Manzese there was an 11 percent drop in enrollment for the same time period for the same standards. The numbers of Buguruni students who did not complete primary school increased 3.4 times from 1980 to 1988.

Girls had a better track record than did boys with respect to school attendance and completing their studies, because they were less likely to be as involved in their own projects. In Buguruni 99 percent of the girls enrolled attended classes, compared with the 80 percent attendance record of boys.[40] Almost 50 percent of boys who had enrolled did not complete their schooling in 1988, compared with 32 percent of girls.

In the 1980s, according to school principals, the main problem affecting children's schoolwork was their preoccupation with small projects. One headmaster commented on these new developments in school attendance:

> Not long ago parents were trying to feed their children. Today, children of Dar es Salaam are feeding their parents [through their projects]. . . . Small businesses are the main problem facing children in school these days. Cigarette hawking, selling chicken, chips, eggs, *maandazi* buns, making local beer, even working at *gongo* [a potent and illegal alcoholic drink] bars. One girl in my school is selling beer at her mother's bar. They learn things that are beyond their age. Those who have small businesses don't do homework. . . . They don't care about school at all. . . . Some children stop going to school completely.[41]

Teachers, parents, and students with whom we spoke agreed that school did little to prepare school leavers to cope after they finished standard 7. Schools in Buguruni and Manzese had virtually no textbooks, notebooks, charts, or even desks and chairs. Nor did they have equipment with which to teach vocational skills. They did not have hoes with which to farm as part of the Education for Self-Reliance program. At one time Uzuri Primary School in Manzese had a fruit garden, but the fruit was stolen. What children learned about domestic science they learned at home. Likewise, those who became skilled artisans went into apprenticeship with their parents, relatives, or someone else. School authorities found parents reluctant to curtail their children's engagement in projects because they were so dependent on their assistance.

Each year 50,000 students graduated from primary schools in Dar es Salaam, only to find no jobs waiting for them. Of the standard-7 leavers in Manzese, 3 percent went to vocational school (in 1985) and 12 percent went to secondary school (in 1987). In Buguruni only 6 percent of standard-7 leavers went to secondary school. The rest went directly into the ranks of the self-employed, into family businesses, or into apprenticeships.[42]

Fending for Yourself

Children had to fend for themselves at an early age. Many found that if they did not find some source of income they would go without various necessities, because their parents simply did not have the means. Their parents may have given them food and occasionally clothes, but anything extra, including school supplies and fees, they would have to work for themselves. These children were involved in virtually every kind of small-scale project. In Manzese some chipped stones and collected buckets of sand to sell to local building contractors. Others collected scraps from the Urafiki textile mill to use in making mattresses or in making wicks for *vibatari* oil lamps.

In order to survive, children had to learn not only ambition but creativity as well. I spoke to one fourteen-year-old boy from Manzese who, with his twelve-year-old brother, took the bus every day after school to the downtown Kigamboni fish market. He would clean fish for people from midday until about 4 P.M. and then return home. He had done this for five years and said he made a great deal of money (TSh 50–100 a day), which he kept himself. He said he was saving to go to secondary school.[43]

Not all children worked for their parents or themselves. Primary-school teachers reported that they would use their students to sell ice cream, soda, *maandazi* buns, peanuts, embroidery, homemade envelopes, and paper bags to other students on a 10 percent commission. Other children, especially street vendors, worked for shopkeepers or patrons, who claimed a percentage of their earnings on a daily basis. One candy-and-cigarette seller reported being allowed to keep TSh 50 out of his TSh 400 a day profits. This gave him just enough to live on, but not enough to accumulate capital to go into business for himself. It also was more than he could have made if he had a minimum-wage-paying job.[44] However, most young vendors and entrepreneurs worked for themselves.

Many of the young vendors in the city center were sent by their rural parents to earn cash to supplement their subsistence farming. These vendors had come for a few years and planned to return home to settle eventually. They traveled back and forth to their rural homes and spent longer lengths of time at home during the harvest season. One typical vendor, a fifteen-year-old, had finished standard 7. He was given capital by his family to come to the city to sell coffee and peanut cakes with his younger brother. He had worked in the city center for two years, selling 300 cups a day at a shilling a cup. He sent money home to his parents, who grew maize in Dodoma.[45]

Although some rural parents sent their children to cities, in recent years young people were beginning to find equally attractive possibilities for business in their home areas. There is evidence that the increase in trade and rural income-generating activities by youth and children has militated against their migrating to the cities after completing standard 7 (M.-L. Swantz 1986, 17). Their parents would use the children's literacy skills to help them carry out trade in fish, cassava, oranges, mangoes, and other produce. When the youth had accumulated enough capital they might go into business for themselves.

The Case of Cigarette Vendors

Vending is one of the most popular income-generating activities among youth because of its low capital and skill requirements. Cigarette vendors are fairly typical of this group of sellers, found at all bus stops, market areas, and outdoor eating places. All of the eleven cigarette vendors we interviewed were in their late teens or early twenties, and all except one had completed primary school. Most had grown up in Dar es Salaam, having come to the city as children with their parents. One vendor who had come three years ago was sent by his parents in Lindi, who were subsistence maize farmers. They wanted him to find a source of income so that he could send cash remittances home.

The vendors had worked an average of three and a half years. Because they were reselling cigarettes at illegally hiked prices, they needed to disguise their activities. They did this by selling something in addition to cigarettes—oranges, candies, peanuts, plastic bags, or soda, for example.

The illegal cigarette market appeared to me to be highly regulated by the national distributors, the shopkeepers, and other legal cigarette agents. Because the most popular Tanzanian brands, Sportsman and Embassy, were in short supply, these traders were able to profit from scarcity premiums by keeping a tight reign on supply sources. Shopkeepers did not sell the cigarettes off their store shelves, as they were supposed to.[46] Instead, they resold the cigarette packets to vendors at hiked prices, usually TSh 20 over the legal price for each packet. They kept the vendors in check by controlling the numbers of cigarette packets a vendor could sell; that is, vendors throughout the city reported that they obtained no more than five packets a day. An agent or shopkeeper could be allocated somewhere between 5,000 and 8,000 packets a month, which he or she would resell to the vendors at hiked prices. Agents could potentially make up to TSh 160,000 a month, whereas if they sold the cigarettes according to official prices, they could only make TSh 20,080 a month for the same quantity. Some agents or their relatives could travel around the country selling cigarettes at even higher prices than they fetched in Dar es Salaam. The vendors, in turn, charged customers TSh 5 for a cigarette that would have cost between TSh 2 and 3 had it been sold at the official price. In this way, the vendors we interviewed made an average of TSh 205 a day. Vendors found the hardest part of their work was putting up with the harassment by the City Council militia, who came by on a regular basis to check for licenses and to extract bribes (from TSh 10 to 50 a day) or cigarettes from them.

One typical vendor we spoke with was born in Dar es Salaam and had been selling cigarettes ever since he finished standard 7 eight years earlier. He had long since stopped looking for work and resigned himself to vending as a means of obtaining a living. His mother supported his family by making pastries and engaging in other small businesses. He explained:

> Life is very hard for the poor in the cities. Only the rich can enjoy life. For others, especially for government civil servants, life is very difficult. They get 1,200 shillings a month. It is better for us who are selling cigarettes. We would prefer to do other jobs, but we can't find them. I would farm if I had a place to live and the means. But you can't just go out and start farming like that. I wouldn't mind cultivating as long as I had enough money to live, to eat, and for clothes. Most people in this business belong to poor families. They did not continue with secondary education. We have no capital; therefore we have to look for other means of survival.[47]

A Precarious Existence

Studies of young people have tended to focus on how they migrated to the city in search of jobs, excitement, fun, easy money, and educational opportunities (Ishumi 1984). The young people we talked to—those born in Dar es Salaam as well as migrants—had a much different picture of city life. They lived a precarious existence and talked mostly about disappointments and fears. Many of them said they had no hope of getting employment. The kinds of jobs they might find did not pay enough to make it worth their while. Others talked about hunger. A nineteen-year-old vendor lamented, "Even though I work I am often hungry. When I am hungry and don't have money all I can live on is 'feelings.' Old men live on feelings, but I am young and I must live on my feelings."[48] Some talked about the problem of thieves. One young orange seller, who started selling at 7 A.M. and left at 9 P.M., said he could not afford to be fearful of walking the city streets at night. "If you are afraid you won't live, you won't eat."[49]

Among the biggest difficulties the young vendors in the city center faced were the almost daily raids by City Council militia. One vendor was apprehensive about being caught by the militia because a friend of his who had been caught had allegedly been beaten. He was afraid of having his day's earnings taken by the militia and of having the candy he was selling confiscated.[50] Another sixteen-year-old candy seller from Dodoma had finished standard 7 and had come to the city to obtain cash, which he would send home to his family, who grew maize. He made TSh 200 a day from his project. In one year he was caught twice: the first time he had to pay an TSh 800 bribe to the militia; the second time the militia overturned his table and took all his money.[51] Virtually every one of the hundred or so vendors we interviewed in the city center complained of such harassment. Unlicensed vendors had to come up with all kinds of tactics of evasion in the cat-and-mouse game they played with the City Council militia. Those who sold fish, oranges, and candy frequently laid their wares on gunny sacks or cardboard boxes on top of small tables. If they saw the militia coming they could quickly fold up the sack or pick up the tray and run. Virtually all shoe shiners sold hiked cigarettes, which they kept hidden inside the stalls from which they worked. Others did not have any fixed premises and carried their peanuts, candies, and cigarettes around in their hands or in cardboard trays to make it easier to evade the militia.

The burden of the crisis is heaviest on children and youth, many of whom at a very early age, even by Tanzanian standards, must fend for themselves. Young entrepreneurs are frequently maligned as idealists who have come to the city, attracted by the bright lights and excitement of city life. But they experience a much different reality. Self-employed youth have been prime targets of state campaigns to eradicate so-called loiterers and unproductive elements. They have been objects of daily harassment by the militia because they operate their businesses without licenses.

Government officials and even academics have often overlooked the conditions that have forced young people to resort to their various income-generating strategies. Rural impoverishment and lack of sources of cash in rural households are two key factors that spur the migration of young people. Lack of jobs in urban areas similarly leaves youth with few options, especially those who have grown up in the city without links to the rural areas. Given these realities, it is important to examine how children themselves see their constraints, opportunities, and futures. What was most remarkable about so many of the children and young people we interviewed was their tenacity, persistence, and inventiveness even in the midst of disillusionment.

THE ELDERLY

Like women and children, old people have also increased their contribution to the household economy. Many who counted on their adult children supporting them as they grew older found themselves supporting their children instead. As I have shown, wages contributed marginally to urban survival, so it comes as no surprise that pensions contributed even less.

Among most of Tanzania's ethnic groups, it is considered an obligation for adult children to assist their parents as much as possible. Today it is difficult for young urban dwellers to find jobs or come up with enough capital to start a small business. Those with jobs cannot survive on their earnings. Many felt badly they could not fulfill their responsibilities as children and be of more assistance to their parents.

Many older people had an advantage over younger adults in that they once had jobs and used their savings to start up a business. Thus we frequently found elderly parents helping their adult children. One man, who had been a primary-school teacher all his life, had taken his severance pay when he retired in 1975 and started a wholesale charcoal business. He brought charcoal to Dar es Salaam from his home area of Kisarawe near the city. He was making TSh 15,000 net profit a month. His plans were to "put a little in the bank and just wait for time to pass" so that he could "go and see *babu* [the old man] in heaven."[52] One of the main things that bothered him was the fact that his son, an employed mechanic, was not self-employed and continually came to him for money. The retired teacher said: "I ask him, when will he stand on his own feet and help his father? But he can't because he is only employed." This man was like many retirees, who used their severance pay to buy land to farm or to set themselves up in a project. The most common projects for the elderly in Manzese and Buguruni included food stalls, retail charcoal sales, fried-fish sales, laundering, and farming.

The elderly face many of the same problems that others do in running their small businesses. But perhaps it is the perspective of time that has made it possible for many elderly to match their bitterness about life today with humor. When we asked one old woman who had sold rice at a beer club for twenty-five years what the main problem in her business was, she replied, without batting an eyelash: "Now that I am an old grandmother when I go downtown on the bus men no longer follow me and shout 'Wait for me!' They just say to me, '*Shikamoo bibi*' [a respectful greeting for an old woman]."[53]

6 Everyday Forms of Resistance and Transformations of Economic Policy

You can't make people go along one narrow road. People have their own minds. They aren't going to go along with force.

CCM ten-cell leader, Dar es Salaam

As the economic crisis deepened in the early 1980s, the conflicts between the government and those involved in the informal economy over how the self-employed were treated, over legalizing their small businesses, and over other policies that were perceived as threatening ordinary people's pursuit of a livelihood reached a new intensity. Urban dwellers' options had become more limited; resources and jobs, more scarce. In the early 1980s the authorities initiated a series of measures targeting people they labeled loiterers, unproductive elements, and economic saboteurs. These and other inflexible policies forced increasing numbers of people to pursue strategies of noncompliance, refusing to abide by laws that violated popular notions of justice.

Meanwhile, the slowdown of the world economy and world trade and the concomitant pressures from external donors and international agencies like the IMF and the World Bank put enormous pressures on governments of low-income countries like Tanzania to respond in ways that weakened their own internal legitimacy. The economic crisis, coupled with these external pressures for restructuring, occurred at the same time that domestic pressures in the form of massive noncompliance with government and CCM regulations became more apparent. This chapter, however, is about changes that were mainly consequences of internal pressures, many of which had little to do with donor conditionality.

After the mid-1980s, open repression of small entrepreneurs gradually gave way to legalization, liberalization, and privatization. Small-business operators who had previously been considered engaged in illegal occupations were now able to apply for licenses. Trade of foodstuffs that had been channeled through parallel markets could now make its way through liberalized open markets. Bus transportation, banks, and medical practices, which had been monopolized by the government, were opened to private ownership. Sometimes, however, the authorities either did not have the capacity to enforce their policies or were not prepared from an ideological standpoint to sanction various practices officially. In these cases they continued to ignore certain illegal economic activities.

The activities discussed in this chapter affected not only the self-employed but also employees in the public and private sectors and their household members. These struggles over the legitimacy of self-employment as a means of obtaining a livelihood and other such conflicts were the main source of tension in the 1980s between those in power and the urban dwellers, including workers and civil servants. With the deepening of the crisis and the state's simultaneous growing inability to maintain adequate wages, the battleground for workers shifted from the official workplace to areas in which the state encroached on people's key sources of income: informal income-generating activities.

People's persistence in their informal income-generating activities in defiance of government restrictions became a form of opposition. These forms of resistance were not formally mobilized, but the collective impact of hundreds of thousands of individuals' resorting to similar kinds of measures clearly was not lost on those in power. They had to respond, often by making policy changes of the kind described in this chapter.

James C. Scott forcefully argued that such "everyday forms of resistance" can be effective, widespread, durable, and highly coordinated, even though they are not formally organized and do not seek "self-consciously" broad policy goals (1987, 421). Although he was referring to peasant resistance, the same conceptualization could equally apply to resistance in the urban setting.

The Tanzanian state's responses to noncompliance were rarely direct. Instead, they involved tacit compromises. The leadership's gradual shift in policy with respect to these small-scale enterprises came about primarily through societal pressures. These pressures initially did not directly threaten the ideological underpinnings of a state that had sought legitimacy from upholding populist and socialist goals of egalitarianism, self-reliance, and communalism. As Scott argues, direct challenges to rulers are more likely to face suppression than are quiet strategies, because a concession to direct challenges necessitates a permanent and acknowledged response, whereas a concession to a quiet pressure can be made informally, without any symbolic or official change in policy. Moreover, the concession can always be retracted. As such, resistance that follows the path of least resistance is often the most effective (Scott 1987, 423). Many of the initial government responses were tacit, but mounting pressures eventually led to policy changes that did, in fact, involve shifts in ideological orientation, as seen in the dismantling of the Arusha Declaration (see chapter 7).

Although forms of noncompliant resistance are sometimes termed passive, empirical analysis of the Tanzanian experience shows that such resistance is by no means characterized by passivity in the literal sense. By pursuing their various survival strategies, people were not just responding to necessity, they were actively remolding their own destinies. They were not only seeking new and innovative ways of obtaining an income, they were consciously and vigorously resisting the state. In the course of defying various anachronistic state policies, they were reshaping the political and economic structures that surrounded them.

People of every class were involved in the informal economy. The poorest vendors might carry out their business in unauthorized locations. At the same time, the upper ranks of civil servants evaded the Arusha Declaration Leadership Code by owning sideline projects and hiring workers to assist them in these businesses. Middle- and upper-income people kept chickens, cows, and pigs in their backyards at a time when city ordinances outlawed such practices. Doctors would illegally moonlight after putting in their hours at the government hospital.

Involvement in projects was characteristic of most classes, but government repression of informal economic activities was not uniform. City Council militia harassed the poorest women, youth, and child vendors on a daily basis, while leaving alone the well-to-do who had sideline incomes and were not paying taxes. During the 1983 Nguvu Kazi repatriation campaign to move so-called loiterers—most of whom were self-employed—to the countryside to farm, one resident of Pemba wrote to the *Daily News* editor: "I would like to question those in authority of their indiscriminate arrests of pedestrians and cyclists in the streets between 10:00 A.M. and 2 P.M. is legal and constitutional. . . . People using cars and trucks during the so-called work hours are not harassed. Why? Can't someone loiter with his car for petty personal business during work hours? Are we creating two classes of citizens in this country—the oppressed and the privileged?"[1]

Examples like this show that although the tactic of noncompliance can be used by many sectors of society, the consequences are not borne equally by all. Rather, the poorest members of society are most likely to suffer the severest consequences, for they generally do not have "friends in the right places" or the mechanisms through which to defend their interests.

The following discussion focuses on some examples of how people involved in various aspects of the informal economy defied government policies through noncompliance and brought about small but important changes. Noncompliance became so pervasive that the cost of coercive enforcement became excessive. The authorities responded by ignoring the activities or by eventually changing the rules in order to give legal sanction to practices that had already, de facto, been in existence. These changes indicated the beginnings of some long overdue adjustments in state-society relations that made the state more responsive to societal needs.

It is important to recognize that noncompliance was not restricted to economic strategies. Other, equally important issues evoked similar noncompliance to government policies. The expansion of unplanned housing settlements is a case in point. Settlement in unplanned areas has mushroomed ever since the city began to expand significantly in 1963, when all freehold land became state land (Stren 1982, 80). For ten years after independence, the government attempted a policy of clearing so-called slums and squatter settlements through the National Housing Corporation.[2] Having had little success with this policy, Tanzanian authorities started a scheme in 1972 to upgrade these areas, and it provided several thousand newly surveyed plots with basic services in planned areas for low-income families. There were some beneficiaries of this plan, but the majority of new urban dwellers continued to settle in unsurveyed and unplanned areas. A 1982 estimate placed the number of illegally built houses at five times that of legally built houses. Town authorities had little choice but to recognize the new illegal settlements as full and recognized town districts (Kulaba 1989, 224–28; Lindberg 1981, 133; Stren 1982, 80).

Richard Stren suggests several reasons why people did not build in surveyed plots in the initial years after independence, even though with a legal plot they had a better chance of obtaining water, garbage-disposal services, and community facilities. Steep legal fees and complex, time-consuming bureaucratic processes involving a maze of paperwork deterred most of the urban poor (1982, 80–81). This was compounded in later years by other disincentives, including the general decline in urban services and officials who were prone to demanding bribes for various necessary certificates. Moreover, the abolition of urban councils during the 1972–1978 period spurred the growth of these settlements, because there was no institution to regulate the informal building of houses (Kulaba 1989).

In housing settlements, as with informal income-generating activities, people resisted government policy because the plans had been made not with their objectives as a starting point but with other preconceived notions of what constituted desirable development, because they had to engage a complicated bureaucracy in order to obtain legal recognition, often requiring the payment of numerous bribes at each step of the way, and, perhaps most importantly, because the urban dwellers did not believe that compliance would result in a fair bargain; that is, their financial input would not result in an exchange for adequate government services.

LEGALIZATION

Defining Productive Work

Both the colonial and postcolonial states made numerous attempts to remove so-called unproductive elements from the city and to repatriate them to the countryside. Often these elements included the self-employed, whose basic conflict with the state thus became one of determining not just how they would obtain a livelihood but also who would control their very means of survival. The resettlement schemes of the postcolonial state had their origins in British vagrancy laws, which date back as far as 1349. They were vigorously enforced by authorities in eighteenth- and nineteenth-century England as a means of securing cheap labor for industry and to round up alleged criminals. These laws were transferred to the colony of Tanganyika in the form of the Penal Code, which targeted prostitutes, beggars, gamblers, suspected thieves, "rogues," and "vagabonds." In addition to this code, the colonial government introduced the Townships (Removal of Undesirable Persons) Ordinance in 1944, which is still in force. Under this ordinance, a district commissioner can order an "undesirable" person who has no regular employment or "reputable means of livelihood" to leave the town (Shaidi 1987).

Another colonial ordinance still in force is the 1923 Destitute Persons Ordinance, which pertains to people found without employment or unable to show that they have a "visible and sufficient means of subsistence." The magistrate can order such "destitute persons" to find work, detain them, or return them to their original place of residence. One of the main aims of these vagrancy statutes was to provide cheap labor for settler communities and to keep people in the rural areas, where they could continue the cash-crop production that was so crucial to the colonial state. In the 1930s the police commissioner and the provincial commissioner (Eastern Province) initiated the first forcible removal of unemployed people from Dar es Salaam to the countryside (Shaidi 1987).

The independent government attempted a number of operations to resettle urban dwellers in the nearby villages, the most important of which was in 1976. It was not long before the majority of the resettled people had returned to the city, some only a few hours after being moved out (Shaidi 1987, 12). In another such initiative the government enacted a Penal Code Amendment in 1983 that banned people involved in so-called unproductive activities from the cities because they were considered "idle and disorderly persons."[3]

Soon after the Penal Code Amendment was enacted, the Human Resources Deployment Act was passed in May 1983, requiring all urban Tanzanians to be registered and issued labor-identification cards.[4] Under this act, also known as Nguvu Kazi, those who could not produce proper identification were to be resettled in the countryside. In the Dar es Salaam region all unlicensed, self-employed people, including fish sellers, shoe repairmen, and tailors, were considered idle and disorderly and treated like loiterers. President Nyerere ordered the prime minister to be "bold" in implementing the Nguvu Kazi act, saying: "If we don't disturb loiterers, they will disturb us." Nyerere compared the "loiterers" with economic saboteurs and racketeers, "whom the nation has declared war on" and depicted this campaign as a strong vehicle for promoting economic production.[5] The leadership justified the operation by the need "to increase productivity and make the country self-sufficient in food."[6]

Immediately after the Deployment Act went into effect on 15 October 1983 the police, national-service soldiers, and people's militia started rounding up thousands of suspected loiterers on a random basis. Even an employed person found walking the streets during working hours could be charged with being "engaged in a frolic of his own at a time he is supposed to be engaged in activities connected or relating to the business of his employment." During the early 1980s Tanzanians experienced severe shortages, and workers frequently left their jobs during work hours to stand in lines to obtain food.

Detainees were taken to one of three centers in Dar es Salaam and had to provide documentation that they were employed and, in the case of women, that they were married. Those who were declared unemployed were sent back to their home villages or to state-run sisal plantations. Three months after the campaign started, 15,611 people had been detained (Shaidi 1984, 86).

The campaign was especially problematic regarding women. The authorities required married women to produce official marriage certificates within seven days of being detained to indicate that they had husbands who were providing for them (Kerner 1988, 53; Shaidi 1984, 86). This policy contained numerous questionable assumptions, including the notion that all women who did not fall into the category of officially married—that is, women who were single, divorced, or widowed or women in common-law marriages—could be suspected of being loiterers and unproductive elements. Moreover, it assumed that the wives were dependent on their husbands, disregarding the fact that married women might have been supporting their families through their own projects.

For a brief period, food vendors and shoe shiners disappeared from the city streets, employed people did not venture away from their jobs during the day, and children going to and coming from school rode buses in groups (Kerner 1988, 49). But it quickly became clear that the campaign was a failure. No sooner were truckloads of people dropped off in rural areas than most of them returned to the city to resume their small-scale enterprises. The illegal trade in identification papers boomed, so that virtually anyone could come up with some form of documentation.

The Nguvu Kazi enterprise had its parallels in other parts of Africa in the late 1970s and early 1980s as various countries sank deeper into economic crisis. In July 1984 Nigeria's military rulers launched a War against Indiscipline, involving the arrests of vendors and the destruction of their stalls along main roads of urban areas. A day or so after the state action the vendors returned to resume business as usual (Eames 1988, 87; Trager 1987, 247–48). In Zambia police attempted to control price hiking during the period of shortages in 1982 by arresting and destroying the wares of women street vendors (Hansen 1989, 148). In Ghana the military government of the Armed Forces Revolutionary Council sought to do away with hoarding and price hiking by market traders during a period of shortages. Soon after their takeover in June 1979, they literally dynamited the central market in Accra to the ground and sold off the trader's stocks at the Kumasi central market. Market sellers continued to sell their goods through friends and from their homes, however. The heightened risk factor meant that the prices of the goods skyrocketed (Clark 1988, 61; Dolphyne 1987, 27).

In Tanzania the Nguvu Kazi campaign was destined to fail when the government resorted to coercion in an offensive against city dwellers, with little regard for the realities faced by the urban poor. It is ironic that while the Nguvu Kazi enterprise aimed at forcing urban dwellers into "productive" agricultural production, by the late 1980s those with farms outside the city or on the outskirts of the city were in an enviable position of having this additional means of livelihood. In principle, most people had no objection to farming and would have welcomed a viable scheme that gave them land and a means to cultivate. As one cigarette vendor who was born and raised in the city told me, "The government just collected us young men and dumped us in the forest to farm. They gave us plots but no capital, no houses, no food. . . . We had no choice but to come back to the city and continue selling cigarettes. If I had a place to live and the means I would have stayed to farm."[7]

Today it is widely recognized that rural life may hold more promise than urban life does, for in cities, in order to eat, one needs cash, which is difficult to come by. As one textile worker who purchased a 1.6-hectare farm in 1976 said: "If I do statistics in my head, life in the villages is better than city life. One has a plot and can sell one's crops. You have no problem if you rely on the crops that you grow. Life in the cities is harder. Where I work many have left their jobs since 1982 and many more since 1985. They have decided to go back to the villages or be self-employed."[8]

The absurdity of the Nguvu Kazi policy was underscored by reports like the one of twenty-two shoe shiners who were arrested on the grounds of being unproductive. Several of them were physically handicapped, and half of them were students at a nearby vocational school who were trying to support their studies through this sideline activity. A city official told them to find jobs and warned them against turning to shoe shining. He announced that people with leather shoes needing regular polishing should learn to do it themselves. The official added, "Otherwise you have to buy safari boots or canvas shoes."[9]

Public response to this campaign was by no means indifferent. The notion that these activities were not productive made little sense to most people. The Tanzanian *Daily News* carried a series of interviews with self-employed people and asked them about the illegal and unproductive nature of their activities.[10] One fishmonger said, "I regard this activity as being gainful. Every day I make a profit of at least 100 and 200 shillings or more at best. I have a wife and five children who are dependent on me. It is a good thing that people should be involved in some gainful activity or other. But there are people who have their businesses who will be harassed for no good reason. I don't see how you will convince me that a certain job is better than what I am doing now. Even if you give me employment in your company, I won't accept it. I just couldn't survive on a monthly salary." A peanut vendor responded, "I tell you I have been able to keep a wife and four children by doing nothing but selling groundnuts. My children are now in school and I rent a house. I have saved 3,000 shillings in a bank. I have even helped people who are employed in offices who came to me to borrow money when in financial trouble." And a knife sharpener answered, "It would not be fair to dismiss this as a useless activity since very many people depend on us. Shopkeepers, hoteliers, butchers and even other individuals bring their knives and *pangas* [machetes] for sharpening. The government should instead give us licenses and a place where we can conduct our activities."

Not surprisingly, rounding up these so-called unproductive elements proved far beyond the capacity of the government. Moreover, it merely served to antagonize the majority of the city's population. It was implemented at a time when virtually no new jobs were available and informal projects had become the main means of subsistence for most urban dwellers. The campaign failed because people simply refused to comply, continuing their daily income-generating activities as they always had. They ignored the new policy because their survival depended on their continuing these activities.

The government was forced to back down from its campaign. By 1984 the mass detentions were curtailed significantly. That same year the City Council began to register people through the ten-house-cell system to verify employment (Kerner 1988, 44). One top City Council official explained to me why the local government changed its position: "The City Council decided to change the 1983 government policy after analyzing the situation. The government could not provide work for all and could not repatriate the people in the countryside. We failed to send them into the regions, and then we failed to send them even to villages near the city."[11]

In 1985, at about the time the new president, Ali Hassan Mwinyi, came to power, the policy softened further, and the government began to license small businesses, thus giving official recognition to them. By the late 1980s, however, there remained disagreement among authorities over whether small projects constitute gainful work. The regional director of administration, who was in charge of seeing that the City Council carried out development policies like Nguvu Kazi, told me: "Some are against such work. They say such jobs could be done by the disabled, the old, not by strong men."[12]

Nevertheless, after 1983 the government began to recognize, even if only minimally, the importance of the small-scale enterprises to the national economy. It "reinterpreted" the Human Resources Deployment Act to see the informal sector in a more positive light. A 1985 study sponsored by the government in cooperation with the ILO Jobs and Skills Programme for Africa explored the possibility of using the Human Resources Deployment Act as the basis for a national human resources scheme to deal, as the author put it, with the "failure of the modern sector to absorb an increasing proportion of the labour force." The new policy toward the informal sector would make it essential that special attention be given to its role in creating employment because of its ability to do so at low levels of capital investment (Aboagye 1985, 1).

The change from 1983 was also evident in the remarks of the director of the National Vocational Training Programme, Morgan Manyanga, who said in a 1986 speech to Parliament that the "informal sector" is a "hidden sector." Services, he said, are provided without valid training licenses, work contracts, or taxation. He urged that such groups come out of "hiding" so that they could greatly help the nation by undertaking productive ventures. Although there is an element of absurdity in the notion that 95 percent of Dar es Salaam's population should "come out of hiding," this official's stance indicates a greater legitimation of these activities than the tone exhibited in 1983.[13] Referring to this change in policy, one young man we interviewed said, "Up to now the government has failed because it wants people to work, but it fails to provide work. They arrested people and sent them to the villages without capital. Even in the past we were not loiterers, we had small businesses, but the government did not want to recognize what we were doing. Now at least they have considered that."[14]

At the national level, the emphasis had clearly changed by the 1990s. The government was beginning, if only haltingly, to assist the informal sector and was encouraging donor support for such activities. By the early 1990s the Human Resources Deployment Act itself was under review. The Ministry of Labour and Youth Development, which was to implement the act, had taken a few concrete measures to address the needs of young people who did not have access to formal education (International Labour Organisation 1992, 7, 8). The Ministry of Industries and Trade had established a Small Scale Industries Promotion Unit to improve the business climate for small-scale industries, and the ministry's Small Industries Development Organization (SIDO) began to address the needs of informal-sector operators in 1988, though budgetary constraints limited the impact of SIDO activities.

By 1994 the government had come up with a national policy to assist informal-sector activities in both rural and urban areas, focusing on the provision of financial services, appropriate technology, markets, and the development of skills. Encouraged by such positive gestures, international donors stepped up their support for the sector. The ILO, for example, launched a major initiative to support the informal sector. This project especially targeted women, children, and youth engaged in low-productivity activities outside "formal regulatory and social protection mechanisms and who have limited access to credit, skills or training." The initiative focused on policy and regulatory reforms and on improving access to credit.[15]

Whereas the 1980s saw a basic acceptance of the right for small businesses to exist, in the late 1980s and 1990s the debate shifted to issues of how municipal authorities dealt with problems of licensing, health violations, and relocating businesses to prevent overcrowding. In particular, small-scale traders were concerned about the abuses that occurred in the enforcement of various laws regarding this sector. In the mid-1990s the City Council militia were continuing their harassment and roundups of street vendors to move them to different business locations. The vendors, whose numbers had swelled in the city center, continued to charge City Council employees with seizing their goods for personal benefit.[16]

Licensing Small Businesses

The key piece of legislation affecting informal-sector operators has been the Urban Authorities Act (1982), which gave the district councils the authority to determine how operators should function. Moreover, it gave them authority to collect revenue and to determine additional fees, such as for garbage collection. In Dar es Salaam two kinds of licenses were issued to small businesses and to market sellers. After 1985, fifty-six different kinds of small-business activities required licenses under the 1985 Dar es Salaam City Council (Hawking and Street Trading) Amendment to the 1982 Local Government (Urban Authorities) Act (see Appendixes D and E).[17] The 1985 law revoked a 1963 law that abolished the urban trading licenses in response to pressure from shopkeepers (Bienefeld 1975, 67).

According to the City Council licensing authorities, only 252 people were found guilty of violating the licensing law in 1987, and all had been fined. Many more, however, had been detained for such violations. They were rounded up by militia hired by the Inspection Committee of the City Council's Manpower Department. The City Council had six inspectors who decided daily where the militia should go. They concentrated on the central part of the city, Kivukoni, Kisutu, and Mchafukoga (Mnazi Moja), rounding up license violators and taking them into custody. In other parts of the city, each ward had its own inspectors who organized similar kinds of raids. Although microentrepreneurs considered legalization of informal-sector activities an improvement over the policy that branded their businesses unproductive, regulation of these small businesses through licensing posed a new set of problems.

City Council officials stated that their concern was making sure that vendors sold their wares in approved locations, yet the officials had no documentation that would indicate precisely where the off-limits areas were. Similarly, they claimed that they were concerned with meeting city health regulations. Yet this was at a time when there was little concern for other, more pressing citywide health issues. For example, shop owners and other people freely dumped large quantities of garbage into downtown streets; drainage systems remained clogged throughout the city; and control of malaria-carrying mosquitoes was virtually nonexistent, although in the past, vigorous campaigns to remove standing water and to spray the city had been undertaken regularly. These factors, along with the harassment of unlicensed small entrepreneurs (rather than the wealthier ones), made urban dwellers suspect that the issue of licensing the entrepreneurs was more than a question of keeping the city clean. Rather, it was aimed at keeping various patronage networks lubricated by extracting bribes from vendors. To a lesser extent, it was a response to shopkeepers' complaints about vendors' selling in unauthorized locations in front of their stores. The actions of the militia did not indicate any real effort to suppress the vendors but, rather, an attempt to intimidate them day after day into handing over a portion of their goods or earnings. It was clearly in the militia's interests to see the vendors return each day.[18]

In 1987–1988, for example, 6,082 small-business licenses were granted out of 10,000 requests. (In Buguruni 325 people out of roughly 30,000 self-employed applied for licenses in 1987.) In 1987 these businesses brought in TSh 3.6 million, or 1 percent of the entire City Council annual revenue. When asked why licensing of the smallest entrepreneurs was so important, given the unpredictability of their income and the fact that most were just barely feeding their families, a top City Council official responded emphatically, "But how are we going to *control* them if we have no licensing system?" He cited the cleanliness of the city and public health that would be jeopardized if people sold wherever and however they pleased. Moreover, he added, the City Council would not be able to do its job properly if it could not control and manage entrepreneurs in this way. City Council officials also suggested to me that people did not obtain licenses because they were selling stolen goods and because they were dishonest.[19]

The self-employed people with whom I spoke had a considerably different perspective on all of these issues. In a country where wages were not adequate, where there were few government welfare provisions, and where the people had to care for their own sick, elderly, disabled, and unemployed, licensing regulations were often seen as an affront to popular notions of economic justice or to the norm of fairness (see Levi 1991). Virtually all of the hundreds of residents and ten-house party-cell leaders we spoke to about this issue saw the licensing of small projects, especially women's projects, as unjust. Many said they had no objection to the licensing of businesspeople engaged in lucrative projects like the sale of charcoal (wholesale), shopkeeping, or operating a restaurant. But for a poor person just trying to get by, they believed, licenses were an injustice because their sources of inputs and markets were too unreliable to make it worthwhile to obtain a license.

Most self-employed in Dar es Salaam operated their businesses without licenses. Ninety-nine percent of all self-employed workers were not licensed in 1988, according to my calculations based on City Council records and the 1988 census. In our survey, 87 percent openly admitted to not having licenses.

Popular sympathy for the self-employed was evident in confrontations between the militia and vendors. Passersby would frequently relay messages to vendors, warning them of the impending arrival of the militia. In May 1991 the *Daily News* reported an incident in which the militia came to arrest vendors who sold meals to workers in downtown office buildings. Passersby joined hands to protect the vendors. Fighting broke out, and the police had to come to the rescue of the militia, who were overpowered by the crowd, which booed the militia and called them thieves.[20] Popular sentiment was underscored in a letter to the *Daily News*, which stated, "The sympathy of the public is always with these . . . people when they are almost daily chased away by guys in the City Council uniforms."[21]

Many City Council officials denied that the militia extracted bribes from the self-employed. Living in the center of the city, I observed the daily cat-and-mouse games of the militia in their pursuit of vendors. I often interviewed the sellers after the raids to find out who had been caught and detained, how much bribe money had been extracted, and whether the militia had confiscated or stolen their wares. Because the militia sometimes came in street clothes, vendors warned each other of an impending raid. Such typical occurrences may explain why City Council officials were so sensitive about the activities of the Nguvu Kazi office in charge of enforcing the purchase of licenses. In fact, they were under orders not to talk to any outsiders (such as journalists or academics) regarding their work and were to refer such people to the city director himself. Only after we interviewed the director did the Nguvu Kazi officials agree to talk to us.

Although the cost of a license was an important factor in explaining why people did not obtain licenses, perhaps even more significant was their rejection of state regulation of a part of life that was considered their own. The most basic right for the urban poor was the right to control their means of subsistence. For this reason, any outside attempts to regulate their means of subsistence was seen as an invitation to further interference, which could prove disastrous at a time when survival was so precarious.

At the same time, the arbitrary assignment of various fees by City Council officials to small businesses only compounded the general frustration with licensing. No study had been made to assess the income obtained from various enterprises. This accounted for the obvious incongruences in the fees relative to the value added of different kinds of enterprises. A woman with eighteen cows making TSh 120,000 a month from milk sales was required to pay the same license fee as was a woman who fried buns and earned TSh 6,000 a month. Tailors, carpenters, and masons, generally at the upper end of the informal-sector income bracket, paid the same license fee as did someone who made and sold paper bags, a low-capital, low-income project. The income of women running hairdressing salons depended on whether they braided hair or used chemicals to treat the hair. These incomes also varied with the size of their clientele, the location of their business, and other factors, yet they were all required to pay the same rate.

Another factor mitigating against obtaining licenses was the fact that in order to pay the license fee one often had to go through the bureaucracy and pay bribes amounting to three or four times the cost of the license itself. As one self-employed carpenter, who in 1982 left employment with the government-owned electricity company, put it:

> Licenses only bring problems. Bribery is so common it isn't even worth mentioning. I have a license, but I had to pay a 10,000-shilling bribe to get it from the City Council. I just paid it because I got tired of coming back day after day and being told that they had not filled out the forms. The militia harass a carpenter for not having a license, but we make more income than they do. A clerk at the City Council makes 2,000 shillings a month. Such authorities know that if they arrest you, you will pay a bribe. It is their means of obtaining revenue. Those in top posts are not hungry because they squeeze the people below.[22]

In addition to the problem of bribery in obtaining a license, many in Buguruni and Manzese reported that they had applied for licenses but had waited for months with no response from the licensing officials. The cumbersome application process for a business license served as an effective deterrent to most potential applicants. The applicants were to first fill out forms obtained from their local ward office, submit the forms to the ward office, and wait until the forms were returned to them. The applicants would then take the forms to a Councillors Committee of the City Council, which would then evaluate the applications. The applicants would have to secure signatures from the responsible City Council Nguvu Kazi officials after having met personally with them (which could require several visits to the downtown City Council offices). In order to obtain a business license, individuals would first have to show evidence of having paid their taxes, of having a building permit, and of having had their business premises inspected for proper hygiene by a health officer (under the 1950 Health Act and the Factories Ordinance). Failure to obtain a license carried a penalty of TSh 2,000 ($20 at 1988 exchange rates) and/or imprisonment for six months.[23] However, it was not uncommon for the application process to take as long as six months. One frustrated applicant applied for a business license, and by the time his forms were processed the license period had expired. When he asked that his application be applied to the following year, he was told to start all over again.[24]

Widespread refusal to obtain licenses eroded the government's credibility and revealed a split among different levels of the government regarding the self-employed. One conflict emerged between local leaders and the City Council; a second, between national and local governments.

Conflicts between Levels of Authority

Payment for small-business licenses was an issue that was vigorously taken up by local CCM leaders and patrons at the lower levels of the party. Historically, the role of local leaders, especially at the cell level, had been to serve as a buffer between the higher state authorities and the people to whom they were accountable (Samoff 1973, 74). Numerous studies have shown how local leaders accommodated their constituents' preferences rather than complying with directives and policies from above (Hyden 1980, 114; Molloy 1971; Samoff 1973). One reason for this greater affinity between ten-cell leaders and local people is that their socioeconomic interests do not differ significantly from those of their neighbors, whom they represent.

Virtually all of the hundreds of CCM cell leaders we spoke to saw the licensing of small projects as unjust for the same reasons citizens opposed the licenses. Although the self-employed opposed payment for licenses for small businesses through quiet noncompliance (that is, refusal to pay), local cell and branch leaders were more vocally against licensing small businesses and, in particular, against the militia harassment of people without licenses. Some branches had sent complaints to ward and district levels of the party, to the City Council, and to Parliament.

One CCM branch leader said that he had taken all steps within his power to raise the issue of licensing with the City Council. Nothing had come of his efforts to try to abolish the licensing of small businesses. He explained that "Those who can't farm have to do small businesses, but they have to do these with difficulty and without freedom. The City Council militia can come and harass them for not having licenses and then take away their wares from them. If I know the authorities, it won't be easy to get them to do away with licenses. These small businesses should not be licensed. The local governments should find another source of revenue and leave the people alone. They don't get much revenue, but still the City authorities harass them." [25]

Local CCM leaders were especially impassioned about this issue because many had small businesses themselves and had experienced harassment. One cell leader said that her children, who sold pastries for her, had been harassed three times by the militia. "We have to run because we can't bribe them always. You run, leave your goods, everything, to save yourself." [26] Another cell leader in Manzese who sold coconuts at the market said: We pay 200 shillings a month to the City Council for the market space and 500 shillings a year for the license, but the City Council does nothing for us. All we have is what God has given us and boards to build a stall. There is no medicine in the hospitals, and you end up going to the private hospitals anyway. If you do not have a license the militia come and harass you and take away your goods and money. We get angry when they come. What kind of government do we have? Where is our freedom?" [27]

Local party organizations were all too often the recipients of orders from above rather than forums for expressing interests that were filtered up to higher levels of leadership, as they were intended. Nevertheless, these organizations were the main forum urban dwellers attempted to use, not only in settling local issues but also in attempting to confront higher bodies within the party and the government.

Urban dwellers also sought local patrons to defend them against militia raids and other encroachments on the interests of local people by the authorities. [28] In fact, some of our most critical comments of party policy came from these patrons, many of whom sought positions as local party-cell leaders or on the elders' council of the party branch. They saw themselves as champions of the poor and the disadvantaged against the intrusions of the party and the government. The patrons' flexibility and willingness to lend money and provide other social and economic arrangements made them indispensable in the community.

One such patron we interviewed was a Zaramo cell leader and businessman who had established a thriving wood trade. He had a little office with a desk and two chairs at the end facing each other, just like the local CCM offices. On the wall he had hung a party calendar and two large pictures of the then party chairman, Nyerere, and President Mwinyi. Outside the office, from which he ran his wood business, he flew the green CCM flag. He proudly explained to us that when the City Council militia came to harass the women selling pastries along the side of the road, they ran to his office with their pots and pans to hide. Thus, while surrounding himself with the symbols of the CCM, this patron was at the same time perpetuating another set of power relations.[29]

In another CCM branch, a hotel owner established himself as a patron. Although he was active in the CCM, he was also critical of it and put distance between himself and the CCM and the government. He remarked, "If they change the [top] leadership of the party, life will be better. My life goes on because I don't sleep. I am a businessman and don't depend on the government. I have a hotel, so I don't wait for the government to help me."[30] The CCM secretary of this branch said that when she needed help in party matters she went to the hotel owner because she respected him and "considered him her father." The terms of kinship are frequently extended to nonfamilial patron-client relations as a means of further solidifying these relations. Clients often refer to the patron as "father" and to themselves as "his children."

The City Council was not only at odds with local leaders over the harassment of vendors without licenses. It also had differences with the national government on the issue. Since 1986 national leaders have won popular support in criticizing the City Council for its harassment of vendors, especially of women. In the late 1980s President Mwinyi several times openly decried the harassment of street vendors "whether licensed or not." In spite of his appeals, City Council representatives continued their harassment of unlicensed entrepreneurs, reflecting, perhaps, some of the competing interests between local and central governments. In one of the appeals, Mwinyi vowed that "stern action" would be taken against any police or militia found harassing vendors. The president said that "the traders were actually engaged in *legal* activities, trying to struggle against harsh economic conditions facing everybody. . . . He said that all urban councils should help the people engaged in petty businesses because that was one way of easing their economic burden."[31]

After Mwinyi's November 1987 condemnation of the City Council militia harassment, I heard vendors express enthusiasm for his statements. The *Daily News* quoted one woman who sold buns as saying: "We have been saved by the President from the hands of the City Council militiamen who have been a constant menace."[32] Vendors also had their reservations, skeptical that this appeal would be heeded by the City Council. Their suspicions were confirmed a few days later when the militia resumed its raids.

Other national leaders also decried the harassment of street sellers. Cleopa Msuya, when he was minister of industries and trade, addressed a 1994 seminar of small-scale women entrepreneurs in Mwanga, which I attended. He responded to their concerns about militia raids on businesses and property to check on licenses and location: "It is something negative to destroy these huts without informing the people. First, after all, these businesses must be allowed, period, because they help people. Second, people must be clear about where they should carry out their business. There must be well planned areas where people can run their businesses. Third, there must be an effort all the time to make sure that people are not interfered with in their places of business and that we should avoid the idea of going and breaking their huts and taking their license payments."[33]

For some leaders, appeals to the rights of street vendors became a quick and shrewd way of gaining popularity. One controversial national figure, Augustine Mrema, became a vocal champion of the causes of the urban street sellers and women. As former deputy prime minister and home affairs minister, he was one of the fiercest critics of corruption from within the CCM. He defended street hawkers from attacks by the City Council and personally intervened with husbands who beat their wives. When he was thrown out of his ministerial post in February 1995, he joined the opposition National Convention for Constitution and Reform (Mageuzi) and became its presidential candidate. His popularity increased, and for the first time the opposition was able to pose a credible threat to CCM's dominance.

The fact that common city dwellers saw the national leaders as allies against the City Council on this issue was evident after an intense period of raids against vendors in 1986. In one particular incident a group of vendors who sold in and around the Kigamboni fish market formed a demonstration and marched to the State House to register their grievances with the president. They told reporters that the City Council was threatening their "struggle to survive." Police diverted the march to the Central Police Station, where the vendors were told to bring their complaints to the City Council or the party.[34] The national government's concern in keeping City

Council militia from harassing poor vendors was a way of responding directly to the problem of not having the resources to adequately pay workers. The continuation of these projects became a means of garnering greater legitimacy.

The differences between the national leaders and the City Council authorities appear to stem from the different interests they hoped to appease. National leaders were responding to pressures from labor to ease the conditions under which workers and their household members carried out projects. The City Council itself was probably divided. On one hand, there was concern to increase council revenue and to maintain good ties with the official business community by keeping vendors off their property. At the same time, the continuing practice of bribery by the militia and by people in charge of granting licenses suggests that the council had individual interests to satisfy within the institution itself.

Dodging the Development Levy

Refusal to obtain business licenses is related to the issue of tax evasion, for licensing and registration require the payment of taxes. Tax evasion has been one of the classic forms of noncompliance worldwide, according to Scott. He argues that although taxes were one of the most frequent causes of riots and revolts in early modern Europe and elsewhere, the main form of tax resistance was through "flight, evasion, misreporting, false declarations, and so on" (1987, 423). Certainly these quiet forms of opposition characterize resistance to taxation in urban Tanzania, where city dwellers have always been artful tax dodgers.

J. A. K. Leslie, writing about Dar es Salaam in the late 1950s, observed that new migrants during their first few days in town made it a priority to visit relatives and meet new people who could, among other things, provide a place to hide from tax clerks. People often used several names in order to make it difficult for the authorities to trace them in the event that they would be sought for not paying their taxes. Moreover, in the colonial period Leslie was describing, people commonly withheld their names or someone else's name from a foreigner or government representative for the same reason. Colonial authorities eventually set up tax drives because voluntary payment had failed. They blocked off streets, asking comers for evidence of payment. Even here, tax dodgers had little difficulty finding back routes to their homes (1963, 58, 60, 250). Those who were caught faced prison or labor camps, where they worked to pay the tax.

As in the 1950s, urban dwellers dodged the collection of the Development Levy, the poll tax of the 1980s and 1990s. The Development Levy, in fact, had its antecedents in the poll tax. The British colonial administration created this tax under the Native Authorities Ordinance of 1926, which established indirect rule through local African institutions and leadership. Under this ordinance, local authorities collected taxes for the use of central government. The poll tax, known as local rates, was a flat rate collected from all adult men over the age of eighteen. Women were exempted from the tax unless they were employed or had an independent source of income. The tax had the effect of forcing Africans into wage-earning jobs in order to pay the tax. Later ordinances gave local authorities the authority to collect taxes for their own use (Bukurura 1991, 77–78).

The local rates were abolished in 1969, partly in response to public opposition to harsh tactics used by authorities in collecting the tax but also because of the association of the tax with colonial practices (Kulaba 1989, 219). The abolition of the tax left local governments completely dependent on the central government, without a major independent source of revenue. This move to eliminate independent sources of revenue was followed by the disbanding of local governments in 1972. Although the dissolution of local governments was heralded as a move to decentralize government, it in fact placed greater decision-making power in the hands of the central government. Regional- and district-level authorities, funded by the national treasury, gained power but were now accountable to the central government rather than to the localities, which had little control over personnel or the way in which funds were allocated. Conditions in the urban areas deteriorated quickly, including the provision of basic services like water and electricity, sewage disposal, and garbage collection (Kulaba 1989).

In 1982 two measures were enacted to rectify this situation. The Local Government Act was passed to reestablish the urban councils that had been abolished in 1972, and the Local Government Finances Act No. 9 was enacted to empower local councils to collect revenue. The passage of these acts meant that the central government dealt with taxes that were easy to collect, such as income taxes, duties, and licenses for larger businesses, whereas the local authorities were responsible for collecting fees that were more difficult to collect from an administrative and political standpoint (Kulaba 1989, 221, 231).

The Development Levy was instituted soon thereafter, though by a narrow margin of two votes in Parliament and after much heated debate.[35] This law required all individuals between the ages of eighteen and sixty-five to pay a flat rate if they were low-income earners or farmers, while wage earners paid a graduated rate that was deducted automatically from their paychecks. Self-employed workers in Dar es Salaam were required to pay a personal Development Levy and a Development Levy on their enterprise the first year they were in business. After that they paid only the business Development Levy, which was a percentage of their yearly business license (30 percent in Dar es Salaam).

People whom I interviewed bitterly resented the Development Levy, regarding it much like the colonial poll tax. They designed means of evading it that were as surreptitious as those of the evaders of the colonial taxes.[36] In some instances, tax collectors resorted to tactics reminiscent of colonial practices, such as road blocks, massive swoops, and detainment of defaulters.[37] Even employees who had the Development Levy automatically deducted from their paychecks were subject to harassment.[38] In July 1987 local governments began to use ten-house cell leaders and village governments to collect the levy in order to minimize confrontations between the people and the authorities, which had at times become violent, especially in urban areas. But this practice often backfired because it was not only taxpayers who evaded payment but also the local authorities assigned the task of providing lists of taxpayers who refused to comply because of the responsibility they felt to their constituents.

Some have argued that the major evasion of the Development Levy has been due to the inability to pay and to a lack of clarity regarding duties, obligations, and reasons to pay. They argue that the government has not done a good job of educating people about the purposes of the Development Levy and convincing them of the necessity of paying the tax (Bukurura 1991, 91). Certainly these factors have contributed to the massive noncompliance in paying the Development Levy. However, it is also instructive to consider what people themselves have to say about the levy, especially given the fact that although for some the fee is too high, for most self-employed urban dwellers the sum is relatively small. The objections I encountered were varied but hinged around the issue of the lack of state legitimacy.

First, residents believed that they received little from the government in return for payment of the levy. They saw few tangible benefits, while the very poorest individuals were forced to meet the most basic welfare provisions on their own.[39] Moreover, residents strongly resented what they believed were excessive misappropriations of funds by government authorities.[40] Second, they feared that one tax would lead to endless demands for money by the government and the CCM. Income tax, house tax, tuition fees, and contributions for school and various fund-raising campaigns of the CCM were mentioned most frequently in this regard. People feared that agreeing to pay for one state tax was an invitation to raise taxes and to find new reasons to demand money from citizens. They made no distinctions between local governments and the central government with regard to these various taxes. Yet another concern was the harassment that accompanied the collection of the levy. In the Coast Region, residents appealed in 1988 to regional authorities to halt mistreatment of people in checking for payment of the levy. The government responded by passing the Local Government (Collection of Rates Procedure) Rules to reduce and eliminate default and do away with harassment by having village and cell leaders collect the levy (Bukurura 1991, 88–89).

Finally, the issue of women's paying the levy was especially controversial. Supporters of the levy on women argued that they were equal to men according to the law and theoretically could own their own property. Opponents argued that women in the rural areas rarely owned their own property and therefore should be exempted. In fact, prior to 1969 most women were exempted from paying the levy, and only those who had their own earnings were required to pay (Bukurura 1991, 80–81). In urban areas, low-income women argued that the tax was unjust because the economic crisis had placed heavy burdens on women and because they had thus been shouldering on their own the burden of caring for the young, old, and sick and of feeding the employed members of the household with income from their own small enterprises. As one woman I interviewed in Manzese, a low-income part of Dar es Salaam, put it, "Life is hard, but they don't understand that these fees just harass us. They are very strict with the Development Levy in the rural areas. A woman with a one-month-old baby was arrested for a whole day because of the Development Levy. Other women like Mrs. Kawawa [former chairperson of the Union of Tanzanian Women] and Kate Kamba [former secretary general of the Union of Tanzanian Women] and the rest marched in support of Development Levy. They do not know the problems of ordinary women. I am just an ordinary citizen."[41]

Clearly the Development Levy brought to the fore the conflicting perspectives of low-income and wealthier, better-educated women, who were concerned with gender equality and the implications of exempting women from the levy. The issue was hotly debated in Parliament for years, with some members of the National Assembly arguing that women need not pay the levy because they are "naturally weak." Women members of Parliament firmly opposed the exemption, but they were overridden by Prime Minister John Malecela when he announced in 1991 that the local councils could exempt women from the tax and look for other sources of income. Still, the conflict between upper- and lower-income women over the levy

Table 7 Local Sources of Revenue of Tanzanian Urban
Councils, 1985–1986

Source	Amount in TSh	Percentage
Development levy	246,690,000	55
Taxes on dwellings	73,244,400	16
Trading licenses	60,915	0
Market dues and fees	29,923,900	7
Other taxes	96,713,900	22
Total	446,633,115	100

SOURCE: Kulaba 1989, 222.

reflected how women experienced their alienation from the state in different ways (Tripp 1994b).

Local authorities fared even worse with the small-business tax (Kulaba 1989, 219, 231). Self-employed producers avoided registration not only to evade the Development Levy but also so that they could operate their businesses without being subject to sales taxes and price controls. Taxes on produced goods ranged from 25 to 200 percent, and no differentiation was made with respect to the size of the production unit. Thus a small-scale industry paid the same tax as did a large-scale one. Because the sales tax is the most important source of domestic revenue for the government, it is doubtful that these laws will be changed (see Tables 7 and 8). Nevertheless, small-scale industries were so vulnerable financially that even simple taxes could make or break them. For most cooperatives and smaller production units the only way to survive was to avoid registration and hence taxation altogether (Havnevik 1986, 280).

The Battle over Grounds

Part of the conflict over small businesses centered on the issue of business locations. Selling in an unapproved location was one reason the City Council militia harassed vendors. Sometimes they were acting at the behest of shopkeepers who did not want vendors positioned in front of their stores. More often, however, the militia were only interested in the vendors' location as an excuse to harass and extract bribes from them. No one in the Nguvu Kazi office or any other department of the City Council knew where the authorized or unauthorized locations were because they had never been determined. This meant that it was left up to the militia and the inspectors to decide arbitrarily whether people were selling in ap-

Table 8 Domestic Sources of Revenue of the Tanzanian
Central Government, 1989–1990

Source	Amount in millions of TSh	Percentage
Customs duty	13,547	14
Excise duty (imports)	2,683	3
Excise duty (local)	11,140	11
Sales tax (imports)	10,445	11
Sales tax (local)	20,200	21
Income tax	19,123	20
Other taxes	6,940	7
Nontax revenue	13,044	13
Total	97,122	100

SOURCE: Calculated from data in a report of a Ministry of Finance
and Planning commission published in 1991 in *Tanzanian Economic
Trends* 4 (2): 80.

proved locations. These conflicts continued into the mid-1990s. In 1995 organizations like the Organisation of Small Businesspeople (FESBA) and the Dar es Salaam Kiosk Owners' Association criticized the City Council for failing to find places to which street vendors could relocate after the City Council cracked down on them in the central Kariakoo market in February 1995. The association chairman, Issa Mnyaru, said in a statement issued to councillors that they were fed up with false promises by the government: "We are in a multipartyism era. You are required to listen to the people who voted for you."[42]

Indiscriminate militia attempts to move vendors from certain locations by and large failed. For example, the plans to move the central Kigamboni fish market to a less accessible location at Msasani met with little success. The market remains the main fish-auctioning center in the city. The City Council was, however, more successful in moving wood carvers who had set up kiosks along Bagamoyo Road to a central location in Mwenge in 1984. At the time, the City Council demolished some of the carvers' kiosks without prior notification and threatened to demolish more if people did not comply.[43]

One important conflict over location had to do with City Council attempts to channel the wholesale trade through a central market at Kariakoo. The downtown Kariakoo market was rebuilt in 1975, after which all wholesale fruits, vegetables, certain staples, and dried and smoked fish were to be channeled through this City Council–operated market. Its aim was to bring the Dar es Salaam parallel market under its control, because it was believed at the time that only 50 percent of the wholesale trade was going through official channels (Sporrek 1985, 74–82). However, the centralization of the wholesale trade in Kariakoo did little to stem the parallel-market trade in the years that followed. The majority of produce coming into the city continued to be sold through markets like Manzese, which is the largest unofficial wholesale grain market in Tanzania.

The issue of location also concerns those with projects involving the keeping of poultry, cattle, and pigs because animal husbandry had initially been forbidden within townships (Kulaba 1989, 213). Urban dwellers relied on people with such projects for their chickens, eggs, ham, and milk, however. A 40 percent increase in registered livestock was reported in the city between 1987 and 1989 (Stren, Halfani, and Malombe 1994, 191). So pervasive was the practice of animal husbandry in the city itself that the City Council conceded to the practice but told owners to keep their livestock strictly within compounds to engage in zero grazing in 1989. The policy was revised in 1990, when livestock owners were permitted to keep no more than four animals at home zero grazing.[44] Further impetus was given to such practices by Mwinyi's call on workers to start farm, animal-husbandry, and other projects.[45] Nevertheless, small herds of cattle continued to roam the city streets despite numerous City Council warnings, ultimatums, petty fines on cattle owners, and roundups of "loitering" cattle, as they were referred to by the authorities. As many as 2.3 percent of all reported road accidents in Dar es Salaam were caused by these animals (Kironde 1992, cited in Stren, Halfani, and Malombe 1994, 191). Although from time to time the City Council would round up "loitering cattle and goats," as it did in a 1995 raid,[46] for the most part this was one of the least-enforced regulations. Because the majority of animal owners within the city belonged to the class of administrators and professionals, it is conceivable that the authorities in the City Council were more hesitant to enforce strictly a law that would impinge on themselves and their friends and families, who depended on these projects for their sustenance.[47]

PRIVATIZATION

The Daladala Bus Wars

Another indication of policy change toward the informal economy was the privatization of sectors that had previously been controlled by state monopolies. Bus service was one of the first privatization moves. Up until 1986, only government-owned buses could operate legally, and the transport needs of the population far exceeded the available services. Around 1983, as the transport problem began to reach crisis proportions, informal buses called *daladala* or *thumni* came into greater use. The name of these minibuses comes from the price of a ride, which in 1983 was TSh 5, or the equivalent of one dollar, hence the term *daladala*. Individuals also began to use their private vehicles as illegal *taxibubu*, giving people rides for a small fee. Both the drivers of these vehicles and the passengers were liable if caught.

Nyerere had been adamant that the government-owned buses retain their monopoly status, but the desperate economic situation and the existence of the informal sources of transport forced the government to legalize the *daladala* in 1986. Three hundred buses were registered with the government bus company. After 1986, even private transporters like owners of pickup trucks were allowed to carry passengers for a fee if they obtained a contract from the public-transport authority and met various safety requirements (Stren, Halfani, and Malombe 1994, 195). By 1988 only 100 government buses were operating, while the legal *daladala* had dwindled to 183 due to the high agency fee they were required to pay. Both public and private buses were often badly in need of repair. The city, according to experts, needed a minimum of 750 buses to meet the needs of its residents in 1988 (Kulaba 1989, 241).[48] By 1991 the number of passengers using government-owned Usafiri Dar es Salaam (UDA) had dwindled to 13 percent of the number in 1982 (Stren, Halfani, and Malombe 1994, 192).

In sharp contrast, by 1991 the number of *daladala* had increased significantly, but approximately 450 out of 600 were operating without licenses. The government then temporarily suspended registration of *daladala* buses, because they had put the government-owned UDA buses virtually out of business. There were only 50 government buses in operation, and their operating costs by their own admission were higher than those of the *daladala*. The *daladala* were favored by passengers because they would go almost anywhere passengers were heading and did not follow strict routes (partly to avoid being caught). Another type of bus that became popular in the early 1990s was known as *chai maharagwe* (tea and beans) because these dangerous open buses contained long benches that reminded people of seating arrangements in local restaurants.

Vehicles like the *daladala* were legalized in other parts of Africa as well, notably in Kenya, where in 1984 the informal *matatu* buses were licensed after being public carriers for twenty years (Kapila 1987, 21). In Nairobi the initial demand for "pirate taxis" mushroomed from 400 buses in 1970 to more than 2,000 buses by 1982 and possibly up to 10,000 in 1987 after privatization.

Doctors and Chickens

The health sector was another area in which privatization occurred in the 1980s in response to popular pressures. Although the majority of employees affected by party and government policies regarding second incomes and informal economic activities were low-income workers, the policies also impinged on the welfare of professionals and semiprofessionals. One dramatic turnabout in policy resulted from the controversy over sideline incomes in the field of medicine. The conflict eventually led to the lifting of restrictions that had prevented physicians from practicing medicine privately. Physicians had been forbidden to practice medicine privately while off duty from serving in government hospitals and clinics. Most physicians were involved in agricultural production or animal husbandry on the outskirts of the city to supplement their income. They often hired local villagers to tend their farms. Nevertheless, a large part of the doctors' time was taken up in their sideline activities. As one Asian woman physician told me, "When I studied to be a doctor, I never thought I'd learn so much about chickens or end up doing so many other things."[49] Other doctors quietly carried out private practices during their off hours (Joinet 1986).

Many doctors believed that it was a waste of the country's resources to be spending so much time cultivating and doing other projects unrelated to medicine, when they could have been practicing medicine privately and legally after hours. Between 1984 and 1989, 196 physicians had left Tanzania to work in hospitals in neighboring countries (Shaidi 1991, 128). The movement for privatization was spearheaded by the Medical Association of Tanzania (MAT), which argued that the association's intention was not to do away with public service but to allow physicians to engage in private practice on the side.

The then-president of the MAT, Dr. Philemon Sarungi, said at a conference of the association that preventing public-service doctors from having private practices during their free time forced them to divert their energy and professional knowledge to nonmedical pastimes such as rearing chickens or pigs.[50] The minister of health and social welfare at the time, Dr. Aaron Chiduo, opposed the move to permit private care on political grounds, saying that the poor would suffer and not have access to health provisions.[51]

The debate made its way into Parliament, where member of Parliament Dr. Zainab Amir Gama argued forcefully that the ministry would "do justice to both the doctors and to the profession if it allowed doctors to practice on a part-time basis instead of going for poultry keeping." She said that "it was an open secret that some doctors were working with private clinics and hospitals on a part-time basis, although it was illegal. Others engaged in poultry projects so as to augment their 'meager' salaries."[52]

Doctors at Muhimbili Medical Centre struck in mid-1990 (and again in the beginning of 1991) because the government failed to follow up on its promise to increase doctors' allowances. To placate the doctors, the government had allowed them to practice medicine privately during their hours off duty. Doctors employed in government hospitals were allowed to work part-time in private clinics and hospitals, although they were not permitted to operate private hospitals and clinics. The prime minister even admitted that the decision to ban private medical practice in the 1980s was out of tune with present situation in Tanzania.[53] By 1994 health expenditures accounted for only 5 percent of the government budget, as compared with 30 percent in 1984.[54] With the public-health system in disarray, the government finally lifted its twenty-eight-year ban on private medicine in 1993. By 1995 the number of private hospitals and dispensaries had mushroomed to around 950, making up 38 percent of the country's health facilities, catering to about half of the country's outpatient population, and accounting for 30 percent of all hospital beds.

Government monopolies in the provision of basic services like medicine and transport were privatized reluctantly, slowly, and only when the crisis had grown to the point where continuing the monopoly would seriously undermine government legitimacy.

ECONOMIC LIBERALIZATION

Supplying the City with Food

The liberalization of food markets was another arena of microlevel impact on macrolevel policy, as Benno Ndulu describes it (Ndulu and Mwega 1994). By the early 1990s the liberalized trade market was no longer an issue of debate and was taken for granted as being an improvement over the controlled markets of the 1970s and 1980s (Amani and Maro 1991–1992, 36). In this latter period, parallel markets gained in importance, thus creating linkages between rural producers, traders, and urban retailers. Parallel markets provide channels for the sale of crops outside the official state-run crop authorities.

Maliyamkono and Bagachwa (1990) made a useful distinction among the different kinds of informal food-marketing arrangements. The first arrangement involved trade between members of one village or of nearby villages. A second was characterized as a shuttle food market, in which family members took one to three bags of grain by bus or truck to a nearby town where they could fetch higher prices than in their own village. A third arrangement was based on interregional trade, in which food commodities were transported from one region to another by unlicensed traders, either on a regular basis or occasionally on their way back from transporting other goods to a certain locale.[55] A fourth arrangement involved urban open markets, in which urban dwellers sold produce they had grown or grain obtained from regional or national food distributors or from the National Milling Corporation (NMC). Finally, a fifth arrangement could be described as the export market, in which crops were smuggled out of the country. Smuggling occurred mainly in border regions. In all of these cases, the forms of trade were not new, but the scale of activity increased significantly in the 1970s.

The extent of parallel-market activity has always been determined, if not defined, by the official marketing system. Even in the 1960s more food crops were being sold privately and illegally than through official markets. At this time the newly independent government, however, expanded the functions of cooperatives to crop marketing and credit, input supply, and other programs. The cooperatives quickly became overloaded with functions beyond their capacity, while corruption was rampant. Nevertheless, their role was expanded even further after the 1967 Arusha Declaration and especially after the nationalization of wholesale trade in 1969 (Coulson 1982; Raikes 1986).

The cooperatives' inefficiency and corruption increased, so that by 1975 the government found sufficient justification to replace them with crop authorities, which were under direct state control. These crop authorities took over the purchasing, processing, and selling of crops and the provision of extension services. This additional centralization only compounded the inefficiency, corruption, waste, and cost overruns that had plagued the cooperatives, as the crop authorities accrued enormous deficits. In 1982 the cooperatives were reinstated, but they were kept under considerable state supervision. Meanwhile, in the 1970s parallel markets had clearly become an institution in the Tanzanian economy as the inefficiency of the food-crop authority, the NMC, was compounded by food shortages (Raikes

1986, 116–20). For example, a study by Peter Temu (1975) estimated that in the early 1970s twice as much maize was being sold in parallel markets as through the official markets. This unofficial trade expanded in the early 1980s, and the Marketing Development Bureau estimated that by 1983–1984 only 25 percent of the marketed surplus of maize was sold through official channels (Ödegaard 1985, 156).

Only a small portion of the food market was channeled through the NMC. Smallholder subsistence producers, who account for most of the country's food supply, bypassed the marketing systems altogether. In fact, the trade in vegetables and some fruits had always been part of an unregulated, well-organized and effective trade system.

Unofficial producer prices were generally higher than those of the NMC (except during bumper harvest seasons or in areas where there were no competing government purchasers) (Temu 1975). These prices were more flexible, varying with the season and from year to year according to supply and demand, whereas NMC prices were fixed before the season began. Crop authorities also suffered from delays in collecting the harvests, lack of storage facilities, and delays in paying for the produce (Raikes 1986).

The purpose of official markets was to bring food supplies to the urban areas and public institutions. Although parallel markets favored rural producers, the traders had the most to gain. Traders charged urban dwellers exorbitantly high prices for agricultural commodities in scarce supply through official channels. Even so, the profit margins were smaller for private traders than for official marketing authorities (Ndulu and others 1988, 9–10). In some instances the open-market consumer prices were higher than official ones, but for key staples like maize, sorghum, and cassava, they were lower than official prices in 1986–1987.[56] For those commodities for which the official price was lower, it should be noted that most city dwellers did not have access to commodities at the official price because of the shortages in the official marketing system and because people with connections frequently diverted the goods to sell at *ulanguzi* (hiked) prices.

Evidence of the increase in urban purchases from the open market are overwhelming. In the early 1980s per capita official food deliveries were about 15 to 20 percent of the 1970 level (Raikes 1986, 116). Obviously, urban dwellers had not reduced their food requirements by 85 percent during this period. If anything, the food demands of Dar es Salaam increased due to population growth. There is little doubt that the difference between officially marketed produce and consumer needs was met by the parallel markets, even though it is difficult to gauge the actual quantities traded unofficially. According to a Marketing Development Bureau study, 90 percent of marketed maize and 75 percent of marketed rice, the major staples under government control, were sold through parallel markets from 1980 through 1987.

Parallel markets also affected the export sector. Cash-crop producers often favored selling their goods on the unofficial markets because their prices were higher than what the government was offering. One of the biggest changes in agricultural production since the 1970s was the shift from export crops to food crops. The general understanding has been that official prices of government-run crop authorities favored food crops since the mid-1970s, hence this drop in export production. However, economists have more recently noted that the real reason for the shift is the gap between the low official prices for export crops and high unofficial prices for food crops (Raikes 1986, 122).

The policy of panterritorial pricing accounted in large measure for the regional differences in sales through official channels. In Tanga, Kilimanjaro, and Morogoro regions, NMC purchases of maize grain accounted for 28 percent of its regional purchases in 1976–1977; five years later, NMC purchases from these regions amounted to only 1 percent of its regional purchases. Meanwhile, per capita maize production increased in all three regions. In effect, those regions that had the lowest transport costs were subsidizing regions with the highest transport costs. This meant that unofficial prices looked much more attractive to producers in these regions and that they were able to obtain twice the price in informal markets than through formal channels. Meanwhile, sales through official channels in more remote, high-transport-cost areas increased (Maliyamkono and Bagachwa 1990, 75).

The pervasiveness of unofficial marketing made regulation virtually impossible. Ultimately it resulted in the liberalization of food markets. Local markets in staples were recognized in the 1982 National Agricultural Policy. Liberalizing measures included the removal of the 500-kilogram restriction on interregional movement of food in 1984; the abolition of permits to move food inside the country in 1986; the decontrolling of pricing and marketing of millet, sorghum, and cassava at the cooperative level in 1987; and the 1988 measures to make the NMC into a commercial enterprise. Maize was also decontrolled at the cooperative level, and private traders were permitted to trade maize after purchasing it from the cooperatives.[57] Other measures included lifting consumer subsidies, especially for maize, to reduce budgetary deficits arising from official food trade;

raising producer prices at a yearly rate of 5 percent; reducing impediments, like roadblocks, to private trade; and, in March 1987, doing away with restrictions on the quantity of crops that could be transported. Unofficial regional trading was forbidden until 1986–1987, when the government began to move toward acceptance of a trading system that combined the NMC, cooperatives, and the open market. The measures had positive results almost immediately, with significantly increased production, especially for maize and rice. Open-market consumer prices resulted in the subsequent stabilization of prices for rice and a decrease in prices for maize after 1983–1984. Moreover, the gap between open-market prices and official prices narrowed significantly (Ndulu and others 1988, 12–16). Another important function of the liberalization of internal trade was to erode the high-scarcity premiums of some traders.

The primary impetus for this particular policy change came from internal developments at the microlevel. Although these domestic factors were directly responsible for the liberalization of internal food markets, it is important to note that they occurred against the backdrop of pressures on Tanzania to sign an agreement with the IMF, which undoubtedly played a role in speeding up the process of loosening restrictions on domestic trade.

THE LIMITS OF GOVERNMENT CONCESSIONS

Government accommodation to many issues made it easier for people to engage in small private enterprises or trading. On other issues the government tried to exert some control, but it clearly was not strong enough to stem the pervasiveness of various activities. For example, a debate emerged within the teaching profession over whether teachers could legally tutor students after school hours. The Ministry of Education had from time to time issued warnings against the prevalent practice of teachers' holding tutorials, called "tuition," after school because it privileged wealthier students who could pay the extra fees. After years of ambiguity in policy and a tacit acceptance of "tuition" by school principals, the practice of tutorials was finally banned in 1991 by the Ministry for Education and Culture. The ban drew immediate protests by angry parents and teachers, who called or visited the official newspaper *Daily News* to voice their complaints. One columnist who supported the ban nevertheless described it as having touched "a raw nerve" among parents and teachers. "This is the only way we can subsidize our earnings," one teacher told a *Daily News* reporter. Another said: "We cannot survive without tuition."[58] In an opinion poll taken by the newspaper, the majority of people interviewed in Dar es Salaam opposed the ban.[59]

In interviewing students and teachers from seven Dar es Salaam secondary schools and teachers and principals from primary schools in Manzese and Buguruni prior to the ban, I found that the practice of holding tutorials was widespread. In secondary schools it was not uncommon for students to take as many as six hours of tutorials a week, paying around TSh 100–200 a month for classes like math, French, Swahili, biology, and English, while physics tutorials could run as high as TSh 400 to 680 a month. The teachers could double, triple, or quadruple their monthly salaries, depending on how many students they had and the number of tutorials they held.

Students gave a wide variety of reasons for taking tutorials. In some instances, they reported that teachers would come to the regular classes but do little in the way of instruction. This left students who wanted to pass their qualifying exams with little choice but to attend tutorials, where the same instructor made a concerted effort to teach well. Some students sought other teachers for tutorials because the quality of teaching was so poor in their regular classes. Other students had difficulty in certain classes and believed they needed extra help. Still others were competitive and wanted an edge over their fellow students so that they would be admitted to secondary school or university.

In effect, a private educational system had emerged within the public-school system. Teachers paid little heed to the ministry's various directives and continued the tutorials at home, while school principals overlooked the practice. Teachers openly disagreed with the ministry's action. They had their own justifications for holding tutorials. One primary-school teacher explained, "Tutorials help a lot, both for the teachers and the students. In the past, classes had 25 to 30 children and it was easy to teach them. Now with the Universal Primary Education there are 100 students to one teacher. So you can't teach them well. But with tutorial classes you have a few, 10, 12, 15, and it is nice because you have peace and quiet and can teach them well."[60] In this teacher's school the practice of tutorials started in about 1984. She said she used to enjoy teaching but that, after thirty-five years, her salary was only TSh 3,000. She continued, "We have no books or textbooks to use in instruction. My students have no desks or chairs. In an effort to cut back costs, the Government laid off the school watchmen and then all the desks and chairs were stolen. Then the Government lost more money on that."[61] Many teachers like this one felt that the satisfaction and money they obtained from teaching tutorials was some compensation for the frustrations and low wages they faced on the job.

Teachers had many other ways of supplementing their income, too. It was a common practice for them to sell ice cream, soda, *maandazi* buns, peanuts, embroidery, homemade envelopes, and paper bags to students. One teacher rented out school chairs for outside functions at TSh 25 a chair. Some had students selling their products for 10 percent commission. These sales on school premises were forbidden, along with the use of students as intermediaries.

As with the tutorials, teachers refused to curtail their projects, while the local school authorities looked the other way, knowing they could do little until the government was in a position to pay the teachers adequate salaries. Given these realities, it was unlikely that the government ban on tutorials would be honored and in all likelihood larger number of teachers simply moved their tutorials from school premises to their homes or some other location. These examples of teachers' strategies show quite vividly the incompatibility between the reality of survival and the egalitarian aspirations of the government. The alternatives are quite stark. The tuition system perpetuates inequalities, denying access to better education to the poor. At the same time, without significant pay increases, teachers will continue to conduct tutorials to support themselves. Were parents to fund schools more directly, perhaps the "tuition" system could be eliminated, but then it would require government's relinquishing greater control to parents. Either way, the solution to the dilemma is far from simple, and it highlights the difficult choices that emanate from the lack of resources.

CONCLUSIONS

In the mid-1980s the Tanzanian government found itself responding to sharp pressures from international financial institutions and foreign donors to engage in various economic reforms. In some instances, structural-adjustment policies worked at cross-purposes with the interests of urban residents; in other contexts, pressures from the informal economy resulted in reforms that were incorporated into structural-adjustment policies; and, finally, there were informal-sector interests that were distinct from those addressed in the economic-reform packages.

After the mid-1980s, open repression of small entrepreneurs and employees involved in informal sideline activities gradually gave way to legalization, liberalization, and privatization. Small-business operators who had previously been considered as engaging in illegal occupations were now able to apply for licenses. The internal trade of foodstuffs that had been channeled through parallel markets could now make its way through liberalized open markets. After 1993, medical doctors could practice medicine privately. Significant policy changes had been implemented in areas that directly affected the day-to-day survival of both urban and rural dwellers.

As the crisis deepened and as economic-adjustment policies pushed the cost of living even higher, people's persistence in informal economic activities led to debates within Parliament and the CCM over the suppression and restriction of various survival strategies. The government initially ignored many of these practices, either because it did not have the capacity to enforce its restrictions or because it was not prepared to officially sanction various practices for ideological reasons.

People's persistence in their informal income-generating activities in defiance of government restrictions became a form of opposition and of noncompliance. The massive scale of these evasions raised the cost of securing compliance for the government to an extremely high level. In the 1980s, to a greater degree than before, the authorities began to recognize various activities as legal. But in the process of transition they adopted a number of different policies: They often insisted on policies that preserved their ideological commitments yet did not have the capacity to enforce the policy, as the case of tutorials reveals. In the end, however, domestic pressures forced the authorities to dispense even with these key ideological principles. The authorities looked the other way when people violated government regulations that lacked any logical correspondence with reality (such as the ban on sideline activities of doctors prior to 1991). At times they made open accommodation (as in the shift from the 1983 Human Resources Deployment Act to the encouragement of small-scale entrepreneurship in the 1990s). At other times they exerted open opposition to various economic activities and attempted to enforce them (as was the case with the 1991 restrictions on illegal *daladala* buses). The authorities also quietly encouraged other illegal activities like militia bribery of vendors because they provided a source of revenue for government employees. These varied government responses clearly reflect the ambiguity of noncompliant economic resistance, as well as its potential transformative power.

7 From the Arusha Declaration to the Zanzibar Declaration

With the First Phase Government there were many problems, especially with supplies. At that time *miradi* [projects] had to be hidden. The Arusha Declaration said that leaders were not permitted to do *miradi*. If they did this they were violating the Leadership Code. With the Second Phase Government one can support oneself with one's income by doing *miradi*. Mwinyi says that the government doesn't have the ability to provide adequate wages and people should supplement their incomes with other means.

College administrator, Dar es Salaam

The year 1990 marked a significant turning point for Tanzania's ruling Chama Cha Mapinduzi (CCM) Party. That year, for the first time since independence, the party began to contemplate multipartyism and to dismantle policies that had been implemented to bolster one-party rule and enhance statism. By 1992 independent parties were allowed to register. The struggle that emerged in the 1980s between the government and the party over policies affecting the informal economy shaped the timing and nature of the new policies that were adopted. For the most part the party acted as a restraint on the government, which was facing more immediate external and internal pressures to liberalize. Nowhere was this conflict more apparent than in the party's footdragging over revising the Leadership Code of the Arusha Declaration after the government had already adopted measures that contradicted the essence of the Leadership Code.

The CCM finally abandoned the Leadership Code in what came to be known as the Zanzibar Declaration of 1991, which fundamentally modified the 1967 Arusha Declaration and challenged the original objectives of the document. The symbolic importance of these changes cannot be emphasized strongly enough, for the Arusha Declaration was the central document in establishing the egalitarian, self-reliant, and socialist orientation that Tanzania had adopted. The CCM, for example, lifted key restrictions on its members with second incomes. CCM members represented 11 percent of the population (2.5 million members in 1988) in a country where many jobs, especially in the civil service and in parastatals, required party membership.

When the Leadership Code was first implemented, it was aimed at preventing party leaders from becoming part of a privileged group that exploited people through hiring labor or renting property. The code was an attempt to stem the growing gap between the well-to-do and the poorer members of society. It was also an attempt to prevent personalistic forms of rule—that is, the exchange of personal favors for political loyalty—that were widespread in other parts of Africa and were beginning to emerge in Tanzania.

The conditions of the Leadership Code were not only party policy, they were made into an amendment of the country's constitution in 1967. Members of Parliament would have to make a declaration to the Speaker that they had agreed to comply with the Leadership Code and to submit a sworn statement detailing their finances. Those who refused to make the declaration or whose statement failed to meet the requirements of the attorney general could face a court petition to vacate their seats. Only one member of Parliament failed to make the declaration by the time of the deadline (Cliffe 1972, 254).

When the Leadership Code was first implemented it was aimed primarily at senior party and government leaders and high- and middle-ranking civil servants, but gradually it came to apply to all leaders and party members who received a salary of more than TSh 1,060.70. The sum was fixed in 1973 and would have included all government and parastatal employees at high and middle levels at that time. By the early 1990s, with the raising of the minimum wage, this included all employees in government or government-owned enterprises (Shaidi 1991, 125).

According to the Leadership Code, party leaders and their spouses could not be associated with capitalist practices. More specifically, they were forbidden to own shares in any company, hold directorships in privately owned businesses, rent out houses, receive two or more incomes, and hire anyone for the purposes of business, trade, or one's profession.[1] The hiring of casual labor or seasonal labor on small farms was permitted, but not that of permanent or full-time labor. Leaders could, however, transfer property to a trust in their children's name. No mention was made of hiring domestic servants, which was ostensibly permitted because no profits were made from their labor. Leaders were given one year to meet the stipulations of the Arusha Declaration.

Leaders had to sign a declaration agreeing to abide by the conditions of the code. In 1973 a Committee for the Enforcement of the Leadership

Code was formed by parliamentary decree to investigate violations, call on the police to arrest people who did not voluntarily respond to summons, and expel members from the party if found in violation of the code (Shaidi 1991, 126).

Little is known about why Julius Nyerere chose to issue this declaration at the time that he did and why it took the form that it did. There have been widely diverging interpretations of this declaration, including those of Lionel Cliffe (1972), Michaela Von Freyhold (1979), Goran Hyden (1980), Bismarck Mwansasu and Cranford Pratt (1979), Cranford Pratt (1976), John Saul (1979), and Issa Shivji (1976).

In part the Leadership Code appears to have been a legitimating move, for it took place at a time when many other African regimes that had come to power with independence were being toppled in military coups. The form that the declaration took, with its strong emphasis on egalitarianism while undercutting any possibilities for leaders to accumulate wealth, can only be seen as an attempt to give the impression that Tanzanian society was moving toward classlessness. The party leaders hoped that it would give the party the moral authority it felt it needed to claim dominance in Tanzania's political order.

Agreement on the Arusha Declaration was far from unanimous, but very little open opposition was visible at the time of its pronouncement. Part of the explanation for the lack of expressed opposition has to do with the nature of the leadership and the weakness of Tanzanian capital. The leaders came from the group of urban civil servants, teachers, farmers, and traders who had formed the base of TANU's mobilization for independence. They were not capitalists themselves, they did not have strong allegiances to capital in Tanzania, and, for the most part, they did not represent the interests of African capital, which was extremely weak at the time. There were only a few hundred rural capitalists at the time of independence, most of whom were scattered around the country away from Dar es Salaam and did not act as a cohesive interest group, unlike their counterparts in Kenya at the time. It is also possible that some may have seen no reason to oppose a move that reduced the competitiveness of foreigners and Asians because this might open up new business opportunities for them in the future (Mueller 1980, 13, 16). The leaders saw the state not only as the main means through which they could advance the nation but also as the main way in which they could advance personally. Tanzania was not seen as attractive to foreign investment at the time, and the leaders grabbed the idea of self-reliance in what Mueller describes as an attempt to "make an ideological virtue out of what they found to be politically necessary and economically expedient to insure their own survival" (1980, 15).

Disaffection with the declaration was not voiced at the time because any open criticism would have been severely muted. Only twenty years after the promulgation of the Arusha Declaration did people begin to feel free to talk about opposition to the decree. One former member of Parliament, who later became an influential businessman, was with Nyerere when the Arusha Declaration was announced. In an interview in 1988 he explained that "the Arusha Declaration was something dictated. Nyerere did not discuss the program at all, he just announced it. It was like someone holding a sharp knife on one's side in such a way that it could not be pulled away without getting hurt. Some left the country, like Kambona. He criticized from the outside, but that was ineffective. Some really supported the policy at first, but then when they realized what the Arusha Declaration was all about, they became bitter."[2]

This particular former parliamentarian opposed the declaration because of what he feared it would do to the economic future of the country, but it appears that much of the resistance came from members of Parliament who were concerned about the loss of personal economic privilege. This concern over private wealth was evident in a booklet published in 1967, featuring questions by members of Parliament regarding the Arusha Declaration answered by Julius Nyerere (United Republic of Tanzania 1967). Not surprisingly, the majority of questions concerned the Leadership Code. The preoccupation with the code is even noted in the four-sentence preface to the pamphlet, which offers the observation that "unfortunately almost all the questions received related to just one section of the Arusha Declaration—that on qualifications for leadership. There was not even one question on Socialism and Self-Reliance."

At the district- and town-council level about one-quarter of the councillors withdrew from political office as a consequence of the declaration (Cliffe 1972, 255). One junior minister, Mr. Mtaki, resigned to keep his job with an international company. Nine other members of Parliament were expelled from the party in 1968 for opposing "the party line," with no further explanation. Their expulsion ensured their removal from the Parliament. Although their background and circumstances varied, they shared an outspoken opposition to the policies that were being adopted and flagrant resistance to authority (Bienen 1970, 437).

At the same time, Oscar Kambona, the secretary general of TANU and minister of foreign affairs, was also expelled from the party, but by the time of his expulsion he had already gone into self-exile. He claimed then and continued to claim that the basis of his opposition was to the one-party state, the "authoritarian rule of Nyerere," and "the limitation on personal and political freedoms, the decline of the rule of law, the growth of corruption in public life and the widespread maladministration in the public services."[3] His departure is significant in the period after the Arusha Declaration, for he was the second-highest-ranking individual in the country at the time.

Those who did not toe the line suffered various forms of repression and ostracism. According to Kambona, his two brothers served ten years under arrest and were released only after repeated interventions by international human-rights groups.[4] In 1968 the National Assembly member who successfully led a parliamentary struggle to restore some of the income lost by leaders with the Arusha Declaration was purged from the party (Resnick 1981, 101). Bibi Titi Mohammed, Michael Kamaliza, and Paul Rupia were other prominent leaders who were casualties of the Arusha Declaration.

IMPACT OF THE LEADERSHIP CODE

The most serious consequence of the Arusha Declaration was not so much that it undercut the leaders' ability to accumulate wealth but that it discouraged private-capital accumulation and investment by the smallest and largest businesses alike. Not only did it hurt foreign investment, but, more importantly, it put a damper on the formation of national capital. Capitalism, as Mueller argued, was "stunted in its most backward form" (1980, 20). From 1965 to 1970 the private-sector share of all monetary fixed-capital formation fell from 60 percent to 30 percent (Hartmann 1991, 11). Meanwhile, the public sector grew, with parastatals increasing in number from 64 in 1967 to 139 by 1974 (Coulson 1982, 272–74).

The Arusha Declaration also put a serious damper on open discussion and criticism. The members of Parliament had been one of the main sources of criticism on behalf of their constituents when it came to issues of equity regarding prices, incomes, and education. This kind of debate over local equity concerns was gradually suppressed as manifestations of authoritarianism became more prevalent (Resnick 1981, 81). Because dominant ideology was proworker and procultivator, any criticism of this was considered opposition to *ujamaa*, or the broader socialist orientation of the country. Moreover, the Leadership Code was seen as evidence that the leaders themselves were willing to submit to the requirements of *ujamaa*. As Von Freyhold put it, the code provided a rationale for suppressing workers' wage demands and banning strikes, because workers' funds were needed for "socialist construction" in rural areas. The "unemployed" could be thrown into the villages to build *ujamaa*, and wealthier farmers who opposed various bureaucratic measures could be told they were thwarting the country's policies. Similarly, the declaration provided the justification for the villagization campaigns and the suppression of poor farmers (Mueller 1980, 20; Von Freyhold 1979, 120).

In the late 1970s in a rare and bold move, Sosthenes Maliti, a retired lawyer who had worked for the government for ten years, published a book, *Honest to My Country*, under the pen name Candid Scope. In this book he criticized the Arusha Declaration, the Detention Act, the extensive presidential powers, and the lack of press freedom. The deferential way in which the book was written, with page after page of praise for Nyerere, the government, and the party and its leaders, is indicative of the fear he undoubtedly felt in expressing his criticisms. It is a fear he addresses in his discussion of the limits on freedom of expression, in which he captures much of what those who disagreed with the policies of the country must have felt (c. 1978, 22):

> Our people's way of life shows an unfortunate spirit of fear to speak about politicians and politics. Fear to express what one believes in good faith to be the correct opinion on the trend of affairs in the nation. There are fears of ending up in *"keko,"* i.e., detention; fears of *"unamulikwa"*— sort of being spied upon; fears of losing a nice job; fears of missing a promotion; and fears of losing some favour or other, if you dare to air a view which contradicts the authorities or the "official line"; even if you believe very strongly that your opinion would be of vital benefit to the nation as a whole. This unfortunate spirit of fear so badly injures the character of our people to an extent that it may be bad for the national interest as a whole.

The code had other direct consequences. Sheer economic necessity had made the party Leadership Code policy on two incomes untenable for people even in the higher-income brackets, who had also suffered a dramatic reduction of living standard with the crisis, while their salaries were lowered and heavily taxed. By 1989 a top-ranking minister took home little more than $25 a month in a country where the cost of living (especially of consumer goods) was close to that in the United States![5] As the economic situation became more difficult in the late 1970s and early 1980s, managers had the choice of either engaging in corruption (embezzlement, graft, extortion) or starting a sideline business with their savings, with funds diverted from the workplace, or with a little of both. The dilemma managers and government leaders faced was that their households would barely survive if they simply lived off the salary they earned by running a state institution or a company. Although many middle-level and top-ranking managers diverted funds from state companies and institutions to finance their private businesses, others worked hard to sustain modest businesses by making and selling chicken feed, raising cows for milk sales, raising chickens for meat and eggs, tailoring, or engaging in agricultural production on the outskirts of the city. A few were able to pursue even larger businesses and left their positions in the government early on to do so on a full-time basis.

One of the most damaging consequences of these restrictions was to blur the lines between gainful sideline activities and outright corruption because the authorities treated them as the same kind of violation. Party members of all income groups had little choice but to engage in sideline activities, but they were forced to conceal them and lie about them. One woman, a party representative at the foreign-owned company she worked for, was responsible for reprimanding other employees who, preoccupied with their sideline projects, were not putting in a full day's work. At the same time she herself had a sideline chicken business. She finally decided to leave her party post and eventually her job because, as she put it, "I found myself and others doing what we had to do in order to survive."[6] She could not reconcile the conflict between the party directives and the realities of life for herself and her fellow employees.

The code also played a role in forcing professionals to leave the country to seek better incomes in neighboring countries or in the West. Drops in real wages meant that they could no longer live on their salaries, but they were not permitted legally to engage in sideline enterprises or hire others to do so for them. The ranks of Tanzania's physicians and university academics were seriously undermined through the voluntary exile of hundreds if not thousands of professionals.

Instead of eliminating capitalism, the Arusha Declaration and the growing state monopoly of various economic enterprises simply increased opportunities for bribery, rent seeking, and clientelism. As the ex-parliamentarian businessman explained in 1988, "Today, only those unscrupulous leaders who are protected by the system pray for the Arusha Declaration to continue."[7]

In the 1970s and early 1980s employees were harassed, questioned, and spied on. Those who were found to have sideline incomes were also threatened with suspension from their jobs. The majority who were punished for violating the code were ordinary party members, according to Shaidi.

Even when economic liberalization began in the mid-1980s, it was not accompanied by ideological concessions that would have suggested a retreat from socialism. In fact, as late as 1985 Nyerere said in an interview that "as far as socialism is concerned, there is nothing that we would not do in the same way. We announced socialism in the Arusha Declaration. If I was asked to rewrite it, I would change some commas, but nothing else. If possible, I would simply strengthen our recommitment to socialism."[8] These were prominent themes in his speech at the October 1987 party conference at Kizota. There he argued (Nyerere 1987, 7–9):

> Economic differences among our people . . . are beginning to be conspicuous. . . . But more noticeable to people suffering economic hardship (as most honest people now do) is the beginnings of real individual wealth in a poor country like ours. . . . Private wealth in our poor country still brings with it a question mark about the probity of the possessor. We still ask "how is it that this or that Government or Party leader seems to be rich"? And we suspect such people either of taking part in smuggling and breaking the Leadership Code, or of breaking all the Tax Laws of our country. . . . We have begun to get truly wealthy people, and we ask where they got their wealth from for it is not easy here in Tanzania for an honest person— even a trader—to get rich quickly.

Not everyone shared Nyerere's view that capitalism inherently bred corruption. Many viewed the 1970s and 1980s as evidence of how state monopolies themselves fostered corruption, especially as the crisis deepened. With options for legal, private-sector activities increasingly curtailed or discouraged, those who pursued these activities often did so within the context of the informal economy. As the incomes of even the highest government officials fell far below the cost of living, they too began to pursue sideline incomes. By the mid-1980s the government openly encouraged sideline businesses to help people get by, while the party remained staunch in its support of the Leadership Code.

Party leaders were reported saying that people who kept poultry and engaged in other small projects were "enemies of our socialist policies." In a 1987 interview Selemani Kitundu, chairman of the Commission for the Enforcement of the Leadership Code, said that public leaders (which included most employees because by the mid-1980s most workers made more than TSh 1,060) were prohibited from having secret incomes and engaging in businesses that condoned the exploitation of one person over another. Kitundu also criticized leaders who used their relatives to run huge businesses on their behalf.[9]

This view was echoed by a member of the party's Central Committee at the time. I asked whether the policy that prohibited second incomes was not unrealistic, given the present state of the economy. The leader's response was that there was nothing wrong with the policy. People simply were not implementing the policy correctly. He argued that if one were to have two jobs, one's formal job would suffer and one would end up cheating the state. If one employed someone to do one's sideline job, then one would be violating the Leadership Code because one would be making money off the sweat of another person, which was exploitation. He added: "Even if all the Muslims started eating pork, it wouldn't make eating pork right for Muslims."[10]

Many of those who opposed economic reforms were concerned that these measures had been taken at the expense of the poor. They feared that Tanzania would forfeit the gains it had made in narrowing the gap in formal incomes and in fostering an ethic of equality within the country's political culture if economic reforms were implemented.

A CULTURE OF NONCOMPLIANCE

By the mid-1980s the Leadership Code affected most urban employees, because the minimum wage exceeded the 1973 income figure that stipulated who had to abide by the code. The inflexible expectations of the party leadership regarding the code contributed to the widening of the gap between party policy and popular sentiments. A culture of noncompliance, including rumors, gossip, and satire, became more prevalent. The vignette that opens this book, in which minibus passengers transformed themselves into a wedding party to avoid police harassment, actually became a commonplace occurrence in Dar es Salaam in the early 1980s. Even the government-run newspaper *Daily News* ran a column by a popular satirist, Adam Lusekelo, who frequently wrote about the pervasiveness of sideline projects, scams, and their social consequences. The columns were on such topics as "Moonlighting Is Now In," "How We Used to Beat the Ban," "Guarding One's Kraal," and "'*Kukus*' [chickens] Build Houses?"[11]

New Swahili words emerged to describe the various economic activities people engaged in and the way they carried them out. Tanzania itself was popularly referred to as *Bongoland;* that is, the land where one needs smarts to survive. *Mradi,* or project, had its origins in the 1970 Education for Self-Reliance campaign gardening projects for schoolchildren and in the large-scale United Nations projects that were initiated in the same period. The term was appropriated and became the common word for small, income-generating projects in the 1980s. Other terms associated with *miradi* also gained in usage in the 1980s, including *shughuli ndogo ndogo, biashara ndogo ndogo,* and *miradi midogo midogo* (small businesses), and *mitumba* (secondhand clothes). *Mteja* (the patient of a healer) became the common term for customer or client in the 1980s.

In the 1990s other words relating to the informal sector increased in usage. *Mama Ntilie* (literally, Mama, put food on a plate) was used to refer to women who sold pastries and other foodstuffs in roadside *magenge* (kiosks). *Wamachinga* originally referred to Mozambicans who had migrated to Mtwara and then to Dar es Salaam in search of work. By the mid-1990s its meaning had broadened to all young street vendors who sold goods they carried around with them because they had no permanent business location.[12] *Dagaa* (small fish) referred to young street children and vendors.

A word that had been used to describe how a traditional healer walked a patient around, *kulangua,* took on an entirely new meaning as price hiking became commonplace in the early 1980s, and *ulanguzi,* the practice of hiking prices, became part of people's everyday language. It then declined in use by the end of the decade as trade liberalization eliminated the price gouging. Bribery or extortion came to be known as obtaining a little *mchuzi* (gravy). The party's initials, CCM, came to symbolize in popular discourse *Chukua Chako Mapema* (Take yours as fast as you can) or *Chama Cha Majangili* (the party of crooks). These terms represent more than linguistic developments. They also belie a value system and a normative view of what the rules of the game should be.

Many gray areas and ambiguities become apparent in analyzing popular noncompliance with the Leadership Code. It is worth trying to sort them out because not all sideline activities were the same. In the first chapter I made a distinction between licit economic activities, which have a legal counterpart in the society in question and illicit economic activities, in which there is no legal counterpart. This distinction is even made in Swahili between the terms *miradi* and *mipango.* Most informal sideline projects, like raising chickens, operating a kiosk, and tailoring, are considered licit. Even though they are commonly not registered, licensed, or taxed, they can be carried out legally in Tanzania and therefore are referred to as *miradi.* In contrast, illicit activities popularly known as *mipango* usually involved one's place of employment. In the 1980s *mipango,* which previously just meant plans or designs, took on the added meaning of schemes or scams; that is, illicit ways of making money through one's formal job. Where there were shortages of commodities and services, people who worked in parastatals or in the public sector sometimes used their jobs to make "a little extra"—or a great deal extra in the case of well-connected employees in better positions. This "little extra" has sometimes been described as a "'veiled' redistribution from the public sector resources into private pockets" (Ndulu 1988, 8).

Scams, like projects, were usually motivated by the need to make up the difference between the cost of living and one's paltry wage. However, increasing one's income by taking bribes (illicit informal activities) differs significantly from augmenting it by farming, selling services, or making commodities to sell (licit informal activities). A ticket agent who, claiming a shortage of seats, inflates the price of a bus ticket offers no service of his or her own, in contrast to a man I interviewed who made maps with his own inputs and sold them at the government-owned map store where he worked.

The scams varied from one workplace to another in the 1980s. In one hospital the laboratory technicians made a minimum of TSh 200 ($2 at 1988 exchange rates) a day from patients who paid TSh 50 to have their blood-test analysis sped up. They called it *chakula cha daktari* (food for the doctor—anyone donning a white coat risks being loosely referred to as "doctor"). One customs official admitted to me that on a good day he could bring home TSh 3,000 for "facilitating" the clearance of imported goods and claimed that higher-ranking customs officials could make as much as TSh 10,000 a day.[13] A woman who worked in the foreign-exchange section of a bank indicated to patrons where they could have money changed on the black market and in this way received her "cut into the action" of the black marketeers. Especially during peak travel periods, people selling bus, railway, and airline tickets would often ask passengers for a little extra in order to guarantee them a seat.

These kinds of scams were by no means new in Tanzania, nor were they peculiar to Tanzania. However, their pervasiveness in the country was new. When asked why they involved themselves in these forms of petty hustling, people invariably answered that their wages were low and that they had to make up the difference somehow. In many peoples' minds, the "hustle" was a way of claiming what they believed was owed them. In a discussion about business licenses one party secretary told me, "You know our problems. I am asked to check licenses in my area. That day I haven't eaten anything. I come to turn you in and you plead and say, 'Please let me go. I will give you 200 shillings.' Well, I let the person go and take the money. People don't care about the law."[14] Another worker expressed the link between wages and scams in reference to the police, who are notorious for extracting bribes: "There are no police in Tanzania. You have to bribe them. It would be better to pay them money as wages than to pay them bribes."[15]

I spoke with one businessman who was a beer distributor and worked at the Ministry of Interior as a civil servant. He set out to explain to me the complexities of Tanzania's political economy. Believing that I was a naive, young, foreign woman he started with the basics: "Let me tell you, my dear, it could take more than a lifetime to understand Tanzanian politics. It is so complicated. Nothing is as it seems. There is so much involved beneath it all. If you say you want to study economics, you can never really know many things. We all do something to survive. We have to. You can't get anything done in this country if you follow the rules. Like me."[16]

This was my cue to ask what he did, whereupon he proceeded to explain how he and other beer distributors would pay mechanics at the government-owned breweries not to fix the equipment when it broke down. This created artificial shortages and raised the price of beer.

The higher the position one held, the greater the opportunities for such illicit scams. For example, parastatals were riddled with clientelistic practices, as Deborah Bryceson points out. The general manager and supporting managers and accounting staff had the best access to parastatal resources and were in the best position to misuse public vehicles, falsify records of purchases, engage in favoritism in allocating goods, misappropriate Treasury funds, charge the parastatal for questionable imprests (per diem for out-of-town business or conferences), commission projects involving kickbacks, embezzlement, and outright theft (Bryceson 1990, 189).

The emphasis on high-positioned people involved in corruption is not meant to imply that low-ranking employees were not also culpable. However, unlike better-positioned citizens, the poorest members of society were most victimized by these scams and had the least opportunities to engage in them. Unlicensed street vendors frequently had to dole out bribe money to City Council militia who threatened them with arrest; applicants for business licenses often had to pay bribes to obtain the necessary forms and papers.

The poor not only suffered tangible monetary losses as a result of bribes and extortion, they also experienced these practices as a personal affront. Bribery violated societal notions of economic justice in which the poor ought to pay the least for whatever good or service is being sought. Moreover, to demand payment so blatantly was taken as an obvious offense.

In addition to the class dimensions of scams, the strengthening of the legal private sector helped bring pressure to bear on those using their public-sector positions to enhance themselves illegally. For example, in 1991 the Tanzania Drivers Association publicly urged the government to crack down on pirate taxi operators, who were using government and parastatal vehicles in what the association called "lucrative and unlawful business." These operators were charging the same rate as formal taxis but were not paying any tax. Most pirate taxis were said to belong to highly placed government officials.[17]

Given these economic realities, the equation of corruption with licit sideline activities only compounded people's frustrations. As far as the Leadership Code was concerned, urban dwellers saw the issue in pragmatic terms, as a matter of survival rather than as one of adhering to an abstract ideological principle. Moreover, given the fact that most civil servants earned so much more income from their sideline activities than from their jobs, it is surprising that they chose to remain employed at all. Most people who engaged in sideline projects saw them as an honest way to earn a living and found the notion absurd that they might be undermining the government or party in some way.

One typical response to our question concerning what people thought of the party policy on two incomes was that of a messenger working at the Tanzania Harbors Authority who made soap as a sideline activity. "Our party should change its policy on that point," he said. "We have to survive, and our wages are not enough. We don't want to offend the party, but we have no option."[18] In 1987 the messenger was still making the old minimum wage of TSh 810 a month even though the wages were supposed to have been raised by TSh 450.

Several things become apparent when one begins to look at popular perceptions of the issue. The class and status dimensions are strikingly clear in the comments of one Dar es Salaam resident who wrote a letter to the *Daily News* in which he responded to the suspension of 102 Zanzibari workers for carrying out sideline activities:

> The practice of indulging in personal *miradi* has become very common these days. We therefore need to ask the question why? Is it because our workers have suddenly become so greedy, bent on making as much money and as fast as possible? It is true that there are some workers especially the top bureaucrats, who are in a position to accumulate money rapidly through corrupt practices. . . . Most of the Government workers in the middle and lower levels, however, are hardly in a position to accumulate much. . . . The cost of living of the middle and lower income workers has increased nearly twice as fast as their wages since 1969. This is not taking

into consideration the fact that many of the essentials can now be obtained only at "black market prices." [They] have to choose either to reduce their consumption below the minimum necessary for survival, return their families to the rural areas, or find other means of supplementing their incomes through petty corruption or petty personal businesses.[19]

Clearly, to this individual the issue of sideline jobs was not one of corruption for the majority of citizens for whom survival was the key issue. Instead, it was government officials who had opportunities to engage in real corrupt practices and enrich themselves at the expense of the citizens. The hypocrisy of the double standard was underscored by one local college administrator who explained: "Men of politics are cheats. The big shots in the party have three incomes themselves, and they are telling us not to have projects."[20] The administrator, who himself had a kiosk, chicken business, and piggery, took refuge in government policy in arguing against the party policy.

Moreover, ordinary citizens saw themselves as victims of rules for which they had not been consulted. If they did not comply, it was because they felt their bargain with the state, such as it was, had been violated by the state. They had not received adequate wages and therefore had to engage in sideline enterprises; they received woefully inadequate services and therefore evaded taxes.

The nature of this violated "contract" between officials and ordinary citizens is seen clearly in the comments people made about the Leadership Code and about the terms of their employment. For example, one civil servant who worked at a ministry office was asked by a fellow employee why he frequently was late for work. He responded with this rationalization: "If I come to work late, I work only two hours and then leave. What are they paying me? They aren't paying me anything. I have to take care of my projects in the morning. What they are giving me [TSh 4,000 a month] is enough only for two hours work a day."[21] It would not be fair, however, to suggest that all employees engaged in sideline projects at the expense of their jobs in this way. For most industrial workers, leaving one's job early or coming in late was not even an option.

In sum, there were many indistinct boundaries between licit informal activities like small-scale enterprises and the use of formal jobs to profit through illicit activities. Nevertheless, it is important to distinguish between ordinary citizens and higher-ranking officials and government employees. These distinctions should be made in the disparities in opportunities to engage in corrupt practices and in the scale of corruption. It should also be noted that the poor usually suffered disproportionately from corrupt practices, which meant that low-income citizens generally experienced more intensely the hypocrisy, double standards, and injustice of a system in which they were told to abide by rules that were not followed by those who made the rules. This kind of hypocrisy led to the belief among ordinary citizens that the leaders had not lived up to their end of the bargain, having established the rules.

THE STRUGGLE BETWEEN PARTY AND GOVERNMENT OVER THE LEADERSHIP CODE

By the mid-1980s illicit and, particularly, licit informal economic activities became so pervasive that they could no longer be ignored by the government, while the CCM remained intransigent on its policy. Dean McHenry refers to this conflict between the CCM and government leadership as one between ideological and pragmatic socialists (1994, 23). The CCM leaders lumped both licit and illicit activities into the same category of "capitalist exploitative" practices and refused to separate the two, thus offending many people who felt they were engaged in legitimate, albeit unlicensed, income-generating activities. Moreover, when efforts were made to curb corruption, they started out with the pretense of targeting the wealthier culprits, but invariably ended up going after the poorer members of society, thus exacerbating tensions between those tied to and protected by the state and those outside those networks. For example, an Economic Sabotage Act was passed in 1983 and revised in 1984 and a National Anti-Economic Sabotage Tribunal was set up to investigate and try offenders of economic crimes like price hiking, hoarding, and smuggling. Initially the efforts of this tribunal were welcomed, but they quickly lost popular support when they became directed against ordinary people, most of whom participated to some degree in these parallel markets. What compounded frustrations was the fact that the largest operators, who were taking advantage of the crisis to make large profit margins, were left untouched by the anticorruption campaign. These actors undoubtedly influenced the shift in the focus of its attack on poor members of society. Similar efforts by the Anti-Corruption Squad to eliminate bribery, embezzlement, and other forms of corruption in the late 1980s drew cynical responses from urban dwellers, who commonly referred to them as the "Corruption Squad."

In contrast to party policy, the government began to encourage workers' projects. In May 1987 President Mwinyi called on workers to start farms, gardens, cattle rearing, and other projects. He said this was a good trend and hoped that more workers would go into such projects. These projects would help to lessen the burden on workers and at the same time help the national economic recovery efforts.[22] The government's changing position was evident also from Mwinyi's comments to university leaders when he said that academics were now permitted to supplement their incomes by cultivating, raising chickens and cows, and other such projects.[23]

Further evidence of a change in government policy came with the issuing of the 1988–1989 budget in June 1988. At that time Finance Minister Cleopa Msuya also mentioned that the government might consider taxing owners of hair salons and other such businesses, apparently referring to the projects of the middle- and upper-income earners. "Don't be surprised if we come to your businesses demanding tax," Msuya warned his fellow members of Parliament as the assembly broke out in laughter.[24] This was yet another indication that the government was softening its position and implicitly acknowledging that most projects of those in middle-income brackets were neither licensed nor taxed because they were skirting the Leadership Code. Frequently civil servants and middle and upper employees underreported their real incomes in paying taxes in order to evade the party's Leadership Code. Admitting to a second income for tax purposes would have been an open admission that they were violating the code.

Although employees were supposed to work at their jobs half a day on Saturdays, it was common knowledge that most considered the weekend a time to catch up on their projects. Attendance at office jobs was especially low on Saturdays. Some workers just made an appearance and then left to attend to their projects. Parliament asked the government to introduce a five-day work week so that workers could undertake activities to supplement their incomes.[25] In May 1991 the president announced a five-day work week, a move that was readily backed by the national trade union.[26] Thus societal noncompliance forced the government to begin acknowledging the real situation, in which the majority of wage earners were pursuing informal sideline incomes and were relying primarily on these incomes as real wages declined.

While the government took pragmatic measures to address the survival needs of workers, the party moved more slowly and cautiously and was more concerned about what was at stake ideologically. Until 1992 the party remained reluctant to condone sideline activities. In response to persistent rumblings within the CCM over the Leadership Code in 1987, Party Chairman Nyerere denied that the party planned to revise the code. One CCM member had asked him whether party and government leaders ought not be able to operate self-help projects like shops and farms to supplement inadequate incomes. Nyerere, sidestepping the issue, responded by saying that leaders would prostitute their offices even if they were allowed to earn side incomes.[27] Herein lay the crux of the difference between the party and government leadership over these sideline incomes: The party leadership equated all second incomes with corruption, whereas the government tended to see sideline jobs as legitimate and necessary activities, given the state of the economy.

Pressures were mounting within the party to review the Leadership Code in light of the changes in the country. Instead, the party leadership launched an aggressive campaign against "corruption" in February 1990. The campaign forced party leaders to list their properties and submit this list to a commission appointed by the Central Committee.[28]

THE ZANZIBAR DECLARATION

Although there had been debates within the CCM regarding the Leadership Code in the late 1980s, it was not until the beginning of the 1990s that internal party differences finally forced the CCM to back down from its ban on second incomes. The code had become an albatross on the backs of many leaders, argue Max Mmuya and Amon Chaligha. Many public officials no longer were involved only in small sideline projects, they had moved on to become large-scale entrepreneurs in the hotel and restaurant business, in the import and export business, in the transport, clearing, and forwarding of traded goods, in retail and wholesale trade, and in manufacturing. The debates over second incomes were part of broader discussions that took place behind closed doors over the continuance of Tanzania's *ujamaa* orientation, the future of parastatals, whether to allow party members to employ workers, property ownership, and other such issues that had been at the heart of the Arusha Declaration (Mmuya and Chaligha 1992, 44, 129).

Finally, in Zanzibar in February 1991, the National Executive Committee of the CCM revised the Arusha Declaration, stating that a party member could draw more than one salary, rent out houses in order to pay back the mortgage, and acquire shares in a private company. The committee's statement, which came to be known as the Zanzibar Declaration, stressed that party members were encouraged to keep livestock, farm, fish, and carry out petty trade. A CCM member could also be employed as a director in a private firm on a full-time basis, and that same person could earn more than one salary if he or she held more than one job.[29] Although it was presented as a "clarification" of the Arusha Declaration rather than a revision of it and as an "adaptation to new social and economic conditions," there is little doubt that the policy change represented a significant shift in ideological orientation. The Zanzibar Declaration was an attempt by the CCM to gain popularity at a time when the debate over multiparty politics was in full force and the future of the CCM was increasingly coming into question.

The Arusha Declaration had been designed to check self-aggrandizement among party ranks at a time when people could buy food and save part of their earnings, the president said in a February 1991 speech. He pointed out that "due to prevailing economic difficulties in the country, the government could not afford to give civil servants, parastatal employees and party leaders adequate pay." Therefore, according to the president, it was illogical to restrict people who engaged in income-generating activities after their official working time.

The public debate that followed the abandonment of the Leadership Code indicated that there were still significant forces in the party that did not approve of the changes and believed that this new orientation would lead to the widening of the gap between the rich and the poor in Tanzania. Many felt that it was tantamount to the dismantling of the Arusha Declaration. Others welcomed the move and called on the party to apologize to people who had been removed from leadership for opposing the declaration.[30] For the most part, however, it was simply a matter of legitimating what had already been going on for years and of doing away with the hypocrisy.

Apart from merely legalizing activities that were already widespread, the rejection of the Leadership Code also paved the way for the taxation of second incomes that previously could not be reported because people were hiding their businesses to avoid losing their formal jobs. Soon after the Leadership Code was dropped, new measures were taken to curb tax evaders. But most importantly, the Zanzibar Declaration represented a clear ideological retreat and helped lay the basis for the move toward multiparty politics.

CONCLUSIONS

The most important consequence of the Zanzibar Declaration was the practical acknowledgement that not all informal activities to supplement incomes were undermining the political order and the economy and that many activities involved the creation of new products and services vital to the survival of urban dwellers. Economic liberalization more generally had the effect of beginning to undermine state monopolies that had been a breeding ground for the illicit informal economy, although as long as there was a gross imbalance between formal wages and the cost of living it is unlikely that these activities would subside significantly. The distinction between *mipango* and *miradi* is not clear-cut, but the experience of the 1980s and 1990s in Tanzania has shown that failure to try to disaggregate various activities within the informal economy led to policies that did not correspond to the economic realities people faced. Moreover, it exacerbated feelings among local people that leaders were perpetuating a state of hypocrisy by demanding that people not engage in licit informal activities while they themselves engaged not only in licit activities but also illicit informal economic activities. The differences between *mipango* and *miradi* also had class dimensions, because those who were best situated in the public sector or government-owned companies had the greatest opportunity to engage in *mipango* involving bribery, embezzlement, and other forms of corruption at the expense of the poor.

8 Conflicting Visions

There are three kinds of laws in this world. The first one is spiritual. These are God's laws. These can't be changed. The second kind of law is of the government, and these laws can be changed since they are made by people. The third kind of law is that of *utu* [humanity]. These laws are obviously lacking when you see this kind of behavior by the militia.

> Charcoal trader, commenting on the
> City Council militia's harassment of women vendors

I had boarded a minibus after waiting the usual hour in the hot sun and then scrambled, along with everyone else, to climb on. The bus was over-crowded, as always, and we were anxious to take off so that a little air could circulate through the glassless windows. On this particular day a woman with a basketful of fish also boarded the bus. She had bought the fish at the nearby "ferry" fish market. She was taking them home, the way hundreds of women do every day, to fry and sell along the roadside in the evening at a little stall lit with a small *kibatari* kerosene lamp. The ticket collector told her to get off the bus immediately because "his" minibus was not allowed to take passengers with fish. The woman refused to get off. The rest of us were all standing and sweating in the bus, which was not moving.

To my amazement, people in various corners of the bus started to make little speeches. None of the speakers could see the woman—or even the ticket collector, for that matter. "Who do you think you are?" shouted one passenger at the ticket collector. "You think you're someone big and important," another passenger said. "You act as though you owned the bus." People shouted: "You're just like the rest of us. You're no different." "Let the woman stay on the bus! She's just trying to feed her children like the rest of us." After five minutes of such criticism from the passengers, the conductor relented, and the woman with the fish was allowed to stay on the bus. The passengers cheered, and the bus took off.

When Tanzania embarked on its path of socialism based on equality, self-reliance, and communalism, it began to tap into various principles shared by the population. As the story above suggests, the urban poor share many norms of fairness, justice, and egalitarianism. Indeed, Nyerere garnered much of the initial popular support for his *ujamaa* policies by addressing some of these fundamental societal values, with which people could easily identify. But gradually many Tanzanians began to believe that these stated ideals were nothing more than a veneer for party and government dominance and an assertion of control in ways they felt were unwarranted. Where the government's policies interfered with their ability to earn a living or to grow food, as we have seen in this study, people refused to comply.

This resistance did not mean that people rejected the basic underlying intent or ideals of *ujamaa*. But they did oppose the way it was implemented, and they did reject it when it violated principles of economic justice and their basic right to subsistence. For example, many expressed to me that the harassment of youth and women vendors by the City Council militia over licenses was simply unacceptable. It challenged the most basic notions of what it is to be human, as the quotation at the beginning of the chapter suggests. And so what one increasingly found by the end of the 1980s was a conflict between the state and sectors of society over what the "norms of fairness" should be; that is, a conflict over the rules of the game. The norm had been violated, and the violation was manifested in noncompliance, especially when it had to do with economic activities.

THE LIMITS OF REFORM

As the government began to respond to external and internal pressures for reform, it had to weigh the relative costs it would incur in popular support as well as in the backing of key players, including the party leaders, parastatal managers, and others who potentially had the most to lose from such changes. The pace, direction, and prioritization of the reforms reflect these competing pressures. The first measures adopted in the 1980s involved merely relaxing the enforcement of various policies that most directly affected urban dwellers' pursuit of a livelihood. Often the laws were not amended on the books but simply were no longer enforced. Some of the first steps included efforts to help make people's day-to-day lives a measure easier: for example, the privatization of buses in 1986, which helped people travel to work; lifting restrictions on the interregional movement of small quantities of food in 1984, which led to the greater availability of food in the cities; external trade liberalization in 1984, which gave people the psychological boost of seeing goods on the shelves again after years with few consumer items and few inputs for their projects; ending enforcement of the Human Resources Deployment Campaign in 1984; and licensing small businesses in 1985. Had these measures not been taken prior to the austerity measures of the 1986 Economic Recovery Programme and the IMF agreement, the government's reforms would have faced considerably greater resistance.

The reforms that were slower in being adopted included the dismantling of some parastatals, the privatization of others, and the granting of permission to private investors to build companies that would directly compete with government-owned companies that had enjoyed monopoly status (such as tourist hotels and breweries). The reluctance came from those tied into patronage networks who had personally benefited and profited from maintaining the monopoly status of the parastatals. The other area in which there had been reluctance to change was in relinquishing policies that were closely associated with the ideological premises of the party leadership. Nevertheless, in the end even the Leadership Code of the Arusha Declaration, one of the linchpins of the socialist orientation of the country, was dismantled.

Although it was relatively simple for the government to ease up on the enforcement of various prohibitions and for the president to encourage people to engage in projects, few positive measures were taken to actually assist people in their endeavors. The government's continuing emphasis on large-scale industry at the expense of small-scale industry reflected the way in which local interests and self-help efforts were overlooked. Large-scale industry, for example, registered negative growth rates throughout the 1980s and was operating at 20 percent capacity in the late 1980s, largely due to its dependence on foreign exchange. In the early 1990s industry fared slightly better, but its -0.5 percent contribution to the growth of the GDP in 1993 still fell below its 0.4 percent contribution two decades earlier, in 1973 (World Bank 1995, 38–39). Large-scale industry suffered from machine breakdowns, frequent power cuts, lack of spare parts and raw materials, declining working capital, and delays in importing inputs. Economic analyses were quick to point out these weaknesses in Tanzania's economy, while ignoring some of the most important developments in small-scale industry that would have revealed some of the strengths of production in Tanzania.

While large-scale industrial production declined, small-scale production was growing at an unprecedented rate, accommodating markets that the formal industry could no longer serve, offering more affordable goods, and providing individuals with work and livable incomes that large-scale manufacturers could no longer sustain. Because small-scale production depended largely on local resources and technology, not on imports, it was less vulnerable to external shocks. Thus, while the formal industrial sector experienced the worst declines in the history of Tanzania, the small-scale producers were increasing in numbers and expanding their businesses.

However, for most, the broader liberalization and privatization measures did not include policies that would have created an environment more conducive to the forms of small-scale production in which they engaged. Instead, the policies were aimed at the more visible and large-scale industries. People continued to operate under considerable constraints in an environment that did not encourage small, income-generating activities. They faced licensing and tax disincentives (paying such fees necessitated paying bribes, for example), and then they faced militia harassment because they did not have licenses. Moreover, taxes on produced goods could be high, with no differentiation made with respect to the size of the production unit. Many of these businesses, especially those of the poor, were so new and precarious that taxes of this kind could destroy them altogether. Access to credit for micro- and small-scale entrepreneurs was virtually nonexistent in urban areas. People who generally bought small quantities of inputs or equipment frequently had to pay for them at very high prices, unlike those operating in the formal sector, who had greater access to inputs at low prices because they could buy in bulk or were well connected. All of these factors served as disincentives for the urban self-employed, who were showing remarkable staying power through their own self-reliant efforts.

One of the main restraints on economic liberalization throughout the 1980s was the party, which by the early 1990s had retreated from an overt position of dominance by opening the door to multipartyism. But prior to this, as the government began responding to the interests of some sectors while leaving others out in the cold, conflicts emerged between those who favored reforms and those who were opposed to them. The sharpest rift that had emerged in the 1980s was between the party and the government leadership, although for the most part the tensions were defused by the announcement of a multiparty system in 1992. Government leaders believed that it would be virtually impossible to reverse the liberalizing trends set in motion in the mid-1980s. At the same time, they had not entirely abandoned Nyerere's ideal of egalitarianism and concern for the redistribution of wealth, but they believed it should be done through taxation. They believed that the Leadership Code needed revision and that second incomes needed to be accepted as a reality of life for Tanzanian urban dwellers. Private enterprises should be officially acknowledged, making it possible to tax and regulate these businesses, some of which were quite lucrative. As long as people had to hide them for fear of being reported to the party and subsequently losing their job or a promotion, they were unlikely to report them to tax officials.

In contrast, the party leadership generally attributed the growing income differentials in Tanzania to corruption. Although there is no question that corruption increased during the crisis years, the party's stance obscured an important dimension of the dilemma regarding informal incomes. In fact, at least two broad categories of activities constituted the informal economy. One involved licit activities in the creation of products, in the provision of services, and in sales, trade, and transport, for which there were legal counterparts. In contrast to these activities, which involved the creation of new resources, illicit informal economic activities involved the diversion of resources from state institutions and the abuse of one's position (usually a public one) for one's own advantage through corrupt practices. By lumping together the two kinds of economic activities, there was a tendency to ignore the economic potential of various informal economic activities and at the same time neglect measures that would eliminate the sources of corruption.

With the view that corruption was at the heart of the widening income differences, the party initiated a clampdown on leaders who had sideline businesses in March 1990 and forced them to declare their sources of income. The government, on the other hand, believing state monopoly and heavy handed restrictions on economic activity to be the main source of corruption, targeted managers of unprofitable and inefficient government institutions and parastatals. They also undercut the parallel currency markets by devaluing the shilling and undercut those smuggling gold out of the country by paying miners prices higher than the official exchange rate. By the mid-1980s the party and the government had veered in diametrically opposed directions, but by the early 1990s the party began to loosen control.

Many of those who opposed economic reforms were concerned that these measures had been taken at the expense of the poor. They feared that Tanzania would forfeit the gains it had made in narrowing the gap in formal incomes and in fostering an ethic of equality within the country's political culture.

In spite of the state's professed concern for the poor and for equality, ordinary urban dwellers continued to find themselves in constant conflict with the state over how to ensure economic justice and a more equitable distribution of resources. Class divisions had become exacerbated, and there was a growing sense of "us poor people at the bottom," as people frequently referred to themselves in relation to those who were better off. This was reflected in the story at the beginning of the chapter about the passengers on the bus, which shows the strong sense of empathy and identification of interests among urban workers, agricultural producers, and those active in the informal sector. Most workers and self-employed people understood in a profound way what the daily struggle to find food for one's family was all about.

When people chose to violate laws that infringed on their ability to obtain a living, they were acting out of a moral imperative that they believed gave them the right to subsistence regardless of the dictates of state policy. Many believed that the "norm of fairness" that Margaret Levi (1990) described had been violated and that the least the government could do was to let them pursue an honest living. Thus the dilemma for those involved in the informal economy in the 1990s was how to create economic, political, and moral climates and institutions that would be more conducive to their interests.

ECONOMIC AND POLITICAL LIBERALIZATION IN TANZANIA

The conflict over economic institutions culminated at the beginning of the 1990s in Tanzania in a conflict over political liberalization. The persistence of various forms of informal economic activities and the transformation of associational life in Tanzania provided pressure points that formally and informally, openly and through noncompliance, forced the state to change or reconsider its rules.

In some instances the government reversed its curtailment of various organizations. Crop authorities, for example, were returned to cooperatives in 1982, although they were still constrained by the government. The Local Government Act reinstituted the urban authorities in 1982, and local governments were strengthened by a 1984 revision of the nation's constitution. The central government, however, continued its supervision of local governments by overseeing the selection of administrators who ran local governments and by approving tax raises and budget proposals (Kulaba 1989, 229). By the late 1980s associations were given greater leeway to form or reconstitute themselves as the party began to loosen its ties to the labor, cooperative, women's, parents, and youth associations it had controlled.

Individuals believed that the atmosphere was more open, and they were not as afraid of being spied on and reported on by the wide network of spies (*shushu*). As one retired business executive remarked in 1988: "In the past two years we have felt freer to express ourselves. If we read the newspaper we see things explained the way they are. Not like in the past where we read an account of something and knew it was a lie."[1] The press opened up considerably, and many new publications emerged for sale on the streets of Dar es Salaam. Perhaps most significantly, the party began to relinquish its hold.

Meanwhile, the top leadership of the party and the government began to veer in opposite directions, largely over disputes regarding the Arusha Declaration, over economic-reform policies, and over privatization. Julius Nyerere had been both president and party chairman until he relinquished the presidency to Ali Hassan Mwinyi in 1985, while retaining the party chairmanship. After stepping down, he became increasingly critical of complacency in his own party and corruption in government, attributing much of the corruption to the economic-reform policies being pursued by his successor. High-level corruption and the erosion of CCM legitimacy intensified during Mwinyi's presidency, and Nyerere was eager to stem these trends.

Conflicts between the party and the government leadership over the country's economic policies took an unexpected turn in 1990, when Nyerere started an open debate about the possibility of creating a multiparty regime. Nyerere, who had been adamant in his insistence on one-party rule in the past, suggested in February 1990 that Tanzania become a multiparty state, claiming that the party leaders were closer to their offices and desks than to the people.[2] His remarks were followed by a debate in the newspapers over the future of the one-party system.

Later in the year, frustrated in his efforts to put a break on economic reform, Nyerere announced his early retirement from the chairmanship of the party in August 1990. By 1992 the party had announced that it would relinquish its dominance as the sole party in Tanzania, and the first national multiparty elections were scheduled for 1995. In order to move toward multipartyism, the party had to disentangle the many ties that blended party and government functions. For example, members of defense and security forces no longer would be required to belong to the party. Similarly, the National Executive Committee of the party decided to separate the dual functions of district and regional commissions and those of the party to pave the way for a multiparty political system. The abandonment of the Leadership Code was also necessary in order to separate service in public institutions and government-owned companies from party control.

It is interesting to note that this opening toward political liberalization was spearheaded by opponents of vigorous economic reform in the CCM. Nyerere believed that multipartyism might inject a greater level of accountability into the political process. However, government leaders who had backed economic-reform policies reluctantly went along with the political-reform measures, and they showed little interest in taking the process of political reform farther after the 1992 decision to register opposition parties. These government leaders hoped they would be able to garner greater support by exhibiting tolerance toward opposition at a time when pressures were mounting for multipartyism throughout Africa. They also banked on being able to maintain control of the political-reform process. But the general lack of commitment by the Mwinyi administration to political reform became evident as religious, media, legal, women's, and other such associations began to push to expand the scope of the reforms beyond multipartyism to include greater freedom of speech and association. Thus the impetus for political reform initially arose out of an intraelite conflict over economic reform and the future of private capital in Tanzania.

STATE AND SOCIETY IN AFRICA

Until the 1990s much of the literature dealing with state-society relations in Africa focused on questions having to do with why the state was unable to enforce its regulations, to make decisions independent of social forces, to secure clear-cut hegemony over intermediary and local political actors, to extract resources from most agricultural producers, and to claim ideological legitimacy (Forrest 1988, 423). The discussion frequently centered on the "soft" or "weak" state, on how to achieve greater "state autonomy," and on problems of "state penetration of society" (see, for example, Callaghy 1984; Lemarchand 1988; Rothchild 1987).

Many of the issues were framed from the point of view of the state, with the view that state capacity was contingent simply on the state's autonomy from internal and external actors rather than also on why people refused to grant legitimacy to the state. Yet, in a country like Tanzania, the more the state tried to assert its autonomy by adopting an interventionist posture, the less it was able to affect change in the intended direction. Although part of this apparent paradox can be explained by taking into account the limitations imposed by the world economy on the Tanzanian state's capacity to act, a close study of the policies the government failed to implement also shows a state that was becoming increasingly irrelevant to the society it sought to rule. Thus the debate about state weakness failed to address a key component of the question because it did not sufficiently consider the problem from a societal perspective, asking why and how majorities of people refuse to comply with state regulations. Societal noncompliance was seen simply as eroding state capacity, making the state's efforts to bring about development even more arduous, and a reflection of the deepseatedness of a "primordial" and "affective" ethos.

With the deepening economic crisis and the concomitant decline in state capacity, many Africanists began to shift their focus and place greater emphasis on society and its responses to state decline (Azarya 1988; Bratton 1989; Chazan 1982; Hyden 1983; Kasfir 1984; MacGaffey 198; C. Newbury 1986; Nzongola-Ntalaja 1986). This approach broadened the scope of actors and of what could be called political participation. One of the reasons for this shift in analysis was the movement toward redefining politics and power relations in a more reciprocal and interactive fashion. Naomi Chazan and Donald Rothchild, for example, argue that to understand politics it is necessary to reject a mechanistic view that pits state against society. Rather, it is necessary to look at the weblike structure of the social landscape and go beyond the official and visible, focusing on the interactive and dynamic (1987). Goran Hyden, similarly, began to develop a "governance" view of political development in which it becomes "significant when political actors challenge existing structures and succeed in transforming them." Governance, according to Hyden, expands opportunities for constructive reciprocities between the rulers and the ruled rather than perpetuating power relations in a hierarchical, asymmetrical fashion (1992).

My study of the relationship between the informal economy and the state shares with this body of literature a focus on state-society interactions and reciprocities. It looked at the impact of the informal economy on changing state agendas at a time when the state was particularly vulnerable to mounting internal and external pressures. By making these linkages between international and domestic events, micro- and macrolevel developments, this study explored the complex mechanisms of state-society accommodations and changing boundaries of state control. The web of significant actors that I wove into this discussion of economic reform included individual household members, ethnic groups, classes, nongovernmental and voluntary organizations, the government, the ruling party, the private sector, international financial institutions, and foreign donors.

IN PURSUIT OF CIVIL SOCIETY

More recently, the study of state-society relations has shifted to a discourse that emphasizes the engagement of the state with various sectors of society, namely civil society. This debate was reinforced in the late 1990s as country after country in Africa began to show signs of political liberalization in the form of administrative, constitutional, party, and other reforms. Problems of democratic transition (Bratton and van de Walle 1994; Chege 1992), movements for democratic reforms (Bratton and van de Walle 1992), governance (Hyden and Bratton 1992; Joseph 1990), civil society (Bayart 1986; Chazan 1994; Fatton 1992; Harbeson and others 1994; Lewis 1992), and societal limits on political liberalization (Lemarchand 1992) began to dominate the intellectual agenda.

This study departs in crucial ways from many of the concerns of the literature on civil society and democratization in Africa. In fact, the informal economy operates within an associational context that challenges many of the assumptions being made about civil society and its potential as a generator of political liberalization. In the civil society debate it appears that the modernization barometer has been revived as African associational life is frequently described as fragmented, defensive, parochial, sectional, factional, marginal, lacking accountability, and in need of promoting "habits of conciliation and compromise" (Lewis 1992, 45, 47, 52–53). The assumption that associational life is defensive and marginal raises the questions, marginal to whom? Defensive by whose standards? Certainly not to the people who depend on their associational links to sustain themselves and who have to actively find their own means of subsistence each day.

Some have mistakenly sought in Africa a civil society that resembles Western organizational forms. One Finnish scholar visited Tanzania in the early 1990s in pursuit of associations that could be said to constitute a civil society. He was sorely disappointed and returned to Finland believing that there were none to be found. If civil society means Western-style organizations, they are indeed few and far between in Tanzania. But does that mean that the changes in associational life, especially in informal organizations and the expansion of the informal economy, have no political significance?

Equally problematic is the search for a civil society that could not possibly exist anywhere in the world. In other words, the standards for what constitutes a civil society are so extreme that no society could live up to such expectations. Jean-François Bayart, for example, has argued that "civil society exists only in so far as there is a self-consciousness of its existence and of its opposition to the state" (Bayart 1986, 117). It is difficult to imagine that there is any civil society anywhere that is conscious of itself, let alone of its opposition to the state.

Civil society, by most accounts, is the sector of society (such as businesses, associations) that interacts most closely with the state but remains independent of it. The problem with focusing on civil society is the tendency to define the whole of society by a group of people who have been most associated with patronage practices because of their proximity to positions of power. For example, René Lemarchand has argued that "the personal rule that characterizes Africa's neopatrimonial states tends by its very nature to impede the formation of any associations not based on personal patronage, ethnic and kinship affiliations, or kickbacks." Patronage creates links between state institutions and families, clans, or ethnoregional groups, thereby making bargaining between state and society a "singularly futile enterprise" (Lemarchand 1992, 104–5). Again, although it is all too obvious that patronage and corruption based on ethnicity and kinship have seriously undermined the effectiveness of the state, it does not follow from this that all associations are based on patronage or a primary affiliation. This does not describe many of the new associations that have emerged at the local level and are tied to the expansion of income-generating activities, especially in the urban areas. Moreover, ethnicity and kinship do not form the only or even the main basis for organizational affiliation in the urban setting, even in a country as polarized along religious and ethnic lines as Uganda (Tripp 1994a).

There is a tendency to assume that all people have access to state resources through patronage ties, when in fact this represents only a fraction of the population, even in the urban areas. Most, however, have to manage using their own resources. As Gavin Williams has pointed out, "What is striking about many African countries is how little trickles down to the worse off through the patronage network and how much sticks to a few hands at the top" (1987, 639).

THE INFORMAL ECONOMY AND LOCAL GOVERNANCE

Although some scholars have begun to make some of the necessary distinctions, I believe we still lack adequate empirical studies of Africa's indigenous entrepreneurs and associations that link micro- and macrolevels of analysis in a way that engenders useful generalizations about the nature of state-society relations. One of the most promising lines of inquiry is an exploration of how this second economy contains a parallel or "second politics," as Frank Kunz puts it, which involves the creation of voluntary neighborhood governments and rural grassroots movements that produce alternative institutions of decision making, drawing on customary notions of justice, fairness, and political obligation (1991, 232–33). The same sentiment is expressed by Bayart, who argues also for looking at politics at the local level: "Africa's potential for democracy is more convincingly revealed by the creation of small collectives established and controlled by rural and urban groups (such as local associations) than by parliaments and parties, instruments of the state, of accumulation and of alienation. These new political mediations will be evolved by Africans themselves, on their own" (1986, 125).

The institutional framework of the informal economy is an attempt by people to govern their economic life, their livelihood, and their destinies. It is an attempt to claim greater political inclusiveness and to participate directly in solving problems of economic hardship. It challenges the authorities to recognize and include them as full, functioning members of a political, economic, and legal order without pushing them back into informality. My concern is that if we look only at the dysfunctional aspects of the informal economy and if we only use the Western yardstick to measure the "level of development of various associations" we may fail to recognize many of the actual transformations that have occurred, which in a country like Tanzania could be considered major social transformations.

A FEW CONCLUDING REMARKS

The changes Tanzania experienced in the 1980s and early 1990s provide opportunities for fresh examination of problems of governance and bringing about state-society accommodations. The government, while operating under enormous external constraints that threatened to undermine the state itself, was forced to respond to quiet pressures from below to lessen the blow of the austerity measures tied to economic reform. Many of these readjustments, in turn, led both to an opening up of the political arena to the possibilities of greater pluralism and to the emergence of societal tensions that had been suppressed.

Much of the discussion throughout this study has dealt with the imbalances and distortions brought about by excessive state centralization and top-down policy making. I have shown how the informal economy diverted demands that otherwise would have been placed on a government which by the 1980s had little to offer in the way of resources. People formed new organizations and networks for self-reliance and cooperation to deal with problems, like local security, that they could no longer rely on the government to provide. At the same time, the government faced enormous pressures from foreign donors and international financial institutions to carry out economic restructuring. These external constraints necessitated vigorous austerity measures that could have cost the leaders an ever-greater loss of legitimacy they could ill afford. With little left to bargain with domestically, the government began to relax its rules and in some cases even changed its rules to allow people more room to pursue their own survival strategies. These survival strategies allowed for broad shifts in government policy, and at times they were even the main motivating factor behind some of the changes toward economic liberalization.

Most important, the informal economy and the associations tied to it were mechanisms to assert self-governance and to challenge the top-down style of governing that treated ordinary people as though they did not have any wisdom to contribute to their own economic and political development. The informal economy is not a residual economic sector to be treated as an afterthought in policy making. Its existence challenges an economic and political order that keeps significant numbers of people from legal involvement in the economy, that bolsters large-scale industry at the expense of small-scale manufacturing in a country where the former has declined while the latter has expanded, and that places unnecessary regulations and tax burdens on a sector that sees these fees as undermining their efforts to survive while they receive little in return for their payments.

This interactive view of state-society relations challenges many of the state-centric views of African politics, which have dwelt simply on the structural constraints leading to state weakness and decline while ignoring actor agency and the dynamic processes that can break through the inertia of the state. The adoption of noncompliant strategies meant that people took charge of the difficult financial predicaments in which they found themselves by ignoring state regulations that interfered with their ability to survive. The impact of hundreds of thousands of people pursuing various "individual" solutions did indeed have a collective impact that the government was forced to recognize. They challenged the rules of the game and by doing so were able to bring about various institutional changes. By involving themselves in informal projects, workers, women, children, the elderly, civil servants, professionals, and other sectors of society changed not only the landscape of a city but also the boundaries of political control.

Research Methods

The objective of the study was to document the growth of new dimensions in Tanzania's urban informal economy in response to the economic crisis of the late 1970s and 1980s. In particular, the study focused on the increase in informal income-generating activities of household members as a result of the decline in real wages. Beyond these empirical changes, the study sought to demonstrate that the informal economy itself was a catalyst for political and economic change, pressuring the state from below.

The bulk of the study was carried out in Dar es Salaam between 1987 and 1988, with subsequent visits to Tanzania in 1990 and 1994. I was assisted by a Tanzanian woman, Salome Mjema, who was working toward her master's degree in political science at the University of Dar es Salaam. Born and raised in Dar es Salaam as a Zaramo, she is intimately familiar with the city's people and culture. I was also raised in Tanzania, having lived and gone to school there from 1960 to 1974. As a youth, I spent considerable time with my mother, Marja-Liisa Swantz, as she carried out anthropological fieldwork in Bunju, a rural village north of Dar es Salaam. I was fortunate to be able to draw on these experiences in carrying out my fieldwork fourteen years later.

The study involved two key sets of actors: those involved in informal economic activities and representatives of the ruling Chama Cha Mapinduzi Party and the government. I believed it was necessary to devise a research design that would combine both quantitative and qualitative methodologies. I was most concerned with trying to unravel people's perceptions of their activities and the decisions they made, especially in relation to the state. Given the sensitivity of the subject, many of these kinds of observations would not have been possible in a survey setting and required informal inquiry and interactions. Even in discussions with government and CCM leaders, some of the most revealing comments were made in informal discussions rather than in formal interviews.

To examine the societal dynamics, we began by carrying out hundreds of unstructured interviews with people involved in informal-sector activities throughout the city. I then developed a more formal questionnaire and used it in a cluster sample survey in Manzese and Buguruni, two large sections of the city populated by workers and people engaged in informal small businesses. We used the same questionnaire to conduct a snowball survey of the households of middle-income employees with sideline jobs, with the aim of better understanding the class component of this informal economy. All of the interviews were conducted in Swahili.

In addition to the formal survey in Buguruni and Manzese, we had numerous impromptu group discussions with young men, elderly and retired men, middle-aged workers, gangsters (identified as such by other residents), housewives, prostitutes, and various other people. These interviews were often quite lively and useful in gaining a perspective on people's lives and concerns.

As part of our effort to study the effect of small businesses on children and youth, we interviewed principals and teachers in Buguruni and Manzese and collected longitudinal data on school enrollment, numbers of standard-7 (seventh grade) school leavers, and numbers of male and female students. We asked teachers about how small businesses affected students' performance in school and how life had changed for young people as a result of new pressures to contribute to the family income. We also asked teachers about their own sideline incomes. In addition, I obtained interviews with nine students and two teachers from six secondary schools throughout the city about the tutorials they had attended or taught over the years. The schools were: Popatlel Secondary School, Kisutu Secondary School, Vituka Technical Secondary School, Kigurunyembe Secondary School, Jangwani Girls School, and Zanaki Secondary School. We asked how much they paid for these tutorials, who paid for them, which classes they had tutorials in, and how the tutorials differed from regular classes in quality.

In Buguruni and Manzese we interviewed religious leaders and other important community figures, as well as leaders and members of local organizations, both formal and informal. These included women involved in projects of the Union of Tanzanian Women; members of the CCM's youth organization, VIJANA; Moslem imams; Ahmadiyya brotherhood leaders;

madarasa Koran school teachers; Catholic and Lutheran ministers and laypeople; organizers of local *sungusungu* defense teams; people running manufacturing and market cooperatives; members of dance societies; the project coordinator of a pilot nutrition center in Uzuri, Manzese (started by the City Council and the Ministry of Agriculture); women involved in *upato* rotating-credit societies; managers of football clubs; and many others. We talked to a young woman in Mferejini, Manzese, who ran an impressive nursery school of eighty children that had been sponsored by the children's parents.

In order to obtain state perspectives on the same phenomenon we interviewed the city director and the regional commissioner, district commissioners, ward leaders, branch leaders, and close to 300 ten-house-cell leaders. At the City Council we spoke to numerous officials, including the city director, the chief economist, and the director of the Nguvu Kazi small-enterprises office. We spoke to leaders of government agencies responsible for assisting small industries, like the Small Industries Development Organization. In addition, I conducted interviews and informal discussions with top-ranking national government and party leaders and their advisers, including two Cabinet members and two party Central Committee members and numerous members of parliament.

To broaden my understanding of the country's recent political and economic changes, I also had extensive discussions with directors and managers of numerous national and multinational corporations, bilateral donor representatives, United Nations Fund for Women (UNIFEM) officials, journalists, editors, academics, foreign diplomats, and other knowledgeable people. I talked to leaders of nongovernmental organizations and networks, voluntary associations, district-development associations, women's associations, professional associations, and business associations.

INITIAL STAGES OF THE STUDY

To familiarize myself with Dar es Salaam's informal sector—with its concerns and problems—I took local buses, with my assistant, to various parts of the city and walked through them. For three months we talked to several hundred people engaged in small businesses in selected areas throughout the city. We went to both heavily and sparsely populated parts of the city, old and newly developed areas, markets, neighborhoods, and business districts to form a picture of some of the variance in the city. We visited Kariakoo, Mnazi Mmoja, Kisutu, Kivukoni, Keko, Changombe, Temeke, Tandika, Buguruni, Ilala, Tandale, Manzese, Mwenge, Kinondoni, and

Mwananyamala. We talked to people involved in countless small businesses, including vendors selling cigarettes, candy, oranges, medicine, shells, brooms, coffee, pastries, ice cream, and fried fish. We also talked to market sellers, signwriters, mechanics, shoe shiners, tailors, tinsmiths, and frame makers and to people operating restaurants, kiosks, food stalls, hair salons, and other such businesses. We asked them, for example, how long they had been in business, about their home area, their education, their ethnic background, the number of their dependents, how they felt their business was doing, the prices of their products or services, their expenses (fixed and working capital), their daily profit, the hours they worked, and how they started their business. The depth of our interviews depended on how receptive the interviewees were. In general, people were willing to talk, but we had an even better response once we started the formal survey, for we were then being introduced to citizens by local cell leaders. Because the cell leaders were generally respected community members, their introductions helped assuage any suspicions people might have had about us.

From these initial interviews we were able to develop a questionnaire to use in our more formal survey. These interviews gave us experience in talking to people in an unstructured setting and enabled us to discover some of their main concerns. It was also important for us to familiarize ourselves with the terminology peculiar to different occupations, such as specific units of measurement, inputs, and equipment. These talks helped give our study focus. We learned that to capture the changes that had taken place in recent years, we would have to take individual household members as the unit of analysis, not simply the activity itself. We decided that we would pay special attention to households with wage employees because the increase in income-generating activities appeared to be strongly related to the decline in real wages. This was not just a phenomenon of the working class but permeated all strata of employed people, so we also had to study middle- and upper-income people (those whose salary in their formal job was more than TSh 3,000) to see what kinds of sideline activities they engaged in to maintain their standard of living.

As it turned out, these informal interviews gave our study a dimension not obtained in the more formal household survey we conducted. We were able to talk to large numbers of young, male street vendors concentrated downtown in the Kisutu, Kariakoo and Kivukoni areas, which are, according to the City Council Nguvu Kazi officials, prime targets of City Council harassment of vendors. Because these youth work long hours, we met few in their home areas while doing the formal survey. For this reason we tried to interview as many vendors as we could downtown, many of whom resided in the same areas we surveyed.

The decision to take household members as the unit of analysis is different from previous informal-sector studies in Tanzania that looked at the activities themselves as the unit of analysis (Aboagye 1985; Bagachwa 1981, 1982; Bagachwa and Ndulu 1989; Bienefeld 1974; Sabot 1974; Sporrek 1985). The surveys by Mboya Bagachwa and A. A. Aboagye used official lists of registered enterprises for their sampling frames. These scholars, however, excluded from the sample all unlicensed, unregistered microenterprises (99 percent in Dar es Salaam), including the sideline businesses of middle-income workers and most enterprises run by women and youth.

When I developed my questionnaire, I realized that I would be using it to find out about many different kinds of activities and decided that I should use the same schedule but remain flexible. It would be better for purposes of comparison to keep one questionnaire. Because my study was exploratory and quantification was only one of my concerns, I would also use the questionnaire as a starting point, where possible, for more in-depth discussions.

The questionnaire was primarily an extension of the questions asked in the informal interviews. It also included some questions drawn from the studies by Manfred Bienefeld and Mboya Bagachwa, which I wanted to compare with my results.

SNOWBALL SURVEY

We initially used the questionnaire in a smaller survey of middle-income civil servants. These people were reluctant to admit their sideline incomes, not only because they were evading taxation and registration but also because the party Leadership Code forbade such enterprises on the part of the employee and his or her spouse. Workers with whom I spoke feared being discovered with a sideline job, even though they were no longer harassed, questioned, or spied on as they had been in the early 1980s. To register their enterprises would have been an admission of having a second income, and it was feared that this admission could jeopardize their formal jobs.

For this reason I chose to conduct a snowball survey with this group of people, because trust was vital to the success and accuracy of these interviews. We would contact one person with a sideline income, interview him or her, and, at the end of the interview, ask for the names of three of his or her friends who were also engaged in sideline activities. We would then contact the three friends, interview them, and obtain additional names from them.

About two-thirds of these interviews were conducted at home. The other third was conducted at work, usually after hours, where it was clear the work environment would not interfere with the interview process. Typically our interviews lasted about an hour. One set of snowball interviews led to a visit from one apartment to the next in a building complex in Oyster Bay. These people all worked at the same place, but each household we visited was involved in its own individual sewing business. The visual impact was striking, to say the least. The projects of most of the people with whom we talked in the snowball interviews differed substantially from those who lived in the working-class–informal-sector areas of the city. They were involved in keeping poultry, animal husbandry, farming, running hair salons, importing chicks, running kiosks, selling cigarettes at inflated prices to street vendors, and teaching tutorials. Because most were university trained, they were familiar with the concept of research and generally were responsive to our questions. They believed that their confidentiality would be respected, so we were able to obtain from them detailed information on their projects and candid opinions of party policy on sideline incomes. Most were proud of their efforts and flattered to be interviewed.

CLUSTER SAMPLE SURVEY

Selection of the Survey Site

We used the same questionnaire in both Buguruni and Manzese. We selected these two areas in order to capture some of the variance in Dar es Salaam. Buguruni is an older part of the city, whereas Manzese, incorporated in 1975, developed as an informal settlement outside the city boundary. Thus the inhabitants of Buguruni generally are more established migrants or children of these older migrants. Some are descendants of the original inhabitants of the area. The area is dominated by the main coastal ethnic group, the Zaramo, who make up about half of the population of Buguruni. Manzese, on the other hand, is the home of more recent arrivals to the city and is a mix of some forty-seven ethnic groups. The Luguru, the largest ethnic group, make up about 20 percent of Manzese's population, according to my survey. The influence of the Luguru, who are energetic farmers, can be seen in the greater number of farmers in Manzese than in Buguruni.

Even though we were especially interested in changes in households with workers, we opted to conduct the interviews in people's homes rather than at their workplaces. A number of factors influenced that decision. It would be too easy for a worker to deny having a sideline income if asked at work, whereas at home, people's projects were usually visible, making denial much more difficult. We found that it was generally easier to talk about a project on location because the surroundings prompted more intelligent questions on our part. It was also easier for the respondents to explain what they did with various equipment at hand. Moreover, it gave us the added visual impact of knowing the scale of the operation, the working conditions, and the general setting. Because many of the projects were carried out by the wife, elderly members of the family, and even the children, the home setting gave us an opportunity to talk with a variety of household members and not just the employee, who was most likely male. Finally, it enabled us to compare employees with those who were not employed and with those who had left jobs to engage in self-employment or farming.

Selection of the Sample and Administration of the Survey

In order to carry out the survey, we obtained permit letters (incidentally, with no difficulty), from the offices of the regional commissioner, the district commissioner, the ward, and the branch. At the branch we obtained a list of cell leaders. We selected every other cell leader on the list and requested an interview with each, along with one resident from the cell. We asked the cell leader to take us to the house to the left of his or her house and interviewed the first resident of that house whom we encountered.

We were accompanied by the party secretary in the branch or, more commonly, by someone from the party youth organization. The individuals who so kindly took us around the branches usually did so for several days at a time. We came to know and trust one another quite well, so that as time went on they often would speak frankly about life in their branch. These people came to be our key informants: they were helpful in letting us know how reliable our interview responses were, in giving us background on the branch and the various individuals we had interviewed, and in explaining the problems people faced in their area.

The cell leaders were also cooperative. Our interviews with them ranged in length from fifteen to ninety minutes. We asked them about the number of houses in their cells, the number of households (these numbers are known because the food-rationing system in the city requires each cell leader to keep track of his or her households), length of service as cell leaders, when they first came to the area, what individual residents in their cells do to make a living, problems in the cells, how well the food-distribution system works, their personal views on licensing and the functioning of the licensing system for small businesses, and the number of women owning houses in the cells and how they obtained them. Not all cell leaders were available when we needed to see them: Some had gone to the countryside to farm; others came back late at night because they not only worked as employees but also were running other businesses. In these instances we would speak to their assistants, wives, or closest relatives—all of whom, we were told, were the responsible representatives if the cell leader was absent. The main purpose of talking to the cell leaders or their representatives was to obtain permission to speak to a resident in the cell. Interviews with cell leaders were of secondary importance, so we did not make more of an effort to talk to the cell leaders themselves. Nevertheless, we did succeed in interviewing about 65 percent of the actual cell leaders.

The interviews lasted an average of about forty-five minutes, and my assistant and I usually conducted them together. One of us would interview while the other took notes. We alternated in these tasks. Because my assistant related better to women than I did (women were often shy and needed to be drawn out), she interviewed more of them. That we worked as a pair was important not only for purposes of the survey but also for cultural reasons. People rarely go out alone, and they would think it especially strange for a woman to go around alone conducting such a study. Even when my assistant carried out the interview and I took notes, it was important for me to be there to expand the interview in various directions and pursue questions that opened up new issues.

Altogether we conducted 180 citizen interviews in Manzese and 107 in Buguruni. In Manzese we visited branches at Mferejini, Mnazi Mmoja, Midizini, Mwungano, Uzuri, Kilimani and Muembeni, and Mvuleni. In Buguruni, we visited branches at Malapa, Mnyamani, Kisiwani, and Madenge.

Almost everywhere we were met with genuine hospitality, which at times could be overwhelming. Interviewees with little means would buy us sodas they could barely afford. They would invariably thank us for having interviewed them and beg us to come back again. When we passed houses that were not part of our sample, people would often call out: "When are you coming to interview me?" or "When are you coming to our cell? We want to talk to you!" Sometimes they would be offended if we did not interview them. In one cell we could not leave until we had interviewed four different people in addition to our selected resident. They insisted on being interviewed. The last one, a mason, made it clear that he would be deeply hurt if we did not interview him. He pulled out a mat, put it down in front of us, and demanded in a jovial manner that we sit down and talk to him.

Problems Encountered

We were generally pleased with the outcomes of the interviews and believed that people had been forthcoming. I had anticipated that interviewees would underreport their informal incomes. As it turned out, these stated incomes were significantly below the figures the interviewees gave for daily food expenditures. In order to gain a more accurate picture of incomes, I estimated, where possible, the value added for various projects based on reported costs and on comparable data from others involved in the same projects. Combining this information with reported amounts spent on food each day (which I felt were quite accurate), I was able to reconstruct more plausible income levels.

The numbers of residents who refused to be interviewed were exceedingly low. Only 3 people declined to be interviewed; the remaining 287 gave their consent, usually quite enthusiastically. The few residents who agreed only because they did not want to offend us betrayed their reluctance by giving short answers.

Some people preferred to be interviewed outside, on their verandas, rather than inside their homes. This posed another problem because passersby, nosy neighbors, and curious children would crowd around. The interviewees rarely seemed to mind all the public attention because that was how things were in their community. We, however, would ask the onlookers for privacy, often enlisting our guide to try to talk people into leaving, but this was not always possible. When people insisted on crowding around despite our polite pleas to be left alone, we would talk quietly so no one around could hear. Sooner or later they would become bored and would leave us alone.

Data Analysis

Our interviews were coded and input into Reflex Plus spreadsheets. I separated the data into sections (hierarchically organized) on general background and employment history, self-employment history and details on current enterprise, details of second and third enterprises, farming, savings, and occupations of other household members. Key variables were cross-tabulated in statistical analyses using the Systat program for microcomputers.

Reliability of the Data

Our survey included 287 residents (145 men and 142 women). I believe the survey adequately represented Dar es Salaam's population. The survey generally corresponded to census data with respect to gender, marital status, and age. I am relatively confident that the figures for self-employment reflect the general picture because they agree with other surveys carried out during the same period with similar questions on occupation (Kulaba 1989, 212; Tibaijuka 1988). My figures for employment, however, were below the 1984 government estimates for Dar es Salaam. This was probably because many employees worked during the hours we carried out our interviews (between 9 A.M. and 6 P.M.), reducing their likelihood of being interviewed. However, I do not think this bias significantly alters the main findings of this study.

The majority of workers in our sample (75 percent) worked for parastatals (state companies) or for government institutions. The largest number were concentrated in the manufacturing sector (51 percent), working in light industries (textiles, shoes, breweries, suitcases, fishnet, farm tools, or mirrors). Other occupations included guards, truck drivers, street cleaners, dockworkers, mechanics, clerks, military, construction workers, domestic servants, teachers, and nurses.

ELITE INTERVIEWS

To learn about CCM views on the informal economy, we interviewed not only ten-house-cell leaders but also local leaders at the party branch level. We carried out extensive interviews with the party secretaries (appointed), party chairmen (elected), and legal counselors. All of the party branch chairmen in Manzese and Buguruni were male elders of the community. The secretaries, generally in their thirties or forties, were also men, except for two women: one in Buguruni and one in Manzese.

We had no problem talking to leaders at the branch level, for many of them were accustomed to having researchers (though not to foreign researchers) visit their areas. Generally we were greeted with the same Tanzanian warmth and hospitality with which the ordinary citizens treated us. In one branch in Manzese, Uzuri, the party chairman called a meeting of the entire branch Elders Council after we completed our survey in his branch. Much to our surprise, we were treated to orange sodas and a two-and-a-half-hour discussion about the problems and issues facing the branch. One council member said that the fact that a person from another country would come, listen to their problems, and find out so much about their life was an honor for them. Another council member thanked us for our research and trusted that our information would be put to good use to help their situation. He said, "If people were rude to you when you talked to them, it was because they didn't understand fully what you were doing. You just have to say as Jesus did, 'Father forgive them, for they know not what they do.'" No one, of course, was rude to us. In fact, our experience in this branch reflected our open reception throughout the study.

CONCLUSION

I believe there were advantages to our being women. Our gender made it easier to talk to women, especially younger women who tended to be shy. Men did not find us threatening and seemed to view the experience of being interviewed by two women as amusing. My being a foreigner also seemed to have been a plus. We were introduced by local authorities, which gave us a certain amount of credibility. I was told that people would have been more hesitant to talk to me had I been a Tanzanian because as a foreigner I could not be associated with the state in any way.

The entire process of interviewing Dar es Salaam residents was a wonderfully rewarding experience. I learned to appreciate that as hard as people had to work to survive, their ingenuity, persistence, and ability to take things in stride and with humor was truly impressive.

Partial List of Interviews

GOVERNMENT OFFICIALS

Mr. Charle, city director

Barbro Johansson, former member of Parliament

Mr. Kafuka, assistant to the director of Nguvu Kazi (with Marja-Liisa Swantz)

J. B. Kitambi, regional director of administration, Coast Region

Beatrice Kunambi, district commissioner, Temeke

Mary Luwilo, district commissioner, Kinondoni

Gertrude Mongella, minister of lands, tourism and natural resources

Cleopa Msuya, minister of finance and economic planning

Amon Nsekela, director, National Bank of Commerce

C. M. N. Ntabajana, manager of planning and strategy, Small Industries Development Organization

Lawrence Saguti, former assistant to the prime minister

Joseph Sawe, director general, National Land Use Planning Commission

Salome Sijaona, chief economist, City Council

NATIONAL-LEVEL CCM LEADERS

Mr. Luhanzi, assistant director, Control and Discipline Commission

Gertrude Mongella, member, Central Committee

Paulo Sozigwa, member, Central Committee

Joan Wicken, personal assistant to the party chairman, Julius Nyerere

BRANCH-LEVEL CCM LEADERS

Adamu Abdalah Ambari, chairman, Madenge, Buguruni
Mohamed K. Berege, chairman, Malapa, Buguruni
Rashidi R. Ibrahim, secretary, Mvuleni, Manzese
A. Kibugila, secretary, Mwungano, Manzese
Rajabu Kikopa, chairman, Mnyamani, Buguruni
Charles Lilamba, chairman, Kilimani, Manzese
Shabani Malewe, secretary, Midizini, Manzese
Charles Marwa, secretary, Kilimani, Manzese
Issa Masondori, chairman, Midizini, Manzese
Shabani S. Mbanga, secretary, Mnazi Mmoja, Manzese
Issa Mgeni, secretary, Uzuri, Manzese
Cheka Juma Mgogo, secretary, Mferejini, Manzese
Amiri Mlawa, chairman, Kisiwani, Buguruni
Thabiti Athuman Mpendakula, secretary, Madenge, Buguruni
F. A. Nyamesha, secretary, Malapa, Buguruni
Halina Saidi, secretary, Mnyamani, Buguruni
Juma Shabani, chairman, Mnazi Mmoja, Manzese
Shomvi, chairman, Uzuri, Manzese
Saidi Simba, chairman, Mwungano, Manzese
Ali Solozi, chairman, Muembeni, Manzese
Ahmadi Ramadhani Yakuti, chairman, Mferejini, Manzese
Ramadhani R. Zomboki, chairman, Mvuleni, Manzese

LEADERS OF THE UNION OF TANZANIAN WOMEN

Mrs. Mbise, general manager, Tanzania Women's Economic Organization
Thecla Mchauro

REPRESENTATIVES OF THE PRIVATE SECTOR

S. K. George, Tanzania representative of Lohnro (multinational corporation)
Mr. Lupembe, exporter, chairman of the Tanganyika Chamber of Commerce
P. B. Matemba, chairman, Tanganyika Tea Growers Association, former chairman of the Tanganyika Employers Association
Juma Mwapachu, JV Group

Paulo J. Mwazyunga, managing director, Industrial Projects Promotion, Ltd. (IPP)

Charles Nsekela, Industrial Projects Promotion, Ltd. (IPP), Pen Company

MISCELLANEOUS INTERVIEWEES

Priest at the Catholic Church, Manzese
Yusa Lui, teacher, Kilimani Primary School, Manzese
Rev. Gehas Malasusa, pastor, Lutheran Church, Buguruni
Mrs. Minyala, headmistress, Ukombozi Primary School
Mzee Maulidi, imam, Malapa, Buguruni
Karama Mlawa, headmaster, Uzuri Primary School
Richard Mwambe, headmaster, Buguruni Primary School
Jafari Nassoro, cell leader, Manzese market

Key Activities in Dar es Salaam's Informal Economy

CRAFTS AND MANUFACTURING

Durable Goods

Tailoring: repairing secondhand clothing, clothes, pillow covers, sofa covers, bags

Blacksmithing: knives, stoves, kitchen utensils, small hoes, *kibatari* kerosene lamps, flutes

Wood processing: furniture, boats, fixtures, mirror and picture frames

Weaving: baskets, mats, baskets to cover food, roofing, rope, fish traps

Leather production: tanning, shoes, leather products

Artisan crafts: carvings, embroidery, ornaments, jewelry, clay pots, musical instruments

Miscellaneous: fishnets, beds, bricks, paper bags, brooms, rubber stamps, varnish, clothes hangers

Nondurable Goods

Food processing: *bagia, vitumbua, maandazi, chapati* pastries, *vibata, vijogoo, visheti* confectioneries, coconut oil (extracted), *mshikaki* shish kebab, fried, chicken, chips, cassava, fish, soup, popcorn, cooked rice, beans, and porridge, milled maize, salt, ice cream, honey

Beverage production: beer and liquor (*dengelua, mbege, komoni, kisonge, mtama, kangale, njimbo, uraka, dadi, wanzuki, gongo*), *tembo* palm wine, liquor, soft drinks like *togwa*

SERVICE

Repairing: shoes, cars, plumbing, machine tools, radios, bicycles, watches, beds

Healing: services of medicine men, herbalists, diviners
Operating: bars, teahouses, hotels, restaurants
Renting: houses, apartments, rooms in house
Others: Tutoring, hairstyling, nail polishing, sign writing, laundering,
   fish cleaning, shoe shining

RETAIL

Stores: general goods, secondhand clothing, *khanga* and *kitenge* cloths,
   charcoal, butcher
Market: vegetables, fruit, herbs and spices, crafts, especially household
   utensils, jewelry, gadgets
Kiosk: household goods, soda
Genge stalls: vegetables and fruit, fried cassava snacks, roasted maize,
   recycled bottles and jars
Street trading: thongs, jewelry, cosmetics, vegetables and fruits, peanuts,
   Arabic coffee, pastries and candies, milk, water, newspapers,
   secondhand books, hair dyes, cigarettes
Home veranda: charcoal, wood, kerosene, flour, vegetables, fruit, peanuts,
   pastries, candies, popcorn, *togwa*

TRADE AND TRANSPORT

Grains, vegetables, fruits, charcoal, wood boards, mangrove poles, fish

AGRICULTURAL PRODUCTION AND ANIMAL HUSBANDRY

Farming: cassava, maize, rice, vegetables, fruits, coconuts
Raising: poultry (layers and broilers), goats, cows (milk), pigs

CONSTRUCTION

FISHING

ILLICIT ACTIVITIES

Prostitution, scams on the job, peddling drugs, begging, smuggling,
   black-market currency exchanges

Rates for Small-Business Licenses in Dar es Salaam, 1988

Annual fee (in TSh)	Description of the business
1,800	Repairing automobile radiators
1,200	Making and/or selling arts and crafts
1,000	Raising cows, pigs, or goats Selling barbecued meat at a bar or a small restaurant Selling fried chips, chicken, eggs, and/or barbecued meat
800	Repairing radios Shining shoes and making minor repairs Vending newspapers and books Welding
600	Vending fruit Vending vegetables Vending fresh fish Operating a food stall in the street or at the workplace Operating a stall for assorted items at a designated place Slaughtering animals at a designated place Preparing food for a festival Shining shoes at tourist hotels Tailoring Repairing bicycles Repairing watches Working as a cobbler Selling soup, including cow's-hoof soup Pulling a cart Raising poultry Entertaining with traditional dances Vending newspapers Working as a carpenter

Working as a mason
Barbering

500   Making bricks
Framing photographs
Tying and dying cloth
Working as a plumber
Selling ice cream or ice cones at a school or a festival
Repairing tires or fixing punctures
Traditional healing
Selling traditional medicine
Writing or painting signs
Selling cosmetics in the street
Making and/or selling paper bags

300   Loading and unloading
Washing automobiles
Making and/or selling household decorations
Fishing
Picking fruit
Vending fried fish
Making and/or selling buns, rice cakes, and pastries
Selling milk, yogurt, and other dairy products
Selling firewood at retail
Selling charcoal at retail
Selling local coffee and/or coffee spiced with ginger
Extracting coconut oil
Laundering
Selling dried cassava

150   Selling water in containers
Cleaning latrines

Holders of Small-Business Licenses in Dar es Salaam, 1988

Number	Description of the Business
1,679	Operating a stall for assorted items at a designated place
794	Tailoring
495	Selling firewood at retail
492	Operating a food stall in the street or at the workplace
303	Making and/or selling buns, rice cakes, and pastries
221	Working as a carpenter
215	Vending fruit
214	Selling fried chips, chicken, eggs, and/or barbecued meat
210	Vending fried fish
204	Working as a cobbler
174	Shining shoes at tourist hotels
153	Selling cosmetics in the street
119	Vending newspapers and books
105	Repairing watches
94	Selling local coffee and/or coffee spiced with ginger
58	Laundering
55	Slaughtering animals at a designated place
52	Selling ice cream or ice cones at a school or a festival
49	Traditional healing
39	Repairing radios
35	Welding
33	Vending fresh fish
31	Repairing bicycles
27	Pulling a cart
26	Selling soup, including cow's-hoof soup
23	Selling traditional medicine
21	Writing or painting signs
21	Barbering
21	Selling dried cassava
19	Washing automobiles

18	Making and/or selling paper bags
14	Working as a mason
12	Framing photographs
12	Making and/or selling arts and crafts
11	Repairing tires or fixing punctures
10	Raising poultry, cows, pigs, or goats
7	Hairdressing and hairbraiding
6	Making bricks
5	Extracting coconut oil
2	Entertaining with traditional dances
1	Preparing food for a party or a festival
1	Loading and unloading
1	Tying and dying cloth
1	Entertaining with music or *taarab* (love songs)
0	Vending vegetables
0	Vending newspapers
0	Making and/or selling household decorations
0	Working as a plumber
0	Fishing
0	Selling flour, cassava, and rice
0	Selling water in containers
0	Cleaning latrines
0	Selling milk, yogurt, and other dairy products
0	Selling charcoal at retail
0	Picking fruit
0	Repairing automobile radiators
0	Selling barbecued meat at a bar or a small restaurant
0	Shining shoes and making minor repairs
6,082	Total

Notes

1. See James C. Scott's work on quiet forms of resistance (1985).
2. Harold Attu, "The Dala Dala War," *Daily News*, 14 September 1991.
3. In a thoughtful piece on the politics of liberalization in Ghana, Zambia, and Nigeria, Callaghy (1989) shows how the capacity of African governments to adjust is determined by their ability to insulate themselves from internal and external pressures. Their capacity depends on how leaders perceive the economic crisis and the level of commitment to reform; the degree to which policy making is based on economic rather than political considerations; the degree of government autonomy from competing sociopolitical forces; state capacity; level of economic development; and the nature, dependence on, and extent of external influence.
4. The ruling Tanganyika African National Union (TANU) merged with the Afro-Shirazi Party of Zanzibar in 1977 to form the Chama Cha Mapinduzi (CCM).
5. No. 7.35, discussion with author, 15 August 1987, Mwenge, Dar es Salaam.
6. Noncompliance has long been on the research agendas of people concerned with gender-related issues, but primarily within the context of interpersonal power relationships (Janeway 1981; Obbo 1980). Others have focused on noncompliance in labor-management relations (Lamphere 1987) or in protest movements of the poor, which include acts of resistance like crime, school truancy, and incendiarism (Piven and Cloward 1979). As Isaacman (1989) has pointed out, African historiography, in particular, draws heavily on the tradition of E. P. Thompson and Eric Hobsbrawm in utilizing the theme of noncompliance and everyday forms of resistance (see Beinart and Bundy 1987; Isaacman and Isaacman 1976; Jewsiewicki 1980; Van Onselen 1976).
7. *Daily News*, 24 July 1991.
8. These organizations included, for example, Karagwe Development Association, Mtwara-Lindi Residents of Dar es Salaam, Kigoma Development Association, Tarime Rural Development Trust Fund, Poverty Africa Shambalai Development Society (Lushoto), Karatu Development Association, and Coast Region Development Association (Kibaha).

9. Lloyd Swantz estimated that in the late 1960s there was a 1:375 ratio of informal medical practitioners to patients if one counts healers (*waganga*) but not herbalists, diviners, and others (1972). In my 1988 survey I estimated a ratio of 1:75 in Manzese and Buguruni. Were one to include all healers involved in informal medical practices, the ratio would be even greater.

10. *Daily News*, 30 May 1988.

CHAPTER 2

1. All dollar amounts given in this chapter correspond to the exchange rate around the beginning of 1988—when I conducted my survey—of $1 = TSh 100.

2. Many artisan and small-scale traders must have been doing quite well, because Leslie found that most houses were owned by them in the 1950s (Leslie 1963, 259). Dar es Salaam medicine men were also fairly comfortable, earning between TSh 120 and 511 a day at a time when the minimum wage was TSh 170 a month (L. Swantz 1972, 149).

3. Data provided by Buguruni schools' secretary, April 1988.

4. Mzee Maulidi, imam, Malapa branch, interview by author, 16 January, 1988, Buguruni, Dar es Salaam; Gehas Malasusa, pastor, Lutheran Church, interview by author, 22 January 1988, Buguruni, Dar es Salaam.

5. *Daily News*, 6 June 1995; 7 June 1995.

6. Data provided on 25 January 1988 by Karama Mlawa, headmaster, Uzuri Primary School, and Mrs. Minyala, headmistress, Ukombozi Primary School.

7. Jafari Nassoro, cell leader of Manzese market, interview by author, 25 November 1987; Mashisa (1978).

8. "Tanzania Economy: Out of Control," Inter Press Service, 21 January 1995.

9. There is considerable variability in these figures. Ödegaard cites Bureau of Statistics 1976/1977 data which suggest that urban food expenditure as a proportion of total expenditure was 33 percent in 1969 and 51 percent in 1977 (ödegaard 1985, 143). If one breaks the Bureau of Statistics data down into income groups, low-income food expenditure was 62 percent of total expenditure.

10. Only 6 percent of the households had two members working for wages, whereas 52 percent were made up solely of members who were self-employed and or farmers.

11. No. 1.66, interview by author, 26 August 1987, Tandika, Dar es Salaam.

12. No. 3.230, interview by author, 16 January 1988, Buguruni, Dar es Salaam.

13. No. 4.117, interview by author, 25 November 1987, Manzese, Dar es Salaam.

14. Comments made at a seminar on "Women Entrepreneurs in the Local Economy," hosted by the Small Entrepreneurs Association of Mwanga, 7–10 March 1994.

15. Benson found that even at the beginning of the present century in England, penny capitalism (small-scale business) was the main source of livelihood for 10 percent of all working-class families and partially supported at least another 40 percent. He argues that it did not disrupt existing relations in the community but helped to ease the dislocation caused by rapid economic and social change (Benson 1983, 134). Male workers mended furniture; sharpened tools and cutlery;

made toffee and ginger beer; made shoes; and caught and sold fish. Female workers cut hair; took in washing and ironing; hawked flowers, fish, fruit, vegetables, and nuts; sewed; and prepared food. Benson suggests that these small-scale and labor-intensive activities were not simply survival strategies for the working class but a central and dynamic component of mid-and late-Victorian growth. The engineering and metal-working needs not met by large industries led to the proliferation of small, labor-intensive units. Some workers who had been able to save sufficient sums left industrial work altogether and went into business full-time as skilled artisans. Another detailed study of working-class living standards in Lancaster and Burrow at the turn of the century found that few married women were employed full-time outside the home. But interviews show that large numbers of women were dressmakers; sold home-made pies and cakes from their homes; helped their husbands in corner shops; took in lodgers; did domestic cleaning; and took in wash and babysat. Between 40 and 43 percent of working-class mothers were involved in penny capitalism (Roberts 1977).

16. No. 7.34, interview by author, 14 October 1987, City Center, Dar es Salaam.

17. No. 2.13, interview by author, 12 June 1988, City Center, Dar es Salaam.

18. Even at this time there were those who believed that rural life was better than urban life. One survey by Market Research, Ltd., "Rural Life in Mpiji River Valley" (1965b) asked rural farmers who had been to Dar es Salaam why they had returned to the countryside. (Twenty-five percent of the farmers had lived in Dar es Salaam for more than twenty years, and 21 percent had spent between ten and twenty years there.) Of these, 92 percent said that rural life was better than life in Dar es Salaam; only 8 percent said it was the same or worse. More food and water were the main reasons given for this preference.

19. No. 4.33, interview by author, 4 November 1987, Manzese, Dar es Salaam.

20. No. 4.14, interview by author, 29 October 1987, Manzese, Dar es Salaam

CHAPTER 3

1. No. 9.9, interview by author, 14 November 1987, Manzese, Dar es Salaam.

2. No. 4.146B, interview by author, 7 December 1987, Manzese, Dar es Salaam.

3. *Daily News*, 29 July 1986; *Africa Events*, September 1986, 40.

4. *Tanzania Economic Trends* 6, nos. 1–2 (1993).

5. "Tanzania-Economy: Donors to Resume Aid after Polls," Inter Press Service, 28 August 1995.

6. *Tanzania Economic Trends* 4, nos. 3–4 (1992): 6.

7. "Tanzania-Economy: Donors to Resume Aid after Polls."

8. Paul Chintowa, "Tanzania Education: SAPs Blamed for Declining Standards," Inter Press Service, 16 March 1995.

CHAPTER 4

1. Because government leaders were also CCM members and because party leaders frequently held government posts, these differences obviously also ran through both bodies, not just between them.

2. *Africa Report,* November–December 1985, 6.
3. *African Business,* October 1985, 27.
4. *Africa Report,* November–December 1985, 4; *Daily News,* 19 May 1985, 1.
5. *Africa Events,* March 1985.
6. *Daily News,* 15 May 1988.
7. Ibid., 14 January 1986, 1.
8. *Africa Confidential,* 21 October 1987.
9. *Daily News,* 2 October 1987.
10. *Africa Report,* March–April 1989, 44.
11. *Daily News,* 13 March 1987.
12. Ibid., 26 January 1985.
13. Ibid., 10 April 1987.
14. *Africa Events* August 1986, 82.
15. *Daily News,* 10 December 1987
16. *Southern African Economist,* December 1989/January 1990, 35.
17. *New African,* October 1987, 11.
18. *Africa Confidential,* 31 March 1989.
19. *Daily News,* 21 May 1995.
20. *Sunday News,* 21 May 1995.
21. *Tanzanian Economic Trends* 2, no. 1 (1989): 2.
22. "What Is Delaying Private Sector Investment," speech by Iddi Simba, chairman of the Confederation of Tanzanian Industries, at a U.S. Agency for International Development conference, Dar es Salaam, February 1994.
23. *Africa Confidential,* 18 March, 1987.
24. No. 7.21, interview by author, 11 June 1988, Upanga, Dar es Salaam.
25. *Daily News,* 5 August 1994.
26. No. 7.26, interview by author, 23 June 1988, Dar es Salaam.
27. No. 7.24, interview by author, 7 June 1988, Mikocheni, Dar es Salaam.
28. No. 7.21, interview by author, 11 June 1988, Dar es Salaam.
29. *African Business,* August 1986.
30. *Daily News,* 2 May 1987.
31. Ibid., 4 June 1992.
32. No. 1.83, interview by author, 17 August 1987, University of Dar es Salaam.

CHAPTER 5

1. An interesting parallel to this argument is made by Carl Chinn in his recent book *They Worked All Their Lives: Women of the Urban Poor in England, 1880–1939,* in which he is concerned with "dispelling the notion that the women of the urban poor were so dispirited by poverty's inexorable advance that they accepted defeat and became its passive victims. The evidence to the contrary is abundant and emphasizes that many women were active; they fought back against privation, and within their communities, against the society which allowed it to spread so wantonly" (1988, 133).
2. In fact, most informal-sector activity in Dar es Salaam by men and women takes place in the home, on the street, in a temporary structure, or in no fixed

location (Planning Commission and Ministry of Labour and Youth Development 1991, 2–5).

3. No. 2.28, interview by author, 18 August 1987, City Center, Dar es Salaam.

4. No. 1.46, interview by author, 8 August 1987, 28 September 1987, Keko, Dar es Salaam.

5. An adult, rather than being referred to by his or her first name, is generally known as the mother or father of the eldest child or the eldest child living at home; hence the appellation "Mama Hamza," or "mother of Hamza."

6. It is not considered appropriate for a woman to work on her veranda on a regular basis, though socializing is acceptable. Although women are not in purdah (seclusion), as they are in other Muslim parts of Africa, they do not want to appear as though they are advertising themselves like loose women or prostitutes. Unlike most women, prostitutes, who usually live together in one house, make a point of doing their household chores and socializing among themselves on the veranda or near the doorway rather than in the back of the house.

7. No. 1.114, interview by author, 29 July 1987, Manzese, Dar es Salaam.

8. No. 4.168, interview by author, 12 December 1987, Manzese, Dar es Salaam.

9. No. 2.16, interview by author, 24 September 1987, Oyster Bay, Dar es Salaam.

10. No. 2.18, interview by author, 17 August 1987, City Center, Dar es Salaam.

11. Premy Kibanga, "Esther Thrives on Exports," *Business Times*, 21 October 1994.

12. No. 2.42, interview by author, 22 August 1987, City Center, Dar es Salaam.

13. No. 3.256, interview by author, 20 January 1988, Buguruni, Dar es Salaam.

14. No. 1.101, interview by Salome Mjema, 3 September 1987, Kurasini, Dar es Salaam.

15. Rev. Gehas Malasusa, interview by author, 22 January 1988, Buguruni, Dar es Salaam.

16. No. 7.18, interview by author, 21 June 1988, City Center, Dar es Salaam.

17. No. 7.30, interview by author, 4 June 1988, City Center, Dar es Salaam.

18. No. 7.30, discussion with Salome Mjema, 10 September 1987, Dar es Salaam.

19. No. 1.63, interview by author, 8 September 1987, Magomeni, Dar es Salaam.

20. No. 2.28, interview by author, 18 August 1987, City Center, Dar es Salaam.

21. No. 2.21, interview by author, 28 September 1988, Oyster Bay, Dar es Salaam.

22. Naomi Amy Kaihula, discussion with author, 10 February 1994, City Center, Dar es Salaam.

23. *New Vision*, 16 October 1991.

24. Comments made at the seminar on "Women Entrepreneurs in the Local Economy," hosted by the Small Entrepreneurs' Association of Mwanga, 7–10 March 1994.

25. No. 3.366, interview by author, 20 January 1988, Buguruni, Dar es Salaam.

26. Of all house owners, only 9 percent had received loans to aid in the construction of their homes from the Tanzanian Housing Bank (THB), the major source of housing finance in Tanzania. The majority built their houses from their

own or their family's savings, often saved from their businesses (Kulaba 1989, 213).

27. No. 1.63, interview by author, 8 September 1987, Magomeni, Dar es Salaam.

28. No. 3.253, interview by author, 20 January 1988, Buguruni, Dar es Salaam.

29. No. 4.41, interview by author, 7 November 1987, Manzese, Dar es Salaam.

30. No. 4.47, interview by author, 11 November 1987, Manzese, Dar es Salaam.

31. Even in advanced industrialized countries, the distinction between production and reproduction has not been completely severed, for women make the same kinds of choices to stay home for similar reasons. In the United States, for example, since the 1970s clerical work, microprocessing, and telecommunications done in the home by women has increased, in part because of new corporate strategies but also because women, especially those with children, find that this kind of work fits well into their life arrangements.

32. No. 2.15, interview by author, 28 September 1987, Oyster Bay, Dar es Salaam.

33. No. 7.18, interview by author, 21 June 1988, City Center, Dar es Salaam.

34. No. 2.42, interview by author, 22 August 1987, City Center, Dar es Salaam.

35. No. 6.64, interview by author, 13 November 1987, Manzese, Dar es Salaam.

36. Comments at the seminar on "Women Entrepreneurs in the Local Economy."

37. Cleopa Msuya, who at that time was minister of trade and industries, attended the closing of the seminar.

38. No. 6.3, interview by author, 26 October 1987, Manzese, Dar es Salaam.

39. No. 3.187, interview by author, 5 January 1988, Buguruni, Dar es Salaam.

40. In the urban Dar es Salaam region 47 percent of the students in primary schools were girls, according to the 1978 census (Bureau of Statistics 1982, 37). The rise in the percentage of girls attending Buguruni and Manzese schools in the 1980s is reflected in regional statistics for public primary schools in Dar es Salaam: 1981, 50 percent girls; 1982, 51 percent; 1983, 53 percent; and 1984, 52 percent girls (Bureau of Statistics 1986). By 1986 50 percent of students in schools nationwide were girls, compared with 44 percent nationwide in 1978 (Bureau of Statistics 1982, 36; *Daily News*, 23 June 1987)

41. Richard Mwambe, headmaster, Buguruni Primary School, interview by author, 22 January 1988, Buguruni, Dar es Salaam.

42. Data for Buguruni and Manzese are based on school records supplied in 1988 by the headmaster of Uzuri Primary School for all five schools in Manzese and by the headmasters of Buguruni's three primary schools: Buguruni Primary, Buguruni Moto, and Buguruni Visiwa.

43. No. 1.81, interview by author, 25 August 1987, Kigamboni, Dar es Salaam.

44. No. 1.3, interview by author, 2 September 1987, City Center, Dar es Salaam.

45. No. 1.39, interview by author, 22 August 1987, City Center, Dar es Salaam.

46. Kenyan and other foreign cigarettes are sold in shops, but they are not in great demand.

47. No. 1.6, interview by author, 21 August 1987, Mnazi Moja, Dar es Salaam.

48. No. 7.33, interview by author, August 1987, City Center, Dar es Salaam.

49. No. 7.31, interview by author, 22 January 1988, City Center, Dar es Salaam.

50. No. 1.3, interview by author, 2 September 1987, City Center, Dar es Salaam.

51. No. 1.162, interview by author, 15 August 1987, City Center, Dar es Salaam.

52. No 3.224, interview by author, 15 January 1988, Buguruni, Dar es Salaam.

53. No. 4.100, interview by author, 24 November 1987, Manzese, Dar es Salaam.

CHAPTER 6

1. *Daily News*, 10 October 1983.

2. Even the use of terms like *slum* and *squatter* by authorities, like their use of *loiterers* and *unproductive elements* for the self-employed, belies the profound gap between government understanding of who these people are and the nature of their experiences, problems, and objectives.

3. The Penal Code amendment expanded the categories of "idle and disorderly persons" to include:

a. any ablebodied person who is not engaged in any productive work and has no visible means of subsistence;

b. any person employed under lawful employment of any description who is, without any lawful excuse, found engaged in a frolic of his own at a time he is supposed to be engaged in activities connected or relating to the business of his employment (Shaidi 1984, 82).

4. The minister of labour, assisted by the labour commissioner and advised by the National Human Resources Deployment Advisory Committee, was in charge of enforcing the act, but the actual implementation was left up to the local authorities (Shaidi 1984, 85).

5. *Daily News*, 26 September 1983.

6. *African Business*, December 1983.

7. No. 1.6, interview by author, 21 August 1987, Mnazi Moja, Dar es Salaam.

8. No. 6.54, interview by author, 11 November 1987, Manzese, Dar es Salaam.

9. *Daily News*, 17 November 1983.

10. Ibid., 2 October 1983.

11. No. 7.18, interview by author, 21 June 1988, Dar es Salaam.

12. J. B. Kitambi, regional director of administration, Coast Region, interview by author, June 1988, Dar es Salaam.

13. *Daily News*, 9 June 1986.

14. No. 1.6, interview by author, 21 August 1987, Mnazi Moja, Dar es Salaam.

15. Alpha Nuhu, "Tanzania-Labour: ILO Comes to the Rescue," Inter Press Service, 31 May 1995.

16. "War on Hawkers to Continue," *Daily News*, 6 June 1995.

17. The other piece of legislation regulating small businesses is the Licensing and Registration Act of 1967, which stipulates that all enterprises employing ten or more workers are required to obtain an industrial license from the Commercial Law, Registration and Industrial Licensing Department, Ministry of Trade and Industries (International Labour Organisation 1992, 21). Few informal-sector operations are large enough to fall into this business category.

18. One person wrote the following letter to the editor of the *Daily News* (3 June 1990): "If the Council is hard up why do they spend whatever little they have (in terms of money) to endlessly chase around the so-called unlicensed street vendors? (By the way is it not a wrong war in the wrong battlefield, and what happens to the 'War Spoils')."

19. No. 7.17, interview by author, 24 June 1988, Dar es Salaam.

20. *Daily News*, 16 May 1991.

21. Ibid., 16 July, 1985.

22. No. 6.72, interview by author, 18 November 1987, Manzese, Dar es Salaam.

23. Government Notice No. 765, 30 October 1987. The Dar es Salaam City Council (Hawking and Street Trading) Amendment, Section 80, No. 8, Bylaw 15.

24. *Daily News*, 23 July 1985.

25. No. 6.61, interview by author, 13 November 1987, Manzese, Dar es Salaam.

26. No. 6.153, interview by author, 8 December 1987, Manzese, Dar es Salaam.

27. No. 7.13, interview by author, 26 October 1987, Manzese, Dar es Salaam.

28. Patron-client relations in Tanzania are rooted in the traditional headman or chief-subject relationship. These local patrons gained prominence in a number of different ways: through the social standing of their families; by marrying into a prominent family; by making a pilgrimage to Mecca and becoming an Al-Hajj; or by becoming a *shehe* (a Muslim sheikh) or imam (prayer leader). Their financial status was usually derived from owning boats, hotels, buses, or taxis or by engaging in trade (M.-L. Swantz 1986, 8–9, 37).

29. Seleimani Chamgulia, interview by author, 9 January 1988, Buguruni, Dar es Salaam.

30. No. 6.46, interview by author, 10 November 1987, Manzese, Dar es Salaam.

31. *Daily News*, 3 May 1989, emphasis mine.

32. Ibid., 14 November 1987.

33. Comments made at a seminar on "Women Entrepreneurs in the Local Economy," hosted by the Small Entrepreneurs Association of Mwanga, 7–10 March 1994.

34. *Daily News*, 4 November 1986.

35. *Africa Research Bulletin*, 15 July–14 August 1982, 6525.

36. Collection of the levy varied from year to year. For example, targets were exceeded in 1984–1985 by many towns, and by the following year, only 53 percent of the targeted amount was collected. Since then, revenue from the development levy has continued to fall (*Daily News*, 7 August 1991).

37. Ibid., 4 January 1985, 3 April 1986, 9 October 1986.

38. Ibid., 25 April 1986.

39. A typical comment by a Dar es Salaam resident: "When it comes to the Development Levy we have . . . seen nothing as a result of the levy we pay. Take Dar es Salaam as a [case in] point: the city is very dirty and the situation is deteriorating day in and day out. Our hospitals in the city are low in standards, [they have] poor hygienic conditions, no soaps, no insecticides and no mosquito nets in the hospitals. What we want to see is how such taxes are being spent" (*Daily News*, 9 June 1985).

40. One Dar es Salaam businessman commented: "The Government is all the time raising taxes. Okay; it needs more revenue, but it has not plugged its own misappropriation of millions of shillings" (ibid., 9 June 1985).

41. No. 6.80, interview by author, 17 November 1987, Manzese, Dar es Salaam.

42. *Daily News*, 8 May 1995.

43. Ibid., 24 January 1984, 31 January 1984.

44. Ibid., 19 December 1990.

45. Ibid., 2 May 1987.

46. Ibid., 5 June 1995.

47. One satirist, Adam Lusekelo, in the government newspaper *Daily News*, had this in mind when he offered the following tongue-in-cheek observation about animal owners in the Oyster Bay suburb populated by professionals, civil servants, and administrators: "Supposing 'City' [Council] is simply ignored by the Oysterbay Ranching Inc. What then? I don't imagine a scenario whereby our personages of great consequence are taken to court. Besides, who will dare take them to court? You can take the Tandika [a poorer area of the city] livestock keepers to court for letting their animals 'fertilise' our roads with their dung. But not kraal owners of Oysterbay. You risk a serious paralysis of Party and Government organs" (ibid., 9 August 1987).

48. Ibid., 3 August 1988.

49. No. 2.9, interview by author, 16 August 1987, City Center, Dar es Salaam.

50. *Daily News*, 18 September 1986.

51. Ibid., 8 April 1987.

52. Ibid., 29 July 1987.

53. Ibid., 19 September 1991.

54. Inter Press Service, 6 February 1995.

55. A 1988 study of Manzese traders provides a useful profile of the traders I encountered in Manzese, one of the two locales in Dar es Salaam where I carried out fieldwork. In the study, Henry Gordon and Paul de Greve found that most trading businesses were single proprietorships run by men, ranging in age from 32 to 49. The lack of younger traders can be attributed to the fact that it takes time to establish contacts and to gain the trading expertise necessary to maintain and expand the business. The largest number of traders were from the Morogoro area. The sale of maize as a grain and of rice and beans was the main source of income for the traders; vegetables and fruit were of secondary importance. Maize and kidney beans are the most heavily traded items at the Manzese market. As is usually the case, the traders did not own transport or storage facilities themselves. For this reason, traders are confined mainly to purchasing the produce at rural markets and bringing it to the urban markets. Similarly, transporters rarely engage in trading.

Instead, they are hired by wholesalers and agricultural producers, both in rural and urban areas. The traders surveyed reported an increase in trade after 1985, some attributing it to changes in the political climate. They also noted that the trade had become more competitive since 1980 (*Tanzanian Economic Trends* 1, no. 3 (1988): 25–33).

One Manzese trader I interviewed had been employed as a guard at Tanzania Breweries but had left in 1985 because his salary of TSh 600 was insufficient. He began trading in 1983, while he was still working at the breweries. He traded with his younger brother and another hired youth, bringing tomatoes, oranges, co-conuts, and pineapples three times a month from Morogoro to the Manzese market. His main concern was timing; for example, getting the tomatoes to Dar es Salaam before they went bad. He was saving to build a house, and he felt his business was going forward.

56. *Tanzanian Economic Trends* 1, no. 1 (1988): 35.

57. Ibid., 1, no. 3 (1988): 26.

58. *Daily News*, 1 March 1991.

59. Ibid., 4 January 1991.

60. Yusa Lui, teacher, Kilimani Primary School, interview by author, 23 January 1988, Manzese, Dar es Salaam.

61. Yusa Lui, interview by author.

CHAPTER 7

1. According to the Arusha Declaration (Nyerere 1968, 36):

1. Every TANU and Government leader must be either a peasant or a worker, and should in no way be associated with the practices of capitalism or feudalism.

2. No TANU or Government leader should hold shares in any company.

3. No TANU or Government leader should hold directorships in any privately owned enterprise.

4. No TANU or Government leader should receive two or more salaries.

5. No TANU or Government leader should own houses which he rents to others.

6. For the purposes of this Resolution the term "leader" should compromise the following:

Members of the TANU National Executive Committee; Ministers; Members of Parliament; senior officials of organizations affiliated to TANU; senior officials of parastatal organizations; all those appointed or elected under any clause of the TANU Constitution; councillors; and civil servants in the high and middle cadres. (In this context 'leader' means a man, or a man and his wife; a woman, or a woman and her husband.)

2. No. 7.21, interview by author, 11 June 1988, Dar es Salaam.

3. *Africa Events*, May 1985, 6.

4. Inter Press Service, 11 December 1990.

5. *Africa Report*, April–March 1989.

6. No. 7.5, interview by author, 5 October 1987, Mikocheni, Dar es Salaam.

7. No. 7.21, interview by author, 11 June 1988, Dar es Salaam.

8. *Africa Report,* November–December 1985, 4.

9. *Daily News,* 29 July 1987.

10. No. 7.28, interview by author, 12 October 1987.

11. *Daily News,* 10 May 1987, 2; 9 August 1987; 20 September 1987.

12. William Mjema, personal communication, 30 August 1995.

13. No. 7.32, discussion with author, 22 January 1988, Dar es Salaam.

14. No. 7.29, interview by author, 6 November 1987, Manzese, Dar es Salaam.

15. No. 4.146B, interview by author, 7 December 1987, Manzese, Dar es Salaam.

16. No. 7.32, interview by author, 25 July 1987, City Center, Dar es Salaam.

17. *Daily News,* 23 June, 1991.

18. No. 1.99, interview by Salome Mjema, 3 October 1987, Kurasini, Dar es Salaam.

19. *Daily News,* 2 September 1981.

20. No. 2.4, interview by author, 10 September 1987, Upanga, Dar es Salaam.

21. No. 7.30, discussion with Salome Mjema, 10 September 1987, Dar es Salaam.

22. *Daily News,* 2 May 1987.

23. *Africa Events,* January 1989.

24. *Daily News,* 25 June 1988.

25. Ibid., 22 July 1987.

26. Ibid., 26 February 1991.

27. Ibid., 8 June 1987.

28. Ibid., 27 February 1990, 1.

29. Ibid., 17 February 1991.

30. Ibid., 8 March 1991, 18 February 1991.

CHAPTER 8

1. No. 7.24, interview by author, 7 June 1988, Mikocheni, Dar es Salaam.

2. *Daily News,* 26 February 1990.

References

NEWSPAPERS AND MAGAZINES

Africa Bulletin
Africa Confidential
Africa Events
African Business
Africa Report
Business Times (Tanzania)
Daily News (Tanzania)
New African
New Vision
New York Times
Southern African Economist
St. Louis Post Dispatch
Sunday News (Tanzania)
Tanzanian Economic Trends

BIBLIOGRAPHICAL REFERENCES

Aboagye, A. A. 1985. "An Analysis of Dar es Salaam's Informal Sector Survey." Addis Ababa: Jobs and Skills Programme for Africa, International Labour Organisation.

Addison, Tony. 1986. "Adjusting to the IMF?" *Africa Report* 31 (May–June): 81–83.

African Census Report 1957. 1963. Dar es Salaam: Government Printer.

Africa Research Bulletin. Africa: Political, Social and Cultural Series. 1982. London: Africa Research, Ltd.

Amani, H. K. R., and W. E. Maro. 1991–1992. "Policies to Promote an Effective Private Trading System in Farm Products and Farm Inputs in Tanzania." *Tanzania Economic Trends* 4 (3–4): 36–54.

Anthony, D. H., III. 1983. "Culture and Society in a Town in Transition: A People's History of Dar es Salaam, 1865–1939." Ph.D. diss., University of Wisconsin–Madison.

Arendt, Hannah. 1986. "Communicative Power." Pp. 59–74 in *Power,* ed. Steven Lukes. New York: New York University Press.

Azarya, Victor. 1988. "Reordering State-Society Relations: Incorporation and Disengagement." Pp. 121–48 in *The Precarious Balance: State and Society in Africa,* ed. Donald Rothchild and Naomi Chazan. Boulder, Colo.: Westview Press.

Azarya, Victor, and Naomi Chazan. 1987. "Disengagement from the State in Africa: Reflections on the Experience of Ghana and Guinea." *Comparative Politics* 29 (1): 106–31.

Bagachwa, Mboya S. D. 1981. "The Urban Informal Enterprise Sector in Tanzania: A Case Study of Arusha Region, No. 81.4." Dar es Salaam: Economics Department, Economic Research Bureau, University of Dar es Salaam.

———. 1982. "The Dar es Salaam Urban Informal Sector Survey, Technical Paper No. 7." Pp. 341–51 in *Basic Needs in Danger: A Basic Needs Oriented Development Strategy for Tanzania.* Addis Ababa: Jobs and Skills Programme for Africa, International Labour Organisation.

———. 1991. "Impact of Adjustment Policies on Small Scale Enterprise Sector." *Tanzania Economic Trends* 4 (2): 43–70.

———. 1992a. "Background, Evolution, Essence and Prospects of Current Economic Reforms in Tanzania." Pp. 19–43 in *Market Reforms and Parastatal Restructuring in Tanzania* M. S. D. Bagachwa, A. V. Y. Mbelle and Brian Van Arkadie, 19–43. Dar es Salaam: Economics Department, Economic Research Bureau, University of Dar es Salaam.

———. 1992b. "The Challenges and Potentials of the New Investment Promotion Policy." Pp. 204–19 in *Market Reforms and Parastatal Restructuring in Tanzania,* ed. M. S. D. Bagachwa, A. V. Y. Mbelle, and Brian Van Arkadie. Dar es Salaam: Economics Department, Economic Research Bureau, University of Dar es Salaam.

———. 1993. "An Analysis of the 1993/1994 Tanzanian Budget." *Tanzanian Economic Trends* 6 (1–2): 42–52.

Bagachwa, Mboya S. D., and Benno J. Ndulu. 1989. "Structure and Potential of the Urban Small-Scale Activities in Tanzania."

Bangura, Yusuf, and Peter Gibbon. 1992. "Adjustment, Authoritarianism and Democracy in Sub-Saharan Africa: An Introduction to Some Conceptual and Empirical Issues." Pp. 7–38 in *Authoritarianism, Democracy and Adjustment: The Politics of Economic Reform in Africa,* ed. Peter Gibbon, Yusuf Bangura, and Arve Ofstad. Uppsala: Scandinavian Institute of African Studies.

Baregu, Mwesiga. 1993. "The Economic Origins of Political Liberalization and Future Prospects." Pp. 105–23 in *Economic Policy under a Multiparty System in Tanzania,* ed. M. S. .D. Bagachwa and A. V. Y. Mbelle. Dar es Salaam: Dar es Salaam University Press.

Barkan, Joel D. 1994. "Divergence and Convergence in Kenya and Tanzania: Pressures for Reform." Pp. 1–45 in *Beyond Capitalism vs. Socialism in Kenya and Tanzania,* ed. Joel D. Barkan. Boulder, Colo.: Lynne Rienner Publishers.

Bashemererwa, Vivian. 1986. "Mlingotini Village." Pp. 81–85 (Appendix 1) in "The Role of Women in Tanzanian Fishing Societies: A Study of the Socioeconomic Context and the Situation of Women in Three Coastal Fishing Villages in Tanzania," by Marja-Liisa Swantz. Unpublished report commissioned by the Royal Norwegian Ministry of Development Cooperation (NORAD).

Bates, Robert H. 1981. *Markets and States in Tropical Africa: The Political Basis of Agricultural Policies.* Berkeley: University of California Press.

Bawly, Dan. 1982. *The Subterranean Economy.* New York: McGraw Hill.

Bayart, Jean-François. 1986. "Civil Society in Africa." Pp. 109–25 in *Political Domination in Africa,* ed. Patrick Chabal. Cambridge, England: Cambridge University Press.

Beidelman, Thomas O. 1967. *The Matrilineal Peoples of Eastern Tanzania.* London: International African Institute.

Beinart, William, and Colin Bundy. 1987. *Hidden Struggles in Rural South Africa.* Berkeley: University of California Press.

Benson, John. 1983. *The Penny Capitalists: A Study of Nineteenth-Century Working-Class Entrepreneurs.* New Brunswick, N.J.: Rutgers University Press.

Berry, Sara. 1978. "Custom, Class and the Informal Sector: Or Why Marginality Is Not Likely to Pay." Working Paper 1. Boston: African Studies Center, Boston University.

Bienefeld, Manfred. 1974. "The Self-Employed of Urban Tanzania. Discussion Paper 54." Dar es Salaam: IDS.

———. 1975. "The Informal Sector and Peripheral Capitalism: The Case of Tanzania." *IDS Bulletin* 6 (3): 53–73.

Bienen, Henry. 1970. *Tanzania: Party Transformation and Economic Development.* Princeton, N.J.: Princeton University Press.

Boesen, Jannik, Kjell J. Havnevik, Juhani Koponen, and Rie Odgaard, eds. 1986. *Tanzania: Crisis and Struggle for Survival.* Uppsala: Scandinavian Institute of African Studies.

Booth, William James. 1994. "On the Idea of the Moral Economy." *American Political Science Review* 88 (3): 653–67.

Boserup, Esther. 1970. *Women's Role in Economic Development.* Brookfield, Vt.: Gower Publishing Company.

Bratton, Michael. 1989. "The Politics of Government-NGO Relations in Africa." *World Development* 17 (4): 569–87.

Bratton, Michael, and Nicholas van de Walle. 1992. "Popular Protest and Political Reform in Africa." *Comparative Politics* 24 (4): 419–41.

———. 1994. "Neopatrimonial Regimes and Political Transitions in Africa." *World Politics* 46 (4): 453–89.

Braudel, Fernand. 1977. *Afterthoughts on Material Civilization and Capitalism.* Baltimore, Md.: Johns Hopkins University Press.

Brett, E. A. 1987. "States and Markets and Private Power in the Developing World: Problems and Possibilities." *IDS Bulletin* 18 (3): 31–38.

Bromley, Ray. 1978. "Introduction—The Urban Informal Sector: Why Is It Worth Discussing?" *World Development* 6: 1033–39.

Bryceson, Deborah F. 1980. "The Proletarianization of Women in Tanzania." *Review of African Political Economy* 17: 4–27.

———. 1985. "Women's Proletarianization and the Family Wage in Tanzania." Pp. 128–52 in *Women, Work and Ideology in the Third World,* ed. H. Afshar. New York: Tavistock Publications.

———. 1987. "A Century of Food Supply in Dar es Salaam: From Sumptuous Suppers for the Sultan to Maize Meal for a Million." Pp. 155–202 in *Feeding African Cities: Studies in Regional Social History,* ed. Jane I. Guyer. Manchester: Manchester University Press.

———. 1990. *Food Insecurity and the Social Division of Labor in Tanzania, 1919–1985.* New York: St. Martin's Press.

Bujra, Janet M. 1978–1979. "Proletarianization and the 'Informal Economy': A Case Study from Nairobi." *African Urban Studies* 3 (Winter): 47–66.

Bukurura, Lufian Hemed. 1991. "Public Participation in Financing Local Development: The Case of Tanzanian Development Levy." *Afrique et Déeveloppement/ Africa Development* 16 3–4): 73–99.

Bureau of Statistics. 1977. *Household Budget Survey: Income and Consumption 1976/1977.* Dar es Salaam: Ministry of Finance, Planning and Economic Affairs.

———. 1982. *1978 Population Census. Volume IV: A Summary of Selected Statistics.* Dar es Salaam: Ministry of Finance, Planning and Economic Affairs.

———. 1986. *Statistical Abstract 1984.* Dar es Salaam: Ministry of Finance, Planning and Economic Affairs.

———. 1989. "Lost between State and Market: The Politics of Economic Adjustment in Ghana, Zambia, and Nigeria." Pp. 257–319 in *Fragile Coalitions: The Politics of Economic Adjustment,* ed. Joan Nelson. Washington, D.C.: Overseas Development Council.

———. 1989. *1988 Population Census: Preliminary Report.* Dar es Salaam: Ministry of Finance, Planning and Economic Affairs.

Callaghy, Thomas M. 1984. *The State-Society Struggle in Zaire in Comparative Perspective.* New York: Columbia University Press.

Castells, Manuel, and Alejandro Portes. 1989a. "Conclusion: The Policy Implications of Informality." Pp. 293–311 in *The Informal Economy: Studies in Advanced and Less Developed Countries,* ed. Alejandro Portes, Manuel Castells, and Lauren A. Benton. Baltimore, Md.: Johns Hopkins University Press.

———. 1989b. "World Underneath: The Origins, Dynamics, and Effects of the Informal Economy." Pp. 11–40 in *The Informal Economy: Studies in Advanced and Less Developed Countries,* ed. Alejandro Portes, Manuel Castells, and Lauren A. Benton. Baltimore, Md.: Johns Hopkins University Press.

Chazan, Naomi. 1982. "The New Politics of Participation in Tropical Africa." *Comparative Politics* 14 (2): 169–89.

———. 1983. *An Anatomy of Ghanaian Politics: Managing Political Recession, 1969–1982.* Boulder, Colo.: Westview Press.

———. 1988. "Patterns of State-Society Incorporation and Disengagement in Africa." Pp. 121–48 in *The Precarious Balance: State and Society in Africa,* ed. Donald Rothchild and Naomi Chazan. Boulder, Colo.: Westview Press.

———. 1994. "Engaging the State: Associational Life in Sub-Saharan Africa." Pp. 255–89 in *State Power and Social Forces: Domination and Transformation in the Third World,* ed. Joel Migdal, Atul Kohli, and Vivienne Shue. Cambridge, England: Cambridge University Press.

Chazan, Naomi, and Donald Rothchild. 1987. "Corporatism and Political Transactions: Some Ruminations on the Ghanaian Experience." Pp. 167–93 in *Corporatism in Africa: Comparative Analysis and Practice,* ed. Julius Nyang'oro and Timothy Shaw. Boulder, Colo.: Westview Press.

Chazan, Naomi, R. Mortimer, J. Ravenhill, and D. Rothchild. 1988. *Politics and Society in Contemporary Africa.* Boulder, Colo.: Lynne Rienner Publishers.

Chege, Michael. 1992. "Remembering Africa." *Foreign Affairs* 71 (1): 146–63.

Chinn, Carl. 1988. *They Worked All Their Lives: Women of the Urban Poor in England, 1880–1939.* Manchester: Manchester University Press.

Clark, Gracia. 1988. "Price Control of Local Foodstuffs in Kumasi, Ghana, 1979." Pp. 57–80 in *Traders versus the State: Anthropological Approaches to Unofficial Economies,* ed. Gracia Clark. Boulder, Colo.: Westview Press.

Cliffe, Lionel. 1972. "Personal or Class Interest: Tanzania's Leadership Conditions." Pp. 254–56 in *Socialism in Tanzania,* vol. 1, *Politics,* ed. Lionel Cliffe and John Saul. Dar es Salaam: East African Publishing House.

Comaroff, Jean L., and John Comaroff. 1987. "The Madman and the Migrant: Work and Labor in the Historical Consciousness of a South African People." *American Ethnologist* 14 (2): 191–209.

Coulson, Andrew. 1982. *Tanzania: A Political Economy.* Oxford: Clarendon Press.

Country Profile. Tanzania, Comoros. 1994–1995. London: The Economist Intelligence Unit.

Dahl, Robert A. 1971. *Polyarchy: Participation and Opposition.* New Haven, Conn.: Yale University Press.

Dalton, George. 1961. "Economic Theory and Primitive Societies." *American Anthropologist* 63 (1): 1–25.

De Soto, Hernando. 1989. *The Other Path.* New York: Harper & Row.

Dolphyne, Florence. 1987. "Market Women of West Africa." *CUSO Journal,* December, 26–28.

Eames, Elizabeth A. 1988. "Why the Women Went to War: Women and Wealth in Ondo Town, Southwestern Nigeria." Pp. 81–98 in *Traders versus the State: Anthropological Approaches to Unofficial Economies,* ed. Gracia Clark. Boulder, Colo.: Westview Press.

Ekeh, Peter. 1975. "Colonialism and the Two Publics in Africa: A Theoretical Statement." *Comparative Studies in Society and History* 17 (1): 91–112.

Ellis, Frank. 1983. "Agricultural Marketing and Peasant-State Transfers in Tanzania." *Journal of Peasant Studies* 10 (4): 214–42.

Fatton, Robert, Jr. 1992. *Predatory Rule: State and Civil Society in Africa.* Boulder, Colo., and London: Lynne Rienner Publishers.

Ferreira, Luisa, and Lucy Goodhart. 1995. "Socio-Economic Growth and Poverty Alleviation in Tanzania." Arusha: Population and Human Resources, East Africa Department, World Bank.

Forrest, Joshua B. 1988. "The Quest for State 'Hardness' in Africa." *Comparative Politics* 20 (4): 423–42.

Foucault, Michel. 1980. *Power/Knowledge: Selected Interviews and Other Writings,* ed. C. Gordon. New York: Pantheon Books.

Frey, B. S., and H. Weck-Hanneman. 1984. "The Hidden Economy as an 'Unobserved' Variable." *European Economic Review* 26: 33–53.

Gerry, Chris. 1977. "Shantytown Production and Shantytown Producers: Some Reflections on Macro- and Micro-linkages." Paper presented at the Bur Wartenstein Symposium No. 73 on Shantytowns in Developing Nations, New York.

Gibbon, Peter. 1984. *The Constitution of Society: Outline of the Theory of Structuration.* Berkeley: University of California.

———. 1994. "Introduction: The New Local-Level Politics in East Africa." Pp. 11–21 in *The New Local Level Politics in East Africa: Studies on Uganda, Tanzania and Kenya,* ed. Peter Gibbon. Uppsala: Scandinavian Institute of African Studies.

———. 1995. "Merchantisation of Production and Privatisation of Development in Post-Ujamaa Tanzania: An Introduction." Pp. 9–36 in *Liberalised Development in Tanzania,* ed. Peter Gibbon. Uppsala: Nordiska Afrikainstitutet.

Giddens, Anthony. 1979. *Central Problems in Social Theory.* London: Macmillan Press.

Green, Reginald. 1981. "Magendo in the Political Economy of Uganda: Pathology, Parallel System or Dominant Sub-mode of Production?" Discussion Paper 164. Sussex: Institute for Development Studies, University of Sussex.

Gutmann, P. M. 1977. "The Subterranean Economy." *Financial Analysts Journal* 34 (November–December): 24–27.

Hansen, Karen. 1989. "The Black Market and Women Traders in Lusaka." Pp. 143–61 in *Women and the State in Africa,* ed. Jane L. Parpart and Kathleen A. Staudt. Boulder, Colo.: Lynne Rienner Publishers.

Harbeson, John W., Donald Rothchild, and Naomi Chazan, eds. 1994. *Civil Society and the State in Africa.* Boulder, Colo.: Lynne Rienner Publishers.

Hart, Keith. 1973. "Informal Income Opportunities in Urban Employment in Ghana." *Journal of Modern African Studies* 11 (1): 61–89.

Hartmann, Jeannette, ed. 1991. "Rethinking the Arusha Declaration." Copenhagen: Centre for Development Research.

Havnevik, Kjell J. 1986. "A Resource Overlooked—Crafts and Small-Scale Industries." Pp. 269–91 in *Tanzania: Crisis and Struggle for Survival,* ed. Jannik Boesen, Kjell J. Havnevik, Juhani Koponen, and Rie Odgaard. Uppsala: Scandinavian Institute of African Studies.

———. 1993. *Tanzania: The Limits to Development from Above.* Uppsala and Dar es Salaam: Nordiska Afrikainstitutet, Sweden, in cooperation with Mkuki na Nyota Publishers, Tanzania.

Hoad, P. 1968. "Report on a Socio-Economic Survey of Kinondoni." Dar es Salaam: Institute of Public Administration, University College.

Howard, Judith A. 1987. "Dilemmas in Feminist Theorizing: Politics and the Academy." Pp. 279–312 in *Current Perspectives in Social Theory,* ed. J. Wilson. Greenwich, Conn.: JAI Press Inc.

Hoy, David C. 1986. *Foucault: A Critical Reader.* New York: Basil Blackwell.

Hyden, Goran. 1980. *Beyond Ujamaa in Tanzania: Underdevelopment and an Uncaptured Peasantry.* London: Heinemann.

———. 1983. *No Shortcuts to Progress: African Development Management in Perspective.* Berkeley and Los Angeles: University of California Press.

———. 1989. "Governance and Liberalization: Tanzania in Comparative Perspective." Paper presented at the 1989 Annual Meeting of the American Political Science Association, Atlanta, Georgia, 31 August–3 September.

———. 1992. "Governance and the Study of Politics." Pp. 1–26 in *Governance and Politics in Africa,* ed. Goran Hyden and Michael Bratton. Boulder, Colo., and London: Lynne Rienner Publishers.

Hyden, Goran, and Michael Bratton, eds. 1992. *Governance and Politics in Africa.* Boulder, Colo.: Lynne Rienner Publishers.

Iliffe, John. 1970. "The History of the Dockworkers of Dar es Salaam." *Tanzania Notes and Records* 71: 119–48.

———. 1979. *A Modern History of Tanganyika,* edited by John M. Lonsdale. African Studies Series, vol. 58. Cambridge, England: Cambridge University Press.

International Labour Organisation. 1972. *Employment, Incomes and Equality: A Strategy for Increasing Productive Employment in Kenya.* Geneva: International Labour Office.

———. 1982. *Basic Needs in Danger: A Basic Needs Oriented Development Strategy for Tanzania.* Addis Ababa: International Labour Office, Jobs and Skills Programme for Africa.

———. 1992. *Policies for Informal Sector Activities in Tanzania: Analysis and Reform Perspectives.* Dar es Salaam: International Labour Organization.

International Monetary Fund. 1989. *IMF Government Finance Statistics Yearbook,* Vol. 13.

Isaacman, Allen. 1989. "Peasants and Rural Social Protest in Africa." Minneapolis: Institute of International Studies, University of Minnesota.

Isaacman, Allen F., and Barbara Isaacman. 1976. *The Tradition of Resistance in Mozambique: The Zambesi Valley 1850–1921.* Berkeley: University of California Press.

Ishumi, Abdel G. M. 1984. *The Urban Jobless in Eastern Africa.* Uppsala: Scandinavian Institute of African Studies.

Jackson, Dudley. 1979. "The Disappearance of Strikes in Tanzania: Incomes Policy and Industrial Democracy." *Journal of Modern African Studies* 17 (2): 219–51.

Janeway, Elizabeth. 1981. *Powers of the Weak.* New York: Morrow Quill Paperbacks.

Jewsiewicki, Bogumil. 1980. "Political Consciousness among African Peasants in the Belgian Congo." *Review of African Political Economy* 19: 23–32.

Joinet, Father Bernard. 1986. "A Letter to My Superiors, No. 8." Dar es Salaam.

Joseph, Richard, ed. 1990. *African Governance in the 1990s.* Atlanta: Carter Center, Emory University.

Kapila, Sunita. 1987. "The Matatu of Nairobi." *CUSO Journal,* December, 21–22.

Kasfir, Nelson. 1984. "State, Magendo, and Class Formation in Uganda." Pp. 84–103 in *State and Class in Africa,* ed. N. Kasfir. London: Frank Cass.

Kerner, Donna O. 1988. "'Hard Work' and the Informal Sector Trade in Tanzania." Pp. 41–56 in *Traders versus the State,* ed. Gracia Clark. Boulder: Westview Press.

Kim, Kwan. 1988. "Issues and Perspectives in Tanzanian Industrial Development with Special Reference to the Role of SADCC." Pp. 92–102 in *Tanzania after Nyerere,* ed. M. Hodd. London: Pinter Publishers.

Kimble, David. 1953. *The Machinery of Self-Government*. London: Penguin West African Series.

Kiondo, Andrew. 1972. "The Nature of Economic Reforms in Tanzania." Pp. 21–42 in *Tanzania and the IMF: The Dynamics of Liberalization*, ed. Horace Campbell and Howard Stein. Boulder, Colo.: Westview Press.

Kironde, J. M. Lusugga. 1992. "Received Concepts and Theories in African Urbanisation and Management Strategies: The Struggle Continues." *Urban Studies* 29 (8): 1277–91.

Kleemeier, L. 1984. "Domestic Policies versus Poverty-Oriented Foreign Assistance in Tanzania." *Journal of Development Studies* 20 (2): 171–201.

Kulaba, Saitel. 1989. "Local Government and the Management of Urban Services in Tanzania." Pp. 203–45 *African Cities in Crisis: Managing Rapid Urban Growth*, ed. Richard E. Stren and Rodney R. White. Boulder, Colo.: Westview Press.

Kunz, Frank. 1991. "Liberalization in Africa—Some Preliminary Reflections." *African Affairs* 90: 223–35.

Lamphere, Louise. 1987. *From Working Daughters to Working Mothers*. Ithaca, N.Y.: Cornell University Press.

Lancaster, Carol. 1990. "Economic Reform in Africa: Is It Working?" *Washington Quarterly* 85 (Winter): 115–28.

———. 1991–1992. "Democracy in Africa." *Foreign Policy* 85 (Winter): 148–65.

Lele, Uma. 1984. "Tanzania: Phoenix or Icarus?" Pp. 159–95 in *World Economic Growth: Case Studies of Developed and Developing Nations*, ed. Arnold C. Harberger. San Francisco: Institute for Contemporary Studies.

Lemarchand, René. 1988. "The State, the Parallel Economy, and the Changing Structure of Patronage Systems." Pp. 121–48 in *The Precarious Balance: State and Society in Africa*, ed. Donald Rothchild and Naomi Chazan. Boulder, Colo.: Westview Press.

———. 1992. "Uncivil States and Civil Societies: How Illusion Became Reality." *Journal of Modern African Studies* 30 (2): 177–91.

Leslie, J. A. K. 1963. *A Survey of Dar es Salaam*. London: Oxford University Press.

Levi, Margaret. 1988. *Of Rule and Revenue*. Berkeley: University of California Press.

———. 1990. "A Logic of Institutional Change." Pp. 402–18 in *The Limits of Rationality*, ed. Karen Schweers Cook and Margaret Levi. Chicago and London: University of Chicago Press.

Lewis, Peter. 1992. "Political Transition and the Dilemma of Civil Society in Africa." *Journal of International Affairs* 46 (1): 31–54.

Leys, Colin. 1973. "Interpreting African Underdevelopment: Reflections on the ILO Report on Employment, Incomes and Equality in Kenya." *African Affairs* 72: 419–29.

Liebenow, J. Gus. 1986. *African Politics: Crises and Challenges*. Bloomington: Indiana University Press.

Lindberg, Olof. 1974. "Survey of Civil Servants' Wives Economic and Occupational Activities." Dar es Salaam: BRALUP, University of Dar es Salaam.

———. 1981. "Development of Settlement in Dar es Salaam, 1967–72." *Fennia* 159 (1): 129–35.

Lipumba, Nguyuru H. I. 1984. "The Economic Crisis in Tanzania." Paper presented at the National Workshop on Economic Stabilization Policies in Tanzania, Dar es Salaam.

Little, Kenneth. 1973. *African Women in Towns: An Aspect of Africa's Social Revolution.* Cambridge, England: Cambridge University Press.

Lofchie, Michael. 1988. "Tanzania's Agricultural Decline." Pp. 144–68 in *Coping with Africa's Food Crisis*, ed. Naomi Chazan and Timothy M. Shaw. Boulder, Colo.: Lynne Rienner Publishers.

Lomnitz, Larissa A. 1988. "Informal Exchange Networks in Formal Systems: A Theoretical Model." *American Anthropology* 90 (1): 42–55.

Lugalla, Joe L. P. 1993. "SAP and Education in Tanzania." Pp. 184–214 in *Social Change and Economic Reform in Africa*, ed. Peter Gibbon. Uppsala: Nordiska Afrikainstitutet.

Lukes, Steven. 1974. *Power: A Radical View.* London: Macmillan Press.

MacGaffey, Janet. 1987. *Entrepreneurs and Parasites: The Struggle for Indigenous Capitalism in Zaire.* African Studies Series, vol. 57. Cambridge, England: Cambridge University Press.

Maliyamkono, T. L., and M. S. D. Bagachwa. 1990. *The Second Economy in Tanzania.* London: James Currey.

Marco, Ltd. "National Capitol Master Plan, 1968."

Market Research, Ltd. 1965a. "Dar es Salaam Social Survey."

———. 1965b. "Rural Life in Mpiji River Valley."

Masaiganah, Mwajuma S. 1986. "Pande Village: A Summary Report." Pp. 86–94 (Appendix 1) in "The Role of Women in Tanzanian Fishing Societies: A Study of the Socioeconomic Context and the Situation of Women in Three Coastal Fishing Villages in Tanzania," by Marja-Liisa Swantz. Unpublished report commissioned by the Royal Norwegian Ministry of Development Cooperation (NORAD).

Mashisa, W. 1978. "Urbanization in Dar es Salaam: The Case of Manzese." M.A. thesis, Department of History, University of Dar es Salaam.

Mattila, Päivi. 1992. "A Study of Women in Informal Markets: Women Traders and Women's Marketing Networks in Mwanga and Moshi Districts in Tanzania." M.A. thesis, University of Helsinki, 1992.

Mbilinyi, Marjorie. 1989. "'This Is an Unforgettable Business': Colonial State Intervention in Urban Tanzania." Pp. 111–29 in *Women and the State in Africa*, ed. Jane L. Parpart and Kathleen A. Staudt. Boulder, Colo.: Lynne Rienner Publishers.

McGee, T. G. 1978. "An Invitation to the 'Ball': Dress Formal or Informal?" Pp. 3–27 in *Food, Shelter and Transport in Southeast Asia and the Pacific*, ed. P. J. Rimmer, D. W. Drakakis-Smith, and T. G. McGee. Canberra: Australian National University.

McHenry, Dean. 1994. *Limited Choices: The Political Struggle for Socialism in Tanzania.* Boulder, Colo.: Lynne Rienner Publishers.

Mganza, D., and H. Bantje. 1980. "Infant Feeding in Dar es Salaam." Dar es Salaam:

Tanzania Food and Nutrition Centre and the Bureau of Resource Assessment and Land Use Planning.

Migdal, Joel S. 1988. *Strong Societies and Weak States.* Princeton, N.J.: Princeton University Press.

Mlimuka, Aggrey K. L. J., and P. J. A. M. Kabudi. 1985. "The State and the Party." Pp. 57–86 in *The State and the Working People in Tanzania,* ed. Issa Shivji. Dakar: Codesria.

Mmuya, Max, and Amon Chaligha. 1992. *Towards Multiparty Politics in Tanzania.* Dar es Salaam: Dar es Salaam University Press.

Mogensen, Gunnar V. 1988. "Black Markets and Welfare in Scandinavia. Some Methodological and Empirical Issues." Paper presented at the 1988 Annual Meeting of the Society for Economic Anthropology, Knoxville, Tennessee, April.

Molloy, J. 1971. "Political Communication in Lushoto District, Tanzania." Ph.D. diss., University of Kent at Canterbury.

Moser, Caroline. 1978. "Informal Sector or Petty Commodity Production: Dualism or Dependence in Urban Development?" *World Development* 6: 1033–39.

Mtatifikolo, F. P. 1988. "Tanzania's Incomes Policy: An Analysis of rends with Proposals for the Future." *African Studies Review* 31 (1): 33–46.

Mueller, Susanne D. 1980. "The Historical Origins of Tanzania's Ruling Class." Brookline, Mass.: African Studies Center, Boston University.

Mwansasu, Bismarck, and Cranford Pratt, eds. 1979. *Towards Socialism in Tanzania.* Toronto: University of Toronto Press.

Mwijarubi, B. E. 1977. "Historical Study of Class Relations in Dar es Salaam: A Case Study of Buguruni." M.A. thesis, University of Dar es Salaam.

Ndulu, Benno J. 1988. *Stabilization and Adjustment Policies and Programmes.* Country Study of Tanzania, no. 17. Helsinki: World Institute for Development Economic Research of the United Nations University.

Ndulu, Benno J., and M. Hyuha. 1984. "Investment Patterns and Resource Gaps in the Tanzanian Economy, 1970–1982." Pp. 47–67 in *Economic Stabilization Policies in Tanzania,* ed. N. H. I. Lipumba. Dar es Salaam: Department of Economics, University of Dar es Salaam.

Ndulu, Benno J., and Francis W. Mwega. 1994. "Economic Adjustment Policies." Pp. 101–28 in *Beyond Capitalism vs. Socialism in Kenya and Tanzania,* ed. Joel D. Barkan. Boulder, Colo.: Lynne Rienner Publishers.

Ndulu, Benno J., H. K. R. Amani, N. H. I Lipumba, and S. M Kapunda. 1988. "Impact of Government Policies on Food Supply in Tanzania." Dar es Salaam: Department of Economics, University of Dar es Salaam.

Nelson, Joan M. 1989. "The Politics of Long-Haul Economic Reform." Pp. 3–26 in *Fragile Coalitions: The Politics of Economic Adjustment,* ed. Joan Nelson, 3–26. Washington, D.C.: Overseas Development Council.

———, ed. 1989. *Fragile Coalitions: The Politics of Economic Adjustment.* Washington, D.C.: Overseas Development Council.

Newbury, Catherine. 1986. "Survival Strategies in Rural Zaire: Realities of Coping with Crisis." Pp. 99–112 in *The Crisis in Zaire: Myths and Realities,* ed. Georges Nzongola-Ntalaja. Trenton, N.J.: Africa World Press.

Newbury, David. 1986. "From 'Frontier to Boundary': Some Historical Roots of

Peasant Strategies of Survival in Zaire." Pp. 87–97 in *The Crisis in Zaire: Myths and Realities,* edited by Georges Nzongola-Ntalaja. Trenton, N.J.: Africa World Press.

Nyerere, Julius K. 1968. *Ujamaa: Essays on Socialism.* Dar es Salaam: Oxford University Press.

———. 1987. "Address by Mwalimu Julius K. Nyerere, Chairman of Chama Cha Mapinduzi, at the Opening of the National Conference, Dodoma, 22 October 1987."

Nzongola-Ntalaja, Georges. 1986. "Crisis and Change in Zaire, 1960–1985." Pp. 3–29 in *The Crisis in Zaire: Myths and Realities,* ed. Georges Nzongola-Ntalaja. Trenton, N.J.: Africa World Press.

———, ed. 1986. *The Crisis in Zaire: Myths and Realities.* Trenton, N.J.: Africa World Press.

Obbo, Christine. 1980. *African Women: Their Struggle for Economic Independence.* London: Zed Press.

Ödegaard, Knut. 1985. *Cash Crop versus Food Crop Production in Tanzania: An Assessment of the Major Post-Colonial Trends.* Lund Economic Series, no. 33. Lund: Studentlitteratur.

Okin, Susan Moller. 1979. *Women in Western Political Thought.* Princeton, N.J.: Princeton University Press.

Ortner, Sherry B. 1984. "Theory in Anthropology since the Sixties." *Comparative Studies in Society and History* 26 (1): 126–66.

Payer, Cheryl. 1982. "Tanzania and the World Bank." Bergen, Norway: Chr. Michelsen Institute, Department of Social Science and Development, Development Research and Action Programme.

Peil, Margaret. 1972. *The Ghanaian Factory Worker.* Cambridge, England: Cambridge University Press.

Pellow, Deborah. 1977. *Women in Accra: Options for Autonomy.* Algonac, Mich.: Reference Publications Inc.

Pfefferman, G. 1968. *Industrial Labor in Senegal.* New York: Praeger.

Pilot Nutrition Project. 1975. "Pilot Nutrition Project Proposal." Dar es Salaam: National Sites and Service Programme.

Piven, Frances F., and Richard A. Cloward. 1979. *Poor People's Movements: How They Succeed, How They Fail.* New York: Vintage Books.

Planning Commission and Ministry of Labour and Youth Development. 1991. *Tanzania: The Informal Sector 1991.* Dar es Salaam: Government Printer.

Polanyi, Karl. 1957. *The Great Transformation.* Boston: Beacon.

Portes, Alejandro, Manuel Castells, and Lauren A. Benton. 1989. *The Informal Economy: Studies in Advanced and Less Developed Countries.* Baltimore, Md.: Johns Hopkins University Press.

Pratt, Cranford. 1976. *The Critical Phase in Tanzania 1945–68: Nyerere and the Emergence of a Socialist Strategy.* Cambridge, England: Cambridge University Press.

———. 1979. "Tanzania's Transition to Democratic Socialism: Reflections of a Democratic Socialist." In *Towards Socialism in Tanzania,* ed. Bismarck Mwansasu and Cranford Pratt. Toronto: University of Toronto Press.

Raikes, Philip. 1986. "Eating the Carrot and Wielding the Stick: The Agricultural

Sector in Tanzania." Pp. 104–42 in *Tanzania: Crisis and Struggle for Survival*, ed. Jannik Boesen, Kjell J. Havnevik, Juhani Koponen, and Rie Odgaard. Uppsala: Scandinavian Institute of African Studies.

Ray, S. K. 1975. *Economics of the Black Market*. Boulder, Colo.: Westview Press.

Resnick, Idrian. 1981. *The Long Transition*. New York: Monthly Review Press.

Roberts, Elizabeth. 1977. "Working-Class Standards of Living in Barrow and Lancaster, 1890–1914." *Economic History Review* 3 (2): 306–19.

Rogers, Susan Geiger. 1982. "Efforts Toward Women's Development in Tanzania: Gender Rhetoric vs. Gender Realities." Pp. 23–41 in *Women in Developing Countries: A Policy Focus*, ed. Kathleen A. Staudt and Jane Jaquette. New York: Haworth Press.

Roitman, Janet. 1990. "The Politics of Informal Markets in Sub-Saharan Africa." *Journal of Modern African Studies* 28 (4): 671–96.

Rothchild, Donald. 1987. "Hegemony and State Softness: Some Variations in Elite Responses." Pp. 117–48 in *The African State in Transition*, ed. Zaki Ergas. London: MacMillan Press.

Sabot, R. H. 1974. "Open Unemployment and the Employed Compound of Urban Surplus Labour." Dar es Salaam: Economic Research Bureau, University of Dar es Salaam.

———. 1979. *Economic Development and Urban Migration: Tanzania 1900–1971*. Oxford: Clarendon Press.

Safa, Helen I. 1987. "Urbanization, the Informal Economy and State Policy in Latin America." Pp. 135–63 in *The Capitalist City*, ed. Michael P. Smith and Joe R. Feagin. Oxford and New York: Basil Blackwell.

Sahlins, Marshall. 1972. *Stone Age Economics*. New York: Aldine.

Samoff, Joel. 1973. "Cell Leaders in Tanzania: A Review of Recent Research." *Taamuli* 4 (1): 63–75.

———. 1974. *Tanzania: Local Politics and the Structure of Power*. Madison: University of Wisconsin Press.

———. 1989. "Popular Initiatives and Local Government in Tanzania." *Journal of Developing Areas* 24 (October): 1–18.

Sampson, Steven L. 1987. "The Second Economy of the Soviet Union and Eastern Europe." *Annals of the American Academy of Political and Social Sciences* 493 (September): 120–36.

Sarris, Alexander H., and Rogier van den Brink. 1993. *Economic Policy and Household Welfare during Crisis and Adjustment in Tanzania*. New York: New York University Press.

Sassen-Koob, Saskia. 1989. "New York City's Informal Economy." Pp. 60–77 in *The Informal Economy: Studies in Advanced and Less Developed Countries*, ed. Alejandro Portes, Manuel Castells, and Lauren A. Benton. Baltimore, Md.: Johns Hopkins University Press.

Saul, John S. 1979. *The State and Revolution in Eastern Africa*. New York: Monthly Review Press.

Schatzberg, Michael G. 1988. *The Dialectics of Oppression in Zaire*. Bloomington and Indianapolis: Indiana University Press.

Schildkrout, Enid. 1982. "Dependence and Autonomy: The Economic Activities of

Secluded Hausa Women in Kano, Nigeria." Pp. 51–81 in *Women and Work in Africa*, ed. Edna Bay. Boulder, Colo.: Westview Press.

Scope, Candid. c. 1978. *Honest to My Country*. Tabora: TMP Book Department.

Scott, James C. 1976. *The Moral Economy of the Peasant*. New Haven, Conn.: Yale University Press.

———. 1985. *Weapons of the Weak: Everyday Forms of Peasant Resistance*. New Haven, Conn.: Yale University Press.

———. 1987. "Resistance without Protest and without Organization: Peasant Opposition to the Islamic Zakat and the Christian Tithe." *Comparative Studies in Society and History* 29 (3): 417–52.

———. 1990. *Domination and the Arts of Resistance*. New Haven, Conn.: Yale University Press.

Shaidi, Leonard P. 1984. "Tanzania: The Human Resources Deployment Act 1983 – A Desperate Measure to Contain a Desperate Situation." *Review of African Political Economy* 31: 82–87.

———. 1987. "Legal Control of Surplus Labour in Tanzania's Urban Centres." Paper presented at the Workshop on Social Problems in Eastern Africa, Arusha.

———. 1991. "The Leadership Code and Corruption." Pp. 125–31 in *Rethinking the Arusha Declaration*, ed. Jeannette Hartmann. Copenhagen: Centre for Development Research.

Sharpley, Jennifer. 1985. "External versus Internal Factors in Tanzania's Macroeconomic Crisis: 1973–1983." *Eastern Africa Economic Review* 1 (1): 71–85.

Shivji, Issa. 1976. *Class Struggles in Tanzania*. New York: Monthly Review Press.

———. 1992. "The Politics of Liberalization in Tanzania: The Crisis of Ideological Hegemony." Pp. 43–58 in *Tanzania and the IMF: The Dynamics of Liberalization*, ed. Horace Campbell and Howard Stein. Boulder, Colo.: Westview Press.

Sporrek, Anders. 1985. *Food Marketing and Urban Growth in Dar es Salaam*. Lund Studies in Geography, Series B, Human Geography, vol. 51. Malmö: Gleerup.

Stein, Howard. 1992. "Deindustrialization, Adjustment, the World Bank and the IMF in Africa." *World Development* 20 (1): 83–95.

Strathern, Marilyn. 1987. "Introduction." Pp. 13–31 in *Dealing with Inequality: Analysing Gender Relations in Melanesia and Beyond*, ed. Marilyn Strathern. Cambridge, England: Cambridge University Press.

Stren, Richard E. 1982. "Underdevelopment, Urban Squatting, and the State Bureaucracy: A Case Study of Tanzania." *Canadian Journal of African Studies* 16 (1): 67–91.

Stren, Richard, Mohamed Halfani, and Joyce Malombe. 1994. "Coping with Urbanization and Urban Policy." Pp. 175–200 in *Beyond Capitalism vs. Socialism in Kenya and Tanzania*, ed. Joel D. Barkan. Boulder, Colo.: Lynne Rienner Publishers.

Sutton, John E. G. 1970. "Dar es Salaam: A Sketch of a Hundred Years." *Tanzania Notes and Records* 71: 1–18.

Svendsen, Knud E. 1986. "The Creation of Macroeconomic Imbalances and a Structural Crisis." Pp. 59–78 in *Tanzania: Crisis and Struggle for Survival*, ed.

Jannik Boesen, Kjell J. Havnevik, Juhani Koponen, and Rie Odgaard. Uppsala: Scandinavian Institute of African Studies.

Swantz, Lloyd. 1969. "Inter-Communication between the Urban and Rural Zaramo in Dar es Salaam Area." Dar es Salaam: Department of Sociology, University College.

———. 1972. "The Role of the Medicine Man among the Zaramo of Dar es Salaam." Ph.D. diss., University of Dar es Salaam.

Swantz, Marja-Liisa. 1970. *Ritual and Symbol in Transitional Zaramo Society.* Uppsala: Almqvist & Wiksells Boktryckeri AB.

———. 1985. *Women in Development: A Creative Role Denied?* London: C. Hurst and Co.

———. 1986. "The Role of Women in Tanzanian Fishing Societies: A Study of the Socioeconomic Context and the Situation of Women in Three Coastal Fishing Villages in Tanzania." Unpublished report commissioned by the Royal Norwegian Ministry of Development Cooperation (NORAD).

———. 1994. "Woman/Body/Knowledge: From Production to Regeneration." Pp. 98–108 in *Feminist Perspectives on Sustainable Development,* ed. Wendy Harcourt. London: Zed Books.

Temu, Peter. 1975. "Marketing Board Pricing and Storage Policy with Particular Reference to Maize in Tanzania." Ph.D. diss., Stanford University.

Tibaijuka, Anna K. 1988. "The Impact of Structural Adjustment Programmes on Women: The Case of Tanzania's Economic Recovery Programme." Report prepared for the Canadian International Development Agency. Dar es Salaam: Economic Research Bureau, University of Dar es Salaam.

Trager, Lillian. 1987. "A Re-Examination of the Urban Informal Sector in West Africa." *Canadian Journal of African Studies* 21 (2): 238–55.

Tripp, Aili M. 1989. "Women and the Changing Household Economy in Urban Tanzania." *Journal of Modern African Studies* 27 (4): 601–23.

———. 1992. "Local Organizations, Participation and the State in Urban Africa." Pp. 221–42 in *Governance and Politics in Africa,* ed. Goran Hyden and Michael Bratton. Boulder, Colo.: Lynne Rienner Publishers.

———. 1994a. "Gender, Political Participation, and the Transformation of Associational Life in Uganda and Tanzania." *African Studies Review* 37 (1): 107–31.

———. 1994b. "Rethinking Civil Society: Gender Implications in Contemporary Tanzania." Pp. 149–68 in *Civil Society and the State in Africa,* ed. John W. Harbeson, Donald Rothchild, and Naomi Chazan. Boulder, Colo. and London: Lynne Rienner Publishers.

Tungaraza, R. D. 1986. "Mbweni Village Summary." Pp. 95–97 (Appendix 1) in "The Role of Women in Tanzanian Fishing Societies: A Study of the Socioeconomic Context and the Situation of Women in Three Coastal Fishing Villages in Tanzania," by Marja-Liisa Swantz. Unpublished report commissioned by the Royal Norwegian Ministry of Development Cooperation (NORAD).

United Republic of Tanzania. 1967. *Arusha Declaration: Answers to Questions.* Dar es Salaam: Government Printer.

———. 1984. *Economic Survey 1983/84.* Dar es Salaam: Government Printer.

Valentine, T. R. 1983. "Wage Adjustments, Progressive Tax Rates, and Accelerated

Inflation: Issues of Equity in the Wage Sector of Tanzania." *African Studies Review* 21 (1): 51–71.

Van Donge, Jan Kees. 1992. "Waluguru Traders in Dar es Salaam." *African Affairs* 91: 181–205.

Van Onselen, C. 1976. *Chibaro*. London: Pluto Press.

Von Bülow, Dorthe. 1993. "Tanzanian Women's Organizations and Networks: Exploring Women's Responses to Socio-Economic Transformation." Paper presented at the Gender and Agrarian Change Seminar, sponsored by the Institute for Development Studies and Centre for Development Research, Copenhagen.

Von Freyhold, Michaela. 1972. "The Workers, the Nizers and the Peasants." Dar es Salaam: Department of Sociology, University of Dar es Salaam.

———. 1979. *Ujamaa Villages in Tanzania: Analysis of a Social Experiment*. New York and London: Monthly Review Press.

Wallerstein, Immanuel. 1964. "Voluntary Associations." Pp. 318–39 in *Political Parties and National Integration in Tropical Africa*, ed. John Coleman and Carl Rosberg. Berkeley: University of California Press.

Weeks, John. 1975. "Policies for Expanding Employment in the Informal Urban Sector of Developing Countries." *International Labour Review* 91 (1): 1–13.

Weiner, Annette. 1976. *Women of Value, Men of Renown*. Austin: University of Texas Press.

Westergaard, Margaret. 1970. "Women and Work in Dar es Salaam." Dar es Salaam: Department of Sociology, University of Dar es Salaam.

Williams, Gavin. 1987. "Primitive Accumulation: The Way to Progress?" *Development and Change* 18: 637–59.

Wilson, Ernest J., III. 1988. "Privatization in Africa: Domestic Origins, Current Status and Future Scenarios." *Issue: A Journal of Opinion* 16 (2): 24–29.

World Bank. 1995. *World Tables*. Baltimore, Md.: Johns Hopkins University Press.

Wunsch, James S., and Dele Olowu. 1991. *The Failure of the Centralized State: Institutions and Self-Governance in Africa*. Boulder, Colo.: Westview Press.

Index

Designer:	Ina Clausen
Compositor:	G & S Typesetters, Inc.
Text:	10/13 Aldus
Display:	Aldus
Printer:	BookCrafters, Inc.
Binder:	BookCrafters, Inc.